CONTENTS

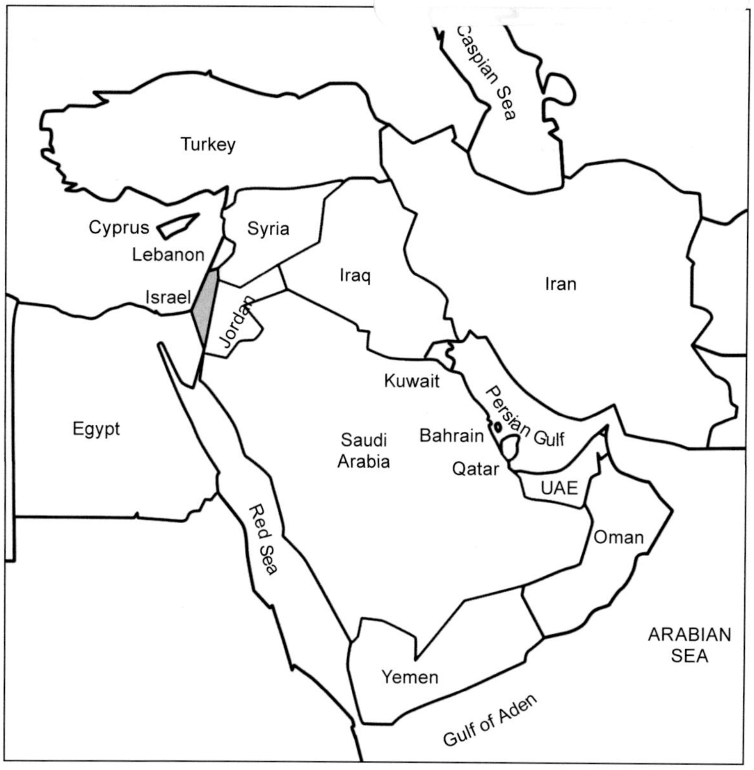

Helion & Company Limited
Unit 8 Amherst Business Centre
Budbrooke Road
Warwick
CV34 5WE
England
Tel. 01926 499 619
Email: info@helion.co.uk
Website: www.helion.co.uk
Twitter: @helionbooks
Visit our blog http://blog.helion.co.uk/

Published by Helion & Company 2020
Designed and typeset by Mach 3 Solutions Ltd (www.mach3solutions.co.uk)
Cover designed by Paul Hewitt, Battlefield Design (www.battlefield-design.co.uk)
Printed by Henry Ling Limited, Dorchester, Dorset

ISBN 978-1-913336-34-9

British Library Cataloguing-in-Publication Data.
A catalogue record for this book is available from the British Library.

Cover Artwork

Spitfire LF.IXe 2008/15 (formerly SL657) arrived in Israel from Czechoslovakia on November 28, 1948, and was put to immediate use. Like its brethren, it carried Royal Air Force camouflage to which the Israelis applied their unit colors and codes. The rudder stripes mark this as a 101 Squadron machine, the red spinner with white back plate from Czech service also adopted. It fought against RAF Spitfires in the January 7, 1949, clash over the southern battle zone during which John McElroy downed one of the British airplanes while suffering some damage in return. It had previously been the mount for two kills of Egyptian Macchi MC.205Vs, making it the highest scoring IAF Spit. It continued to serve until sold to Burma in 1954.

Acronyms and Abbreviations

AA	anti-aircraft
AAA	anti-aircraft artillery
AAM	Air-to-Air Missile
AB	Air Base
ADF	Automatic Direction Finding
AHQ	Air Force Headquarters
AMU	Aircraft Maintenance Unit
AOP	Air Observation Post
APC	armored personnel carrier
AR	aerial refueling
ARM	Anti-Radiation Missile
AS	Air Service
BDA	Bomb Damage Assessment
BVR	beyond-visual-range
C^2	Command and Control
C^3	Command, Control, and Communications
cal	caliber
CAP	Combat Air Patrol
CAS	Close Air Support
casevac	casualty evacuation
CGS	Chief-of-General-Staff
CO	commanding officer
EAF	Egyptian Air Force
ECCM	Electronic Counter-Countermeasures
ECM	Electronic Countermeasures
EW	electronic warfare
FAC	Forward Air Controller
g	acceleration due to gravity
GHQ	General Headquarters
HAS	hardened aircraft shelter
HUD	Head-Up Display
IAF	Israeli Air Force, Israel Air Force
IAI	Israel Aircraft Industries
IDF	Israel Defense Forces
IMI	Israel Military Industries
IR	infrared
kg	kilogram, kilograms
km	kilometer, kilometers
l	liter, liters
LAPES	low-altitude parachute extraction system
lb	pound, pounds
LZ	landing zone
m	meter, meters
MIVA	Mystère IVA
mm	millimeter, millimeters
MoD	Ministry of Defense
Mt.	Mount
ORBAT	order-of-battle
OTU	Operational Training Unit
PGM	Precision-Guided Munition
PLO	Palestine Liberation Organization
PM	Prime Minister
POW	prisoner-of-war
PR	photo reconnaissance
QRA	Quick Reaction Alert
q.v.	*quod vide* (on this, go see)
RAF	Royal Air Force
REAF	Royal Egyptian Air Force
recce	reconnaissance
RPG	rocket-propelled grenade
RPV	Remotely Piloted Vehicle
RWR	Radar Warning Receiver
SyAAF	Syrian Air Force
SAM	Surface-to-Air Missile
SAR	search and rescue
SEAD	Suppression of Enemy Air Defense
SMB2	Super Mystère B2
specops	special operations
St.	Saint
STOL	short take-off and landing
TV	television
u/s	unserviceable
UHF	Ultra High Frequency
UK	United Kingdom
UN	United Nations
US, USA	United States of America
USAF	United States Air Force
USSR	Union of Soviet Socialist Republics
VHF	Very High Frequency
VIP	Very Important Person

Introduction

May 2023 marks the 75th anniversary of the founding of the State of Israel and its air force. The maturation of the Israeli Air Force (IAF, Israel Air and Space Force or IASF from 2005) during its 75 years is a fascinating study in a relatively small military force working to meet shifting obligations under multiple impediments while being repeatedly tested in combat. Many factors over the decades shaped the air fighting capability, not the least being the demands of the evolving battlefield, uncertain funding, available weapons, and quality of personnel. Tactics and doctrine were, in turn, shaped by government policies, international pressures, and confronting adversaries likewise evolving. When the trials in war or combat short of war came, success was a measure in relevance of the service's weapons, adequacy of training, and experience of personnel.

The three volumes in this series document this evolution of the Air Force throughout its history by examination of all of these factors. It stands apart from many other books in performing this examination in a more dispassionate and critical manner, without the common hyperbole. A good deal of space is devoted to describing the shifts in the force's aircraft and other weapons over time. An air force is structured to match its capabilities as defined by its aircraft and associated tactics, and so that structure is examined as well. Accounts of the service's combat operations then show the effectiveness of all the equipment and preparation. A summary of the geopolitical milieu in which Israel and its military institutions dwelled over the 75 years helps to understand the materiel acquisition and tactical choices while placing in context the operations in which they were employed. These volumes are written at a time of historical changes for the air force, and the Israel Defense Forces (IDF) as a whole, and so informs understanding of the service emerging and operating in future years.

These books leverage off of my volume *Air War on the Edge, A History of the Israel Air Force and its Aircraft since 1947* (Midland Publishing, 2004), but with a different focus and, of course, updated. Backed by official and unofficial histories published since, and the unprecedented openness in the past few decades (yet filtered through the military censor), I have worked to make this account more accurate and complete than those of the past, albeit restricted by limited size of the volumes. It is additionally constrained by the inability to conduct conventional research, confirming information via multiple official sources, because of security restrictions and foreign national access limitations. Consequently, errors may have crept in and disinformation unwittingly repeated. Place names and the names of persons are those most commonly referenced, as are Hebrew translations, for example, "Israel Air Force" and "Israeli Air Force" are both found alternatively throughout officially translated literature and signage. Written for the distant future reader, past tense is employed throughout these books.

I thank all those who assisted with research material, additional information and confirmation of facts, and providing photographs. I am also grateful to all those Israeli authors who labored so hard and for so long to record the history of the IAF/IASF in open literature via original research from which this interloper could mine in the writing of this book. A special thanks to my friend Ra'anan Weiss who was the inspiration for these books and their format.

Those readers who would care to comment on these and my other publications, or offer additional research material and photographs, may contact me at williamnorton@earthlink.net.

Bill Norton

Tehachapi, California, 2020

CHAPTER 1

PRE-STATE SUBTERFUGE

The embryo of an air force for the Jewish community in Palestine was grown in the years of tension under British administration of the country. This was made necessary by local Arab resistance to Zionist immigration into the country and Great Britain's efforts to keep the peace and prevent the adversaries from arming themselves. A culture of daring and improvisation was fostered during this period that would serve the force that followed throughout its early years.

Roots of the Conflict

Jewish immigration to Palestine had expanded rapidly in the early 20th century, driven by Zionist zeal and the harsh conditions for Jews in Europe. The size of the *Yishuv*, the Jewish community, went from approximately 25,000 in 1882 to 413,000 by 1938, or some third of the population. The Arab inhabitants saw this as a threat to their way of life and reacted with occasional violent outbursts. The Yishuv formed the underground *Haganah* self-defence force, with the *Palmach* elite strike force, numbering about 3,000-4,000 full-time members plus 50,000 militia. Great Britain then controlled Palestine under a League of Nations mandate. When the Second World War erupted, the British trained Jews for local military service or to go abroad. This provided the Yishuv a core of individuals possessing formal military training and combat experience. A small number returned having served as aircrew, aircraft maintainers, and other functions of a modern air force. The war brought a sizable Royal Air Force (RAF) contingent to the Middle East and many airfields were constructed in Palestine.

The end of the war and the horrors of the Holocaust brought tremendous pressure to form a Jewish state in Palestine. Hundreds of thousands of Jews dispossessed by the war sought to make a new life there. Attempting to strike a balance between a massive influx and emergent Arab nationalism, the British restricted Jewish immigration. This prompted large-scale Haganah clandestine operations to bring in refugees. The Yishuv grew to roughly 650,000 persons by 1947. The 1,200,000 Palestinian Arabs resisted with greater destruction and attacks on Jewish settlements. The Zionists responded with more focused attacks and property damage. Both sides began intensive efforts to smuggle arms into the country.

When more extreme Jewish paramilitary organizations, separate from the Haganah and Palmach, began a terrorist campaign against the British administration, the United Kingdom (UK) responded with a massive infusion of military personnel and materiel. The crackdown on Jewish and Arab militias only hardened attitudes and resistance. The cost of the Mandate and the loss of international goodwill became untenable. Great Britain notified the United Nations that it intended to quit Palestine and requested that the international community find a just solution to the conflict. The UN voted on November 29, 1947, to partition Palestine between the Jewish and Arab communities, with the British mandate ending on May 14, 1948. The Yishuv accepted the decision, but the Arabs saw it as another imposition on their national rights by imperialist powers.

The British resolve to withdraw created a looming power vacuum that local factions and the surrounding Arab states sought to exploit. The end of the Mandate was recognized as the date when open warfare would come to Palestine. The Haganah and the *de facto* Yishuv government, the Jewish Agency with its leader David Ben Gurion, prepared for the crises. Adjacent Arab nations declared their intentions to send armies to aid their Palestinian brethren, but also to seize territory. Weapon smuggling moved into high gear, adding heavy weapons to those sought.

Aviation Baseline

As Arab actions had made it increasingly difficult for the Haganah to maintain ground communications throughout the country, aircraft became a vital link. Fortunately, there were a few commercial aviation firms and aero clubs to draw upon. These provided airplanes and pilots for emergency Haganah flights and a covert means of training future aircrew. Operations consisted mostly of liaison and flying light supplies to remote settlements.

The Jewish Agency had formed the Israeli General Council of Aviation in March 1945 under Joshoa Eshel, who initially lacked aviation experience.[1] It supervised and helped fund aviation activities with an eye to paramilitary applications. It also purchased additional light-planes to be operated from the principal civilian airport at Lydda. But for a few light twin-engine machines, most of the aircraft were trainers or sport airplanes barely able to drag a pilot and a passenger aloft. However, they were easy to fly and maintain, and could operate from short dirt strips. Apart from small airstrips, airports were under the control of the British authorities and so the paramilitary flights had to be conducted covertly. As the emergency deepened, the Haganah's covert flights grew in number.

With the defense situation becoming critical, the Haganah grew into an army and was compelled to accept personnel who had served with the British in the Second World War. These persons had previously been regarded with suspicion. A proposal to form a proper air element was offered in summer 1947 by Alexander Ziloni, previously with the RAF. Heyman Shechtman (later Shamir) and Aharon Remez were tasked with drafting a plan to match. Shechtman had been a navigator in the US Army Air Forces and Remez a fighter pilot with the RAF. These two responded in October with a 15-page outline of the staff structure, functions, and efforts necessary to prepare for war. It included a basic list of requisite materiel and the urgent recommendation to determine the essential manpower resources within the country while bringing in experienced volunteers from abroad. The proposal was accepted and on November 10, 1947, the Air Service (*Sherut Avir* or AS) was ordered into existence, absorbing all air elements in the country. The commanding officer (CO) was Joshoa Eshel. At its creation, the Sherut Avir's small staff was housed in the Aero Club of Israel's Tel Aviv offices.

Achieving the aims of the Shechtman/Remez plan while still under British rule required that acquisitions of equipment and personnel occur abroad, principally Europe and the United States of America (USA), while preparing to move all in at the end of the Mandate. This work had to be conducted under a veil of secrecy and front organizations because of growing international efforts to limit arms flowing to Palestine and so contain the scale of the violence. In the meantime, seven airstrips within Zionist areas were prepared, though many were only marginally safe owing to poor ground, short length, obstructions, and enemy proximity.

All qualified persons within Jewish Palestine were called to enlist in the new air arm. Although many men had returned from the Second World War with some relevant experience, this core was critically small. However, the war had left tens of thousands of personnel around the world with tremendous experience operating

Aero Club members pose before their three neat and clean Taylorcraft, with the nose of an R.W.D.-13 in the foreground. The aircraft were among those owned by Aviron and based at Lydda, the primary civilian field in Palestine. The photograph was taken in November 1947 just before internecine violence skyrocketed and the airplanes were turned to clandestine operations protecting Jewish settlements. (Author's Collection)

and maintaining modern warplanes in foreign lands. They were confident, worldly, and knew what a competent staff and effective air force looked like. Some of these individuals needed work or were eager for further adventure. Many were also motivated to help establish a home for the Jewish people so grievously wronged in the recent world war. Thousands of aircraft from the war were available in storage depots, though they needed some restoration. Getting the men and machines to Israel would require subterfuge, as many laws would be broken.

A move of the Haganah's mish-mash of light-planes from Lydda was necessary when battle lines began to form and the airport fell largely within the Arab sphere. A hasty transfer to the area of Tel Aviv, the Jewish center, was undertaken on December 13, 1947. A disused civilian field on the coast named Sde Dov, in the northern environs of the city, was made operational to take the six serviceable airplanes.

The A or "Tel Aviv" Squadron, possessing all Sherut Avir's aircraft, was formally inaugurated on December 27. The 10 airplanes were flown by 20 pilots and maintained by a small cadre of mechanics.

Sde Dov	
A Squadron	1 Dragon Rapide, 1 Seabee, 2 R.W.D.-13, 1 Autocrat, 2 Tiger Moth, 3 Taylorcraft
	10 total aircraft

These images show the Air Service's meager fleet of airplanes in the early period operations at the austere Sde Dov airfield. Seen at the end of 1947 and beginning of 1948 is the R.W.D.-13, two Tiger Moths, and likely a pair of Taylorcraft. The sandy surface off the runway and the ramshackle buildings are evident. (Shlomo Aloni and Ra'anan Weiss Collections)

A boost to operations came via the purchase as scrap of 20 former RAF Auster Air Observation Post (AOP) light-planes. These were slowly made airworthy beginning in late February 1948.[2] Because these operational airplanes did not officially exist, a scheme of applying civil registrations matching other light-planes had to be maintained. The limited range of the AS airplanes meant it was desirable to keep groups in the north and south to support missions in the environs of the country. The addition of the Austers made it possible during early 1948 to create two new units as semi-autonomous flights of A Squadron.

As hostilities escalated, the light-planes were ceaselessly busy performing liaison, light supply, observation, evacuation of walking wounded, and aerial photography with typical handheld cameras. They also patrolled the vital water conduit running to the Negev settlements. Scouting in advance of resupply convoys was vital to identify roadblocks or ambushes. The light-planes could

The Auster AOPs, bought as scrap, were not supposed to exist as flying aircraft and so the Air Service had to find a means of deceiving the British authorities. The Mk. IIIs looked like the AS's Auster Autocrat and the Mk. Vs their Taylorcraft, those aircraft already bearing registrations. So, the ex-military machines were painted and given markings of those civilian machines. Mission planners then had to work to ensure no two aircraft with the same registration appeared at the same airfield and so alert the British to the illegal activity. This proved difficult and some embarrassing incidents did occur. It is likely that some of the Brits were aware of the deception but turned a blind eye.

This Auster AOP Mk.III, serialed A-7, is seen at the Dorot forward strip in the Negev during summer 1948. By that point, the aircraft had been camouflaged and military markings applied. A large radio antenna protrudes from the top of the aircraft. The armed man may be more than a bystander as some small arms fire were delivered from these light-planes in flight. (Author's Collection)

land close enough to settlements to deliver small quantities of critical supplies, such as ammunition and fuel, and fly out wounded. The AS also made airdrops to inaccessible sites, although this consisted of little more than tossing out the items, wrapped in blankets, at low altitude. Sometimes a parachute could be used or the items dropped onto an area covered with old automobile tires. A portion of the supplies would be destroyed in the drop as a price for getting some into the hands of anxious defenders. The airplanes performed message drops by using a simple drawstring pouch with red streamers. Mail could be collected without landing by snatching the bag, hung from a "clothesline," via a nylon rope with a weight at the end that wrapped itself around the ground line on impact and was then drawn into the aircraft hand-over-hand.

Commander

Joshoa 'Iseek' Eshel took command of the Air Service at its founding on November 10, 1947. He had fought with the British during the First World War and was a long-time Haganah member. Although possessing sound organizational and leadership background, he initially had no aviation experience. Eshel was first assigned to head the Israeli General Council of Aviation in March 1945 by The Jewish Agency and carried on when the AS was formed on November 10, 1947. As the Air Service grew into an air force, a new commander was sought and Eshel stepped aside in April 1948.

This is allegedly a picture of Joshoa Eshel, the first commander of the Air Service before the Israeli Air Force was formally established. It is likely not a contemporary photograph. (*Israeli Air Force*)

The first light attack from an AS aircraft was conducted on December 17, 1947; a gunner fired a machine gun from the cabin and tossed grenades down on the attacking force. Although accuracy left much to be desired, the Arab irregulars frequently withdrew in the face of such unexpected assaults. To surprise the enemy at night and avoid some ground fire, the pilots would pull the throttle to idle and descend towards the target with the engine sound virtually inaudible from the ground. The young air arm's first multi-ship combat mission included three light-planes participating in a January 15 action helping defend the Gush Etzion settlements.

Influx

By the end of 1947 the AS had 66 personnel and was flying 500 hours per month. However, the machines and number of experienced personnel were clearly inadequate for the coming crisis. Efforts outside the country were already underway at recruitment and aircraft procurement. Airplanes that were more substantial began arriving, usually via some deceit and difficult delivery that appears adventurous in hindsight. Many required some overhaul and modification with extended range fuel tanks for delivery – usually facing a long over-water leg and night landing away from British eyes. All were, by necessity, non-combat types at this stage. Among these were rugged Noorduyn C-64A Norseman, listed in the original proposal for a "Hebrew air force." Each carried eight passengers or 3,200 lb (1,452 kg) into unprepared fields. A C-64 crash on May 10, during an attack mission, marked the young Air Service's first combat fatalities.

Possibly more important in the long-term was the Douglas C-47 Dakota ('Dak'). These proved vital in maintaining an air link to Europe after airlines ceased to operate into the increasingly hazardous conflict zone. However, larger aircraft were required for a foreseen airlift of arms.

In April 1948, the Yishuv negotiated the sale of a large quantity of weapons and combat aircraft from Czechoslovakia. The Czechs badly needed the hard currency and had the tacit approval of their patron, the Union of Soviet Socialist Republics (USSR). The Soviets welcomed the socialist character of the nascent Zionist state and hoped it could serve as a foil to Britain's Middle East plans. Over the coming months two Douglas C-54 Skymasters, a Lockheed Constellation, and a dozen Curtiss C-46 Commandos were acquired and turned to the vital airlift of Czech arms. The four-engine C-54s and the "Connie" could fly from Prague to Palestine nonstop with a sizable payload – albeit with an exhausting 11.5-hour flight timed to arrive in country at night, and departing before dawn. The Commandos were large twin-engine transports

Most of the Air Force's early aircraft came to them by odd means. Their first Fairchild Argus was seized from a hashish smuggler, repaired, and pressed into service during April 1948. At that time, it was a great leap in capability for the young force surviving on little "bug-smashers." The Fairchild was soon joined by others brought into the country by the usual subterfuge. (Author's Collection)

The Noorduyn Norseman was a rugged and powerful airplane that could haul a respectable load into some marginal airfields. It was ideal in the difficult circumstances of the period, even serving as an improvised bomber. The earliest example arrived in May 1948, but this particular aircraft, B-53, was delivered to Israel in August 1948. It is seen here during 1949 when it was used to spray DDT on a locust infestation. (The Peter M. Bowers Collection, Museum of Flight)

This photograph reveals some of the mish-mash of civil aircraft being brought into the country and turned to military purposes in the Air Service, and then the IAF. In the foreground is a Dragon Rapide, next a Beech Bonanza, and then a rare DC-5. All were used as improvised bombers in addition to general transport. (David Farer Collection, National Air and Space Museum, Smithsonian Institution)

that needed a refueling stop on the continent – a cumbersome proposition given the quasi-legal nature of the operation. The first mission was executed on the night of March 31/April 1, 1948.

With many aircraft being acquired abroad, volunteers *en route*, and the rapid growth of the AS in the offing, it was seen necessary to guide the expansion toward a desired goal.[3]

The staff drafted the outline of an "aviation force" with four wings consisting of 141 to 180 aircraft of all types making up a modern air force servicing all conceivable missions. Submitted to the Haganah Operations Section on March 9, 1948, it reflected sound planning but unrealistic objectives given the circumstances. Regardless, the exercise in exploring how to meet an Arab offensive held some value.

Civil strife grew in the last months of the Mandate. The combatants vied to take possession of strategic positions and British facilities, including airfields, as UK forces withdrew. The Jews alone suffered 1,200 deaths between January and mid-May 1948. Five AS airplanes were lost in action. With armies from the surrounding states poised to invade, the Yishuv faced an existential threat.

CHAPTER 2
WAR OF INDEPENDENCE

On the day the British Mandate in Palestine ended, David Ben Gurion declared creation of the State of Israel. That day, May 14, 1948, also marked the beginning of what became Israel's War of Independence. The air force grew tremendously throughout that year as it worked strenuously to defending the new state.

Joy and Crisis

In March 1948, the Haganah had begun to plan for securing the Jewish areas of Palestine in the coming war. Israel lacked decisive air capacity as it still awaited combat airplanes from abroad. However, there was pressure across Europe and in the USA to impound aircraft and arrest aircrew suspected to be bound for the war zone. Yet, some countries provided support while keeping the operations low key. The embargo initially had the greatest impact on the Israelis who were attempting to cobble together a modern army while the Arab states had standing forces. Some proper airfields came under Jewish control as the British withdrew, many with excellent facilities. Among these in Galilee was Ramat David and Haifa, and in the center of the country Petah Tiqva, Ramleh, and St. Jean. The fields at Aqir (renamed Ekron), Qastina, and Lydda were occupied only after enemy forces were driven back.

It quickly became clear to the Israelis that a proper military organization had to be adopted. A more formal command and administration structure was established in May. The Air Service was then considered merely a specialized branch of the Army and its officers, some with considerable operational experience,

Many light-planes were brought to Israel by well-meaning donors, but usually without spares and with little appreciation for how they would be employed in a war zone. The Norécrin was one such, though, like the others, the airplane was put to good use. It was found that the wide door could permit a stretcher to be loaded, albeit with difficulty, across the low wing. Flying into semi-prepared fields, it assisted in extracting casualties. (BIAF – Israel Aerospace Magazine)

The new nation faced a collection of local Arab militias plus invasion forces from Egypt, Transjordan, Syria, Lebanon, Iraq (operating from Transjordan), and a few Saudi Arabian elements. While the armed forces of these nations were small, modestly equipped, and lacking in experience, they were trained under British tutelage. Altogether, they possessed about 160 aircraft, but suffered from low serviceability and too few pilots. Only the Royal Egyptian Air Force (REAF) had proper fighters in two squadrons of Spitfires, but had to improvise bombers using C-47s. Their only air base in reach of Israel was El Arish in the northwest corner of the Sinai Peninsula, although it had to be expanded while a nearby base at Bir Hama was built. Towards the end of the war, the REAF introduced Macchi MC205Vs fighters and Stirling bombers.

were excluded from senior planning sessions. When Joshoa Eshel was reassigned in April, it was four weeks before Israel Amir was named successor. Amir was another officer without aviation experience, and senior AS personnel appealed to Ben Gurion. Air Service senior personnel insisted that an air force had unique command and control (C^2) requirements that required a separate air headquarters (AHQ) advising the Chief-of-General-Staff (CGS). This was especially true as the AS positioned itself for rapid growth with more complex aircraft and operations. The Prime Minister (PM) suggested that Amir serve as a director backed by an aviation commander. Amir successfully resisted this division of authority and responsibility. He remained, however, backed-up by a strong aviation staff.

On Israel's first full day of existence, the Sherut Avir had roughly 900 personnel, with about 500 in administration and 350 ground crew. Of 37 aircrew, 11 had been trained locally by the Haganah, 13 by the RAF, and 11 were foreign volunteers of which nine were Jewish.[4] Approximately half the airplanes were unserviceable and there were no combat aircraft.[5] The C-47s were supplemented on occasion with transient aircraft, operated between the time they arrived and then left the country.

Ekron	
	1 C-46
Nir'am and Dorot	
Negev (or 2) Squadron	normally 1 Taylorcraft, 2 AOP
Sde Dov	
A (or 1) Squadron	2 C-47, 1 Dragon Rapide, 2 Norseman, 2 Bonanza, 1 Seabee, 10 AOP, 1 Autocrat, 2 R.W.D.-13, 1 Taylorcraft, 2 Tiger Moth
Yavneel and Mahanayim	
Galilee (or 3) Squadron	normally 1 Taylorcraft, 2 AOP, 1 Argus
Europe	
	1 C-54, 1 C-46
	34 total aircraft

Commander

Reflecting the meager means and confusion of the period, this is all that survives as an image of the Israeli Air Force's first commander. Israel Amir was a transitional figure, a trusted Haganah commander seeing the service through its earliest formative period and the initial fighting during the War of Independence. (Author's Collection)

1st Commander – Israel Amir (originally Zavlodovski) assumed command of the Air Service on May 16, 1948, four weeks after the former commander departed. An early Russian immigrant to Palestine, he was a militia fighter and agricultural laborer from young manhood. As a long-time Haganah senior officer, he held the trust of the general staff. He served only until July 29, but during an important period, with the IAF formally established on May 28, aircraft and personnel acquisition efforts moving into high gear, airfields established, organizational structure formulated, and the War of Independence passing through its first difficult phase. However, Amir had no aviation background and his appointment was met with scorn from the fliers. With the force growing rapidly in numbers and sophistication of missions, a man with more air combat experience was needed. A new commander was brought forward and Amir moved on to other important IDF duties.

Opening Round

The air war began in earnest on May 15 with numerous Egyptian and Syrian air attacks on Israeli areas, including airfields. Several light-planes were damaged or destroyed at Sde Dov. Israeli aircraft had to be hastily camouflaged and dispersed. National markings and serials were devised and applied.

All of Israel was mobilized to fight for its existence, and conscription ordered on the 26th. The situation rapidly grew critical. Transjordanian forces cut off Jerusalem, the Egyptians were advancing up the coast and into the Negev, and the Syrians had isolated many settlements in Galilee. Loss of life on both sides was frightful and sometimes accompanied by atrocities. Arab air attacks included the bombing of both military and civilian targets, with almost daily sorties against Tel Aviv.

The Air Service had no effective answer to the air raids and ceased daylight flights to avoid contact with enemy fighters. This rule was rescinded for emergencies – of which there were many as isolated settlements needed to be reinforced or evacuated by air. Night operations were hazardous given the meager navigation means, especially in wartime blackout conditions, and need to take-off and land on minimally prepared fields. Runways were marked with cans of burning kerosene-soaked sand or truck headlights illuminating the landing path.

Initially lacking real combat aircraft led to improvisation with a number of indigenously assembled bombs and incendiaries. Light weapons were held in the lap of the "bomb chucker" and tossed out the window or door after the detonator pin was removed. Larger aircraft such as Norseman or Dakotas had the bombs passed hand-to-hand to be tossed out the aft door, or heavier ordnance rolled out. Such methods required multiple passes over a target at slow speed, increasing the risk from ground fire. This was reduced with adoption of external bomb racks, fabricated from scratch or cobbled together from RAF junk heaps.[6] None of the ersatz bombers had bombsights and few could dive for more precise aiming. The timed-detonation bombs could explode ineffectively above the ground if the aircraft flew too high. Yet, AS units worked hard at these nocturnal missions, exemplified by Galilee Squadron flying 91 sorties and dropping 4,465 lb (2,025 kg) of bombs during the first half of July.

The Air Service attempted to respond to the enemy superiority with bold action in bombing troop concentrations, enemy headquarters, and transportation nodes. This included strikes on Gaza and on the Syrian tactical headquarters on the Golan Heights. Auxiliary fuel cells within a cabin were improvised for extended range or endurance. Leaflet drops were also executed.

More men and women from within the country were trained for roles in the new Air Service. However, the bulk of the experienced aircrew, armorers, and maintainers came from abroad – 60 to 80 added per week.[7] These foreign volunteers, called *Mahal*, had to be recruited, some manner of legal arrangements made for pay, and some refresher training performed. Training was usually conducted outside the country as the personnel were gathered in Europe awaiting transport. Some individuals had difficulty maintaining a low profile and the world press ran stories about the flow of aircrew and airplanes to Israel. With most Mahal being Americans and Brits, English became the *lingua franca* of the force. However, almost all senior commanders of the army were Israelis.

In the frantic rush to get war materiel to Israel, virtually any kind of airplane was bought in. Some were of marginal value in a war zone and others performed poorly in the Middle Eastern environment. Regardless, all were flown until wrecked or repairs became impractical with parts inaccessible.

The Czechoslovak airlift became vital to the existence of the state. The Czechs offered Avia S-199 fighters with training, spares, weapons, and ammunition, all at exorbitant prices. These could only be moved to Israel rapidly by air transport. A Czech airfield was offered as both a training base and shipping point, with arms and equipment flowing to this hub.

The C-54s and C-46s performed the bulk of the airlift, the first S-199 delivered to Ekron on the night of May 20/21. The tempo of flights increased despite the refueling point shifting with the political tides and application of bribes. These 2,200-mile (3,541-km) flights were only possible thanks to experienced Mahal. Yet, maintenance was far from ideal, loading was haphazard and often over the limit gross weight, little weather information was available and blind-flying instruments lacking, and safety gear was missing. Few of the 50-odd aircrew would have been considered proficient at the start, refresher training being gained on-the-job.

The de Havilland Dragon Rapide was in airline service in Palestine before Israel was formed. It was a respectable aircraft and served well during the 1948 war and beyond. Apart from personnel and freight airlift, it also dropped parcels and bombs. (BIAF – Israel Aerospace Magazine)

The men were usually fatigued and operations in Israel were at night to avoid enemy fighters. Any diversion to other fields *en route* risked the aircraft being impounded and the crew arrested, as occurred several times.

The S-199 fighters were the hoped-for answer to the enemy's air superiority. These were Czech postwar production of an early model Messerschmitt Bf 109, but with Junkers' Jumo engine from the Heinkel He 111 bomber matched to a paddle-blade propeller. The result aggravated the worse characteristics of the old fighter and made ground operations so difficult that accidents were frequent. Once in flight the guns and cannon frequently jammed, and synchronization with the prop was sometimes mis-rigged so as to risk the pilot shooting off the propeller. The fighter pilots were unhappy with the Avia, but there were no alternatives.

A team sent for training in Czechoslovakia included pilots with experience in high performance fighters and those with only time in light-planes. The latter group was quickly eliminated as unsuitable for rapid conversion to the temperamental S-199. With the situation in Israel reaching a crisis, the remaining five pilots traveled back after just a handful of flight hours in the type and never having fired the guns. For a time, pilots continued to be sent to Czechoslovakia for checkout in the type because training flights in Israel on the few Avias could not be risked.

A force of five Avias was gathered at Ekron. To ensure the strictest secrecy and preclude an attack on them, the S-199s were kept under cover. A team of Czech mechanics supervised assembly and testing, although Israelis assumed the task thereafter.

To this point, the war had gone badly for Israel. Much territory allocated to them by the UN had been overrun, settlements cutoff or evacuated, the Jewish enclaves in Jerusalem occupied by the Jordanians, and all with much loss of life. Most worrying, an Egyptian column had thrust north to within 20 miles (32 km) of Tel Aviv, the Jewish center in the country, with little to arrest its progress. Two weeks of REAF airstrikes were especially troubling, yet there was nothing to challenge them. It was hoped the new Sherut Avir fighters could at least slow down the enemy momentum.

The May 28 introduction of the 199s was re-planned from a strike on El Arish air base to hitting the Egyptians column. To ensure surprise, the fighters were rolled out for the mission without the guns being fired or even the engines run. However, only four machines were ready and the first mission saw one lost to anti-aircraft (AA) fire and another damaged during a landing mishap. Two launching the next morning had one damaged by bird strike and the other downed by AA – that pilot becoming the first to bail out of an Israeli airplane. Yet, these missions, followed up by nocturnal bombing and ground actions, caused the Arab advance to lose momentum. They ended the immediate danger from the Egyptian movement north and Iraqi gains that threatened to cut Galilee off from the rest of the country.

On June 1, two Avias were damaged in an attack on Ekron by the REAF. The first Sherut Avir air-to-air kills were made on the 3rd when the only operable 199 brought down two REAF Dakota "bombers" over Tel Aviv. This ended the REAF bombing missions over the city, though fighters continued to drop ordnance for a time longer. The first enemy fighter fell to an S-199 on June 8. However, an REAF Fury probably shot down a Fairchild F-24 Argus during this period to become the first air-to-air loss for the Israelis.

As the AS gained aircraft and skilled personnel, it undertook bolder offensive actions. A pair of light-planes bombed Amman on the night of May 31/June 1 in the first Israeli attack on an Arab capital. The raid was meant to impress the attendees at the Arab League conference meeting in the city. Dakotas struck Damascus on June 10/11. Other missions bombed Gaza, Arab Jerusalem, troop concentrations in the south of the country, and so on. Although the physical damage from such raids were largely inconsequential, the impact on enemy morale and the resulting pressure on their governments were not.

Both sides had by this time reached the limits of their strength and supplies. All accepted the UN-sponsored 28-day ceasefire that came into effect on June 11, 1948. The Israelis had only just

The beefy Curtiss Commando was a vital airplane for the infant state during the War of Independence. Bringing in arms via a strategic airlift, positioning troops and supplies in advance of an offensive, and lifting the first units of paratroopers were roles it contributed to ably. The aft fuselage stripes marks this as a War of Independence image, though the C-46 served until 1952 when the Air Force chose to standardize on the more reliable C-47. (BIAF – Israel Aerospace Magazine)

The Israeli search for fighter airplanes finally hit pay dirt in a deal with the Czechs that included 10 Avia S-199s, later increased to 25. These were a local integration of a German bomber engine with an older Bf 109 airframe that left much to be desired. Nonetheless, they arrived at a critical moment and helped stem the tide of the Arab advance while the military buildup continued before the Israelis could assume the offense. As soon as better equipment was available, the remaining S-199s were set aside – D-123 is shown here at Herzliya. (David Farer Collection, National Air and Space Museum, Smithsonian Institution)

Brought from South Africa and The Netherlands via long and arduous routes, three Beech Bonanzas proved very versatile in early IAF service. They possessed respectable performance and had electrical bomb carriers installed under the fuselage to haul two 200-lb weapons. Targets even included Amman. (BIAF – Israel Aerospace Magazine)

Only one of 12 awards of Israel's highest military award for courage under fire during the war, the *Ot Ha'Gvora*, went to an airman. The recipient was Auster pilot Zvi Zivel who, on June 25, 1948, flew vitally needed supplies into a besieged strongpoint on the road to Jerusalem. After landing at the tiny strip, he began unloading the supplies alone and under constant fire. When the gunfire became quite intense, he enlisted the aid of local forces to pile sandbags onto a tractor. He then drove the tractor to the airplane to serve as a barrier while he finished the unloading and flew out. Zivel was killed months later when an Egyptian fighter shot down his Piper Cub.

managed to bring in sufficient arms and personnel to stabilize the situation at a crucial moment. They had struggled at great cost to stall the Arab campaign, strongly motivated in fighting for their embryonic country and their lives. By contrast, the Arab forces lacked unified command, had divergent goals, and were fighting beyond their borders. The appearance of Israeli fighter airplanes was especially demoralizing. Arab rhetoric in the press was offensive to Western readers and sympathy for the Israeli cause was widespread, thanks also to widespread reporting of heroic stories. Millions of dollars contributed by world Jewry was indispensable in preventing collapse of Israeli defenses by facilitating arms purchasing, especially airplanes.

Respite

The Israeli air arm had suffered serious losses while struggling to maintain equipment and train new personnel under the strain of combat. The hiatus offered the opportunity to organize more comprehensively. On May 26, the Haganah and other military groups were merged as the Israeli Defence Forces (IDF) or *Tsvah Haganah le Israel*, known more commonly by the acronym-derived name *Zahal*. Its air component became *Heyl Ha'Avir* (literally Corps of the Air) or simply the Israeli Air Force (IAF or IDF/AF). Now a defined service, an Air Staff was formed and organizational structure firmed, with the headquarters established in a Tel Aviv hotel.

The combatants violated the ceasefire terms by acquiring more arms and training foreign personnel. The territorial state of affairs was intolerable for Israel and they were unenthusiastic about UN efforts to broker an armistice. The IDF began planning an offensive for the end of the ceasefire, July 8, to push back the Arab forces. In preparation, the 101 Fighter Squadron was moved to an improvised and secret field at Herzliya to avoid enemy attack.

The campaign had been planned with important roles for the IAF, then much better organized and equipped with approximately 2,000 personnel including experienced Mahal. It possessed 60 aircraft of which 40 to 41 were operational. The only true combat type were 14 S-199s, with 10 airworthy. Four Bristol Beaufighters were in such poor shape they contributed very little. Carefully planned opening attacks were canceled either because aircraft were unserviceable or aircrew could not locate the targets. If executed, many of the attacks were not carried out properly. More Avias were lost in combat and accidents. The IAF did execute some successful missions and gained sufficient command of the air to begin carrying the battle to the enemy's home with attacks on Arab air bases. However, the IAF was unable to support battlefield action consistently.

Three Boeing B-17Gs brought from the USA were refurbished in Czechoslovakia, but with much improvised equipment. The trio flew to Israel on July 15 with one bombing Cairo *en route* and the others Rafah in the Sinai Peninsula. They continued to fly throughout the war, greatly increasing bomb delivery tonnage. The B-17s, with defensive guns and a surprisingly good serviceability rate, generally flew daylight missions while the cargo bombers continued to work at night. The Forts operated below 14,000 feet (4,267 m) because they lacked crew oxygen. During the first six and a half days of the offensive, before the Flying Fortresses arrived, the IAF dropped 20,657 lb (9,370 kg) of bombs in 82 sorties. In the last three and a half days, it delivered 107,870 lb (48,929 kg) with the contribution of the B-17s. These included further excursions across the border to include bombing Damascus on July 18. By unspoken mutual agreement, bombing of cities largely ceased by late summer.

A July 19, 1948, ceasefire ended the "Ten Day War" with little gained, although the Israelis had assumed the initiative. The second ceasefire, for an indeterminate period, provided further

The Israeli acquisition of a trio of B-17 heavy bombers was a major coup in the war. The aircraft greatly improved ordnance delivery tonnage, if not accuracy. This low fly-by was performed on May 12, 1949, at Ramat David AB. The bombers survived beyond the war, but were flown seldom, even taking on the maritime patrol mission to sustain proficiency. They were stored in 1954 in anticipation of retirement. (Ron Feldman Collection)

opportunity for reflection and improvement. Ben Gurion had two independent teams, led by foreign senior officer veterans, assess the IAF and make recommendations for improvement.[8] In general they concluded the service was poorly organized and managed, lacked strict structure and discipline, and suffered poor aircraft serviceability. Consequently, some organizational changes and leadership clarifications were introduced. By an order dated July 26, the IAF was explicitly identified as a separate service within the IDF. Aharon Remez was named commander, falling under the CGS while also answering to a Deputy Minister of Defence for the Air Force.[9] The IAF Operations Officer, Heyman Shamir, attended Zahal planning sessions.

The ceasefire only had the effect of limiting combat to small-scale battles, and all combatants contributed to ceasefire violations. Another round seemed inevitable as the Arabs refused to accept a Jewish state and the Israelis were determined to create a nation of rational territorial dimensions. The IAF continued to over-fly enemy territory and engage opposition aircraft when encountered. The combat strength of the Air Force also increased markedly. Recruitment brought highly skilled Mahal combat pilots, including a number of recognized "aces." A September 17 accounting showed 92 aircraft with 49 serviceable. Among these were 20 fighters and the three heavy bombers. Matched with highly experienced aircrew, this force was approaching parity with Israel's adversaries.

During the first month of the war, an average one cargo airplane arrived per night, the freight contributing greatly to Israel's ability to hold on. By July, 118 tons of cargo had been delivered in 30 flights, including 11 S-199s.[10] In early August the Czechs, responding to international pressure, told the Israelis to clear out. During the entire operation the fleet of about 10 aircraft was credited with some 100 flights and 600 tons of freight including the 25 S-199 that helped turn the tide in the air.[11]

The last flare-up had failed to establish a permanent link with the Negev settlements encircled by Egyptian troops. By August, the situation for the civilians and Negev Brigade was growing dire and a plan was laid for relief in advance of another offensive. This was to be a large-scale airlift with the goal of 600 tons over a month. With just 30 miles (48 km) from Ekron to the area, the transports were expected to make multiple flights per night. Apart from food, this was to include weapons and jeeps while flying out exhausted fighters and bringing in fresh troops.

Most of the IAF's heavy transports were then in the country. Their flights would alight at a dirt strip laid on an emergency landing field near Ruhama. The 4,000-foot (1,219-m) runway was restored and equipped with electric runway lights and reliable communications because the missions had to be flown in darkness across Egyptian lines. The 30-minute flights allowed multiple sorties per night.

On August 23, five days after identifying the potential site, the first C-46 landed at Ruhama. That night 29 tons were delivered in four flights, followed by 75 tons in 11 flights the next night. In the September alone, 13 sorties brought in 81 tons. The missions were very stressful owing to the short runway, poor visibility in dust, and difficulties of night operations without proper instruments. Yet, the 170 missions by September 21 delivered about 1,130 tons of supplies including wheeled vehicles and 2,384 persons – far outstripping General Staff expectations.[12]

The need to rest the crews and perform maintenance on the aircraft, plus a protest by Mahal aircrew, interrupted the momentum of the airlift. The personnel dispute involved pay,

Commander

2nd Commander – Aharon Remez was named commander of the IAF on July 29, 1948 after a critical assessment of its early performance during the War of Independence. Just 29 years old, Remez was a sabra (native-born) and during the Second World War he served as a RAF fighter pilot achieving Warrant Officer grade. He helped establish the foundation of the Air Service and IAF with advanced planning, then held various staff posts before and during the early months of the independence fighting. As CO, his grade was Air Marshall, following the British tradition, before the standard IDF rank structure was adopted for all services. Remez resigned before the end of 1950 when his plans for expansion of the IAF was rejected by the government.

Air Marshall Aharon Remez is shown at right in about 1950. He was one of the original architects of a Jewish air force and was assigned commander at the end of July 1948. Remez resigned the post near the end of 1950. (Author's Collection)

This "Dakota" is emblematic of many aircraft brought to Israel to fight the difficult war. It was a former Swissair C-47B illegally flown to Israel in late 1948, approximately the period in which this photograph was taken. It was deceptively and jocularly marked "Al-Shem" (Hebrew or "No Name") for a time during low-profile operations outside the country such as bringing in tens of thousands of Jewish immigrants from predominantly Muslim nations – though most of that airlift was performed by contract outfits. It was operated by the IAF through 1955 when it was transferred to Arkia, the Israeli inland airline. However, it was mobilized for the 1956 war and so operated again, briefly, by the IAF. (BIAF – Israel Aerospace Magazine)

the pace of operations, hazardous working conditions and poor lodging, a required oath of allegiance to the new state on joining the IDF, the disputed need to take on the trappings of a formal military organization, and the integration into the IAF as a squadron rather than becoming the nucleus of a national airline. The acrimony soon passed. The volunteers who remained were given one-year contracts and not required to formally join the IDF.[13]

Operations resumed in early October. The Egyptians eventually discovered the activities around Ruhama. This and desire to increase the operation's tempo was cause to prepare a second airstrip near Urim. It was a bit farther removed from the enemy lines and was given a longer runway to accommodate heavier airplanes. With both destinations active, the average flight rate rose to 10 per night. By the end, on October 21, the 417 airlift flights had delivered 1,911 passengers and 2,224 tons of cargo including 520 tons of food, 500 tons of fuel, and 200 tons of ammunition, while bringing out 3,187 persons.[14] The IAF had finally done something earning praise from the General HQ (GHQ).

This general area map shows the locations of the primary and secondary Israeli airfields as they evolved during the War of Independence. The names are those commonly used by the IAF at that time. The nearest Egyptian base affecting the war is also depicted. (Author)

Final Acts

Israel was ready to undertake a major effort at dislodging the Egyptians from the Negev. Kicked-off on October 15, this was the first combined-arms operation with missions for the ground forces, Air Force, and Navy supporting the same objectives. The IAF portion involved unrelenting pressure on the enemy's command structure and REAF assets in the area while also supporting the ground campaign.

Significant changes were occurring in the IAF fleet by this point, supported by additional experienced Mahal. In May, 20 Piper Cubs began assuming the usual light attack missions, but also casualty evacuation (casevac) aided by a pallet rigged in the aft fuselage to accommodate a stretcher. Five AT-6s Harvards were smuggled in, but only a few were assembled and placed into action by the end of the war. These served as trainers as well as light attack machines. Of greater importance were five P-51D Mustangs that began arriving in August, but much time was required to make them operational. One was put to immediate use, including shooting down an RAF Mosquito photo reconnaissance (PR) ship that had repeatedly violated Israeli airspace. Mechanics also cobbled together two Spitfires from RAF scrap heaps and downed REAF aircraft. A handful of Lockheed Hudson light bombers began arriving in November. Like others, they had to be re-militarized and so introduction was slow.

The Israelis eagerly concluded a deal in June to buy 50 secondhand Spitfires from Czechoslovakia. Conversion training, weapons, ammunition, and spares were included. At first, it appeared to be a coup just to acquire Spitfires at any price. They could unquestionably tip the balance of power in the air in Israel's favor. However, an expeditious way had to be found to get the aircraft to Israel. Another airlift was out of the question. Although many were shipped overland and then by sea, it was urgent that some be flown to Israel as soon as possible. External slipper tanks and modifications for S-199 drop tanks permitted the ferry with all non-essential equipment removed. Yugoslavia permitted a refueling stop in

Two Spitfires of indeterminate model were cobbled together by the Israelis from wreckage and derelicts left behind by the British, plus parts collected from Egyptian Spitfires shot down inside Israel. The run-up of D-130 at Herzliya in September 1948 reveals the crude surroundings and a mirror above the canopy brow taken from an automobile. This aircraft and its companion D-131 almost became the Air Force's first operational fighters, but they flew only after the S-199s arrived. (Author's Collection)

The Piper Cub came late to the war but was very welcome in taking on the roles played by the much-abused pre-war light-planes. This example has light bomb hangers attached off the bottom corners of the fuselage and a large radio antenna above. A marking of 3 Squadron "Galilee" has been painted below the observer station. (Author's Collection)

Spitfires from Czechoslovakia were immediately effective when introduced and gave the Israelis a sense of more assertiveness in the air. This pair of 101 Squadron fighters out of Hatzor AB (the former Qastina) was photographed over the Negev from a B-17 during a January 1949 bombing mission over Faluja (note bomb shackles). (Ron Feldman Collection)

their territory, but that still left a 740-mile (1,181-km) leg of more than seven hours, and in a period during which heavy weather could be expected. A C-54 with navigator served as a pathfinder, Israeli vessels were posted along the over-water portion, and other transports stood by to drop life rafts to any pilots who were forced to ditch. Avia S-199s would meet the unarmed airplanes over the Mediterranean and escort them into Israeli airspace. Still, the delivery flights were hazardous.

The first half dozen Spitfires departed on September 24, but only three reached Ramat David. One was landed gear-up in Yugoslavia by one of the inexperienced pilots and two were interned when the crews diverted with fuel emergencies. The three Spitfires were put to speedy and valuable use in the October offensive.

By this point, the Heyl Ha'Avir was arguably the most potent air force in the region. It flew 230 sorties during the weeklong campaign, with 60 on October 16 alone, and delivered 151 tons of bombs.[15] These included visual and photo reconnaissance, patrol, bomber escort, scrambles, and dive-bombing. The service lost three airplanes and two pilots in combat, but claimed three enemy aircraft in the air and five on the ground. At one point a formation of 13 bombers attacked the Gaza railway station – the largest "strike package" the IAF assembled during the war and for many years to come. An offensive in the north successfully cleared Galilee of enemy forces by the time of the ceasefire and even penetrated 20 miles (32 km) into Lebanon. The IAF contributed 34 sorties and 27 tons of bombs to that effort. Overall, the service performed well, although its immaturity was still evident. The greatly improved situation relieved the Air Force of a great deal of its freight-hauling obligations.

With the final offensive of the war planned for late December, strenuous efforts were undertaken to bring 15 more Czech Spitfires to Israel. Some of the aircrew were very low time pilots with no experience in a Spitfire and virtually none in such a high performance warplane. Some had not earned wings in any air arm. Training in Czechoslovakia included just seven to eight hours in type before being considered sufficiently trained for the ferry mission. Navigation training was so meager that the inexperienced pilots were told to bail out if they became separated from the leader – the only pilot in the flight with a radio and a chart.

The first ferry attempt on December 18, failed when four Spitfires turned back in the face of a snowstorm and two crashed with a pilot perishing. One of the Skymasters was also lost supporting the Spitfire deliveries when it returned to Israel at night to find full blackout and no one responding to radio calls. The crew was forced to ditch in the surf off Tel Aviv. Another 10 fighters made it by the end of the month with less drama.

By the time of the third truce on October 31, the Israelis had largely neutralized the immediate threat and opened a road into the Negev, though Egyptians still occupied vital areas. The final large-scale operations were to hopefully force the Egyptian army out of Palestine and compel Arab negotiations to end the war. Commencing on December 22, the IDF pressed the Egyptian forces into what became the Gaza Strip, further isolated those in the "Faluja Pocket," and relieved the threat to Beersheba. The IAF supported the effort with 243 sorties of all kinds, 126 contributed by the newly arrived Spitfires, and delivered 226 tons of bombs.[16] Threatening to cut off the Egyptians still in Palestine, IDF troops crossed into the Sinai. With Israeli troops overrunning El Arish auxiliary landing strips and threatened

One Air Force leader during the War of Independence became a legend. Modi Alon was the first commander of the IAF's first fighter squadron, the 101. He had been trained as a fighter pilot by the British during the Second World War, but was a modest and quiet man, and a husband with a child on the way. He seldom joined the Mahal pilots in their nocturnal Tel Aviv drinking bouts. Those men also lived in hotels and were paid for their duty in addition to generally being *prima donnas* – quite a contrast from the rough-hewn socialist Yishuv Jew. Yet, Alon held their respect with his tough leadership. He captured the affection of Israelis by shooting down two Egyptian C-47 "bombers" over Tel Aviv on June 3, 1948 – the IAF's first aerial victories and in full view of the populace. The product of a frontier kibbutz and a Haganah veteran, the handsome 27 year old Sabra had military bearing befitting the billing of hero. Alon was killed in the crash of an S-199 on October 16, 1948.

Modi Alon (wearing sunglasses), commander of 101 Squadron, escorts the Israeli Prime Minister and Defence Minister, David Ben Gurion (right), during a visit to the unit at Maabarot on August 10, 1948. Also shown to the left of Alon is Giddy Lichtman and behind to the right is Syd Cohen. (Author's Collection)

Bir Hama following IAF attacks, the REAF was forced to evacuate. A paratroops drop was prepared to help assault the base, but the mission proved unnecessary. On January 5, under unrelenting air and ground attacks, the Egyptians signaled to the UN their desire for an immediate ceasefire and armistice negotiations.

The REAF had been reinforced with fresh equipment and personnel and they acted with renewed vigor – though still suffering poor serviceability and a pilot deficit. Countering with their Spitfire and Mustang fighters, Israeli pilots were very aggressive – a trait for which they would be known thereafter. They did not hesitate on the day before the ceasefire, January 7, when encountering REAF and RAF fighters over Zahal troops. The British were concerned about Israeli incursions into Sinai, potentially signaling a threat to the Suez Canal, plus the grave condition of their allies Egypt and Transjordan. The RAF sent fighters into the war zone and encountered a rare four-ship IAF formation. The British suffered four destroyed, two pilots killed and two captured, while the REAF lost two airplanes and pilots. This action brought the UK to the verge of direct conflict with Israel. They issued an ultimatum for Israel to withdraw its forces from Sinai. This the IDF did after a few days. The tension between the two countries would persist for several years after.

A concluding effort in the Negev on March 6-10, 1949, established an Israeli presence on the Gulf of Aqaba by seizing the tiny port of Om Rashrash, the future Eilat. This could be strategically vital to Israel in the future. To prevent the troop movement re-igniting the war, it was conducted quickly, quietly, and without violence. Two brigades began the trek south to push out the few Transjordanian troops. Because the area was almost trackless, aerial resupply and relief was required. An airlift of materiel to Avraham Field, 35 miles (56 km) north of Om Rashrash, was undertaken.

Assessment

When the final ceasefire came into effect, Israel had secured most of Palestine. A narrow waist of land opposite Jerusalem joined the fertile Galilee and the vast wilderness of the Negev. The ancient city was divided, with Transjordan (soon renamed Jordan) holding half as well as a sizable portion of Palestine west of the Jordan River (the "West Bank") which it soon annexed. Egypt maintained control of what became the Gaza Strip and home to many of the 750,000 or so Palestinian Arab refugees. Many of these people were housed in camps supervised by the UN. Although armistices (not formal peace treaties) were signed during 1949 with Egypt, Syria, Jordan, and Lebanon, Iraq refused to participate. Technically, a state of war still existed between Israel and these Arab nations whose resentment meant the confrontation would continue.

The young Israeli Air Force had achieved much. Despite the pressures of combat operations and a fragile national infrastructure, the Israelis had built and operated a modern air arm. By the time of the third ceasefire, the IAF was executing operations in a thoroughly professional and reliable manner, although the immaturity of the team with hastily assembled resources remained evident. A command structure was in place and equipment was adequate to meet the immediate threat. Squadrons had successfully relocated to forward bases in anticipation of intense operations. Growing a force under the pressure of combat and an international embargo meant many corners cut. Some missions were not well executed and the makeshift nature of the operations caught up with them on several occasions through ground and flight mishaps costing lives. Some 34 to 38 machines were wrecked in operational accidents and two captured – more than were lost in combat. However, confidence was gained in the success of innovation and bold action. These attributes would be fostered for decades to come.

At the peak of operations, there were 193 pilots, 164 other aircrew, about 2,000 ground personnel and some 4,000 more support staff. Of the 525 aircrew that flew during the war, 70 percent were Mahal (42 percent Americans) and 75 percent of those Jewish. Foreigners also filled most of the squadron-level command positions and operational planning postings. Over a one-year period, the Air Force had acquired 178 aircraft of 30 different types while maintaining and operating them under very difficult circumstances. At one point in December 1948, the IAF had 113 aircraft, although only 60 were serviceable and of these

Another warplane smuggled into Israel with great difficulty against the international embargo, the first IAF Mustang is shown being prepared for its initial flight in early October 1948. One of just two made operational during the war, they were plagued by shortage of spares and repair manuals. Yet the P-51s shared or scored several kills and ended RAF photo reconnaissance flights over the country. (Shlomo Aloni Collection)

only 28 were true warplanes. In air engagements, the teams shot down 27 airplanes and perhaps six more destroyed by AA fire or on the ground.[17] Some 15 to 18 Israeli aircraft had been downed or destroyed on the ground, with two known to have been shot down by enemy fighters. A total of 23 pilots, 10 other aircrewmen – about half Mahal – and perhaps 10 ground personnel had been killed, while two pilots were listed as missing and four other aircrew captured. These were counted among the total 6,000 Israeli dead and 12,000 wounded.

At the end of 1948, the IAF order-of-battle (ORBAT) had grown three-fold over nine months, though half the aircraft were unserviceable.

Ekron	
Station Flight	1 Taylorcraft
35 Flight	2 Norseman, 7 Harvard
69 The Hammers	3 B-17
Air Transport Command (soon 106)	9 C-46, 2 C-54, 1 C-69 (in Czechoslovakia), 1 Lodestar, 1 Hudson, 1 Anson ?
Nir'am/Dorot	
2 Camel	4 Cub, 1 AOP
Ramat David	
3 Galilee	1 Rapide, 3 Cub, 2 AOP, 1 Taylorcraft
101 First Fighter	14 Spitfire including 1 photo reconnaissance, 2 P-51, 6 S-199 (stored), 1 BT-13, 1 Seabee
103 Transport	6 C-47, 1 DC-5, 1 Mosquito PR.16, 2 Beaufighter
Sde Dov	
1 Tel Aviv	5 Dragon Rapide, 2 Argus, 3 Bonanza, 2 Norécrin, 12 Cub, 1 RWD-13, 9 AOP
	107-108 total aircraft

Israel had spent many millions of dollars acquiring aircraft and operating the rapidly evolving air force, proportionally much more than for the other IDF corps. Yet, important though their contributions had been, the IAF was not a decisive factor in the war. The GHQ repeatedly complained about this, and especially the IAF's inability to prevent enemy aircraft harassing ground forces and bombing population centers. Before each of the three offensives, the airmen asked for a delay to permit the latest combat aircraft to be brought in. Each was refused, reflecting the low benefit the leadership anticipated. Only aerial transport had been clearly critical in the war's outcome by sustaining civilian settlements, delivering materiel from outside the country, and ensuring the success of offensives through replenishment across enemy lines. Bombing was so poor that its employment in advance of an offensive, or flying close-air-support, was largely ineffectual. The strikes beyond the borders sent a message but were otherwise unimportant to the outcome of the war. Whether the IAF had truly established air superiority could be disputed. To the last days the REAF bombers and fighters were active in the combat zone, though the IAF continued to out-perform them.

Although the Israeli Air Force grew from just a handful of airplanes, the Arab air arms were quite small as well. As the international embargo took hold, both sides struggled to remain suitably equipped. Downed or wrecked aircraft were salvaged if possible or parts removed for reuse. Some former-enemy aircraft were placed into friendly service. An Israeli Dragon Rapide that made a forced landing behind Egyptian lines was repaired and flown by the REAF until the IAF reclaimed it when they overran El Arish airfield. A Jordanian Arab Airways Rapide had repeatedly cut across the Negev *en route* to Egypt until forced down at Beersheba in 1950. The passengers were repatriated while the aircraft became the property of the IAF.

A handful of North American AT-6s "Harvards" arrived near the end of the war and deployed as dive bombers and strafers. These machines were also applied to flight training even as the war continued. This example from the middle of 1949 has had yellow bands applied denoting training, though also differentiating them from Syrian Harvards. (Jay Miller Collection)

CHAPTER 3
CHARTING A COURSE

The years following the war were an exciting time of nation building and assimilating the hundreds of thousands of Jews immigrating to Israel. From about 650,000 persons in 1948, the population more than doubled by 1952. The strain of settling the many new citizens and solidifying the national infrastructure put tremendous fiscal pressure on the government. The country was in debt and experiencing a depression. Consequently, the IDF suffered from low funding. The Arab-Israeli conflict continued to simmer in the presence of lingering Arab resentment and in an area with many multinational interests. Another round of fighting seemed likely and so Israel had to maintain a ready military at a high cost for the new nation.

Character Development

The IDF/AF lost its edge quickly following the war as volunteers returned home and money for training withered. A few Mahal remained under contract, or foreign experts hired, to guide and train the fledgling force until local personnel were sufficiently proficient and a reliable structure established. Of the Israeli pilots flying during the war, 76 percent had been hastily trained during the emergency and so required remedial instruction. The IDF became known for some of the youngest officers, and especially generals, in the world as it sought to grow its internal talent. The service was able to draw upon the best examples of foreign air arms and its own small experience to create unique doctrine and tactics.

The Air Force was headquartered in Jaffa and was responsible for all military aviation. Separate Army or Navy air arms were clearly unaffordable and probably unnecessary. The severe fiscal limitations led Israel to select a large reserve structure for her armed forces, with citizens performing 30 to 45 days of military duty per year. Conscription was maintained and draftees could volunteer for specialized training to enter elite corps, such as Air Force pilot. In this way, the best of the inductees could be directed to the more demanding duties. Only a relatively small number of regular elements were maintained on active duty. The IAF had to be ready instantly to protect the tiny state during the 48 to 72 hours required for full mobilization of the reservists and their equipment. The small country did not permit trading territory for time in the event of an enemy offensive. Consequently, the Air Force had a higher ratio of full-time personnel (approximately a third of the force) and trained more frequently. An uninterrupted mobilization and deployment demanded complete control of the skies. This was the IAF's foremost mission, leading to a strong emphasis on fighter airplanes and air-to-air combat, plus the goal of a high ratio of pilots-to-aircraft to sustain a high sortie rate with the small number of aircraft. The secondary mission was suppressing enemy air power followed by support of the Army and Navy missions.

Israel possessed a relatively small armed forces in which many officers knew each other despite being in different branches. Army, Navy, and Air Force personnel alike were referred to as soldiers. Despite being declared a separate service, years of struggle by the IAF was required to establish truly independent functions within the IDF. Much work was done on inter-service cooperation, especially the Air Force supporting ground operations. The IAF was among the first small air forces to adopt Forward Air Controllers (FAC) embedded with IDF units to at least the battalion level.

Some IDF leaders used the contention that none of the battles of the war had been decided by airpower to keep postwar investment in the Air Force at low level. The IAF was restricted to just 4,500 personnel and some bases were closed. Much heavy maintenance was performed abroad. There was little money to sustain the service properly and it resembled many of the second-rate air arms so prevalent following the Second World War. Training and readiness was poor, and materiel was on hand for only a few days of hard fighting. Command and control was hindered by the sad state of the communications infrastructure. In June 1949, the IAF reported an aircraft serviceability rate of just 40 percent with shallow spares stock. Discipline and morale were low, combat skills marginal, the staff bloated, and accident rates high owing to undisciplined flying.

A large-scale joint IDF exercise during October 1950 did not go well for the Air Force. It was judged to have no overall operational plan, possessed poor equipment, lacked discipline, and personnel had low morale.[18] Air Marshall Remez pointed to the transitional state of the force as one factor in the low performance. He fought to ensure that the IAF had an operational structure separate from the IDF GHQ so it could respond quickly enough to gain air superiority and protect mobilization. He offered a plan to grow the IAF to a force of seven wings (air bases, AB) with 15 squadrons possessing 292 aircraft.[19] This was clearly beyond the means of the state and inconsistent with political reality. His plan rejected, Remez resigned to be replaced at the end of 1950 with Shlomo Shamir.

Shamir was a career Army officer who had also commanded the Navy. His assignment as Air Force CO was felt necessary given his breadth of command experience. His stated goal was to bring the IAF command more closely under the GHQ umbrella as a technical force supporting Army operations. Consequently, he was so resented that most Air Force senior staff resigned.[20] He reorganized the rank structure from that reflecting the RAF system to one aligned with the IDF, emphasizing unity with the greater force. The Air Force CO then became a Major General. Shamir also moved the AHQ to Ramleh AB in 1951. However, he fell ill and relinquished command to Haim Laskov in August 1951.

Also Army with no aviation background, Laskov worked to reorganize the IAF into a more rational structure and instill more discipline. He trimmed staff by more than half to make more funds available for operations. He, too, unsuccessfully sought greater organizational independence. It was only in 1953 that IDF leadership felt the time was right for an aviator to take the IAF's reins. Dan Tolkowsky was named, although the General Staff still had reservations whether an officer with only a flying background was suitable.[21] It also resisted appointing Air Force officers to

Commander

3rd Commander – Shlomo Shamir assumed command of the IAF in December 1950. He was an immigrant who worked in the Haganah throughout his adult life. During the Second World War, he served with the British Army and achieved the rank of Major. In the War of Independence, he led an infantry brigade and later commanded the Navy. Although he held a pilot's license, he had no air force exposure. His assignment to lead the IAF was felt necessary by the General Staff given his broad command experience compared with the available youthful aviators. He worked to ensure a harmonious integration of the IAF and Zahal, especially in growing the Air Defence Forces. He also established Hatzor as a full air base and set in motion important acquisition efforts. However, Shamir's appointment was so resented that most Air Force senior staff resigned. Shamir fell ill and relinquished command in August 1951.

Shlomo Shamir is pictured as the Navy commander prior to his assignment as Air Force CO at the end of 1950. His service in the air post was relatively brief, but not without note. The growth of Hatzor as an air base and development of the Air Defence Forces owe themselves to Shamir's efforts. (Israel GPO)

Commander

Haim Laskov was a soldier at heart who took the post of Air Force commander when his nation called. His time as CO was one of reorganization, discipline, and growing the aerial reconnaissance capabilities. Serving from 1951 into 1953, he went on to many other military duties benefitting his country. (Author's Collection)

4th Commander – Haim Laskov took up the reins in August 1951. He was an immigrant that grew up in Palestine, was part of the Haganah from his youth, and fought with the British during the Second World War where he rose to the rank of Major. He returned to perform training and combat command duties during the War of Independence. He held other staff duties in the IDF before being called to serve as Air Force CO. Laskov lacked an aviation background but understood command and military structure. He worked to trim the IAF staff and reorganize it to a more rational form while instilling greater discipline. He also grew the photo reconnaissance capabilities as an intelligence resource. Most importantly, Laskov strove to bring the first jet fighters to Israel. However, he never felt comfortable as IAF commander and asked to be relieved after two years. He continued a distinguished career in the Army that included Chief-of-General-Staff between 1958 and 1961.

positions on the General Staff, and this caused a ruckus in 1954, although eventually resolved.

The fundamental Air Staff structure is shown in the accompanying illustration, this morphing over the decades.[22] At times there were Group Commanders over fighter, transport, and helicopter echelons. Eventually, airfields with squadrons of just one aircraft class (e.g., fighters) were identified as numbered Wings while those with multiple classes (e.g., fighters and transports) were identified as numbered Bases. The squadron commanders (with two deputies) answered to the wing or base commander on operational matters. He determined the means for executing combat taskings directed from AHQ. Combat employments and management of air battles was directed by the headquarters. The Base infrastructure and Wings provided administrative and technical support with intermediate maintenance, while each squadron (save for station flights of liaison aircraft) had flightline maintenance, flight operations, safety, meteorological, and intelligence resources.[23]

As airfields came due for extensive sustainment work or improvements, several were abandoned, including St. Jean, as affordability measures. A few became minimal forward airfields, dispersal fields, or emergency landing strips. Some portions of highways inside the country were constructed to be converted to runways in an emergency, and exercises occasionally employed these. Technical School 21 was established in Haifa that came to also operate two technical high schools. Eventually, an Aviation Professional School was created to train air traffic controllers, intelligence, communications, and administration specialists. Officers were sent abroad to attend staff colleges, some working up similar functions upon returning home. A Staff School at Tel Nof AB (the former Ekron, reflecting a penchant to rename locales) eventually became an IAF Command and Staff College while an IDF Defence College was also created. An Air Depot was established at Kfar Sirkin (formerly Petah Tiqva), but moved to Zrifin when Sirkin was closed.[24] Sde Dov was turned over to civilian control and the Air Force transferred aviation squadrons to other bases. The Aircraft Maintenance Unit (AMU) 22 was at Tel Nof to perform repairs, overhauls, and modifications while bases performed inspections and squadrons the routine aircraft servicing activities.[25] Bedek, subsidized by the government,

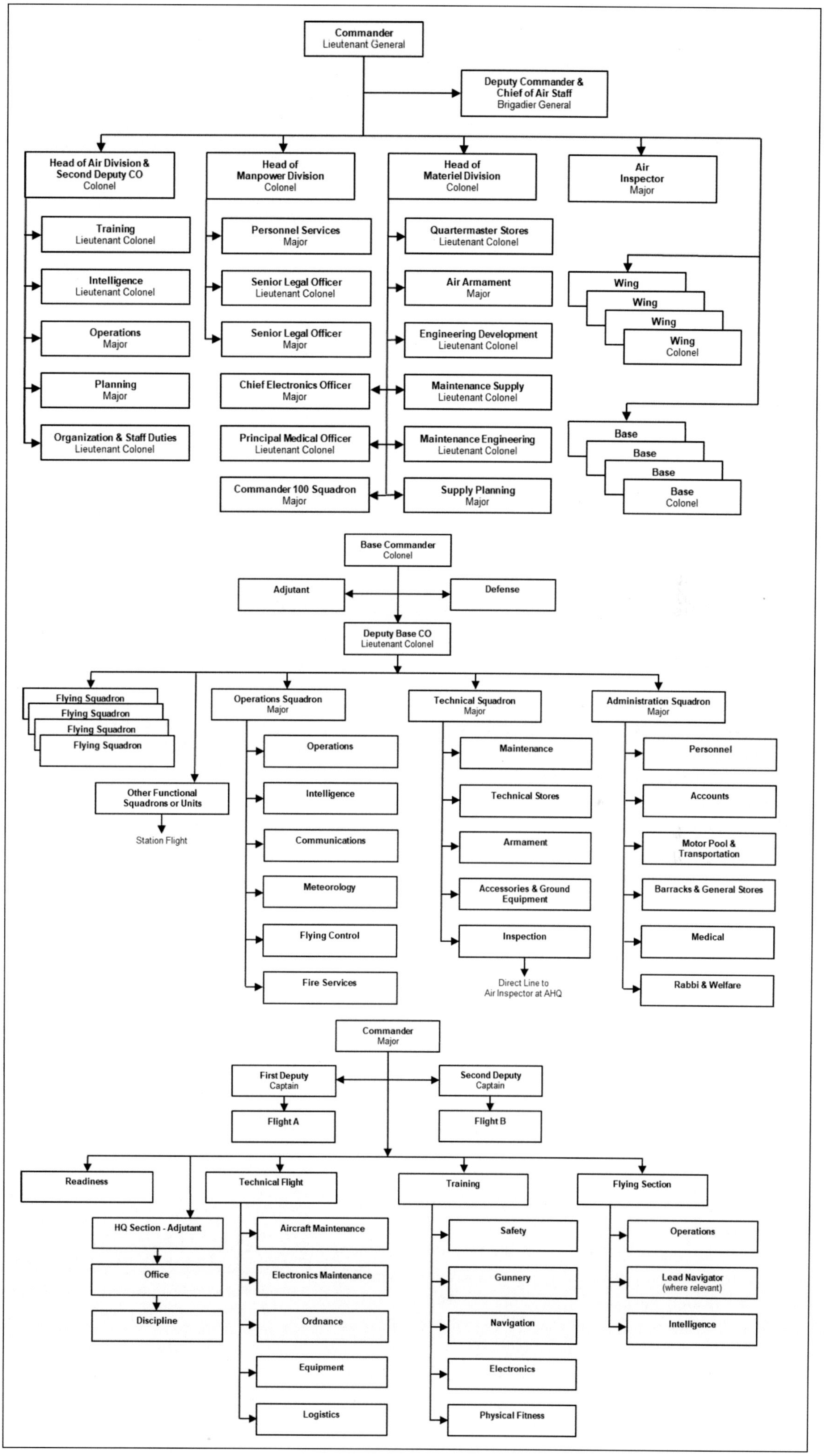

At top is the IAF Air Headquarters (AHQ) organization circa 1950s. In the middle the IAF Wing /Air Base organization circa 1950s and 1960s. At the bottom is the IAF aviation squadron organization circa 1950s and 1960s. Flying Squadron commander rank changed from Major to Lieutenant Colonel following the 1967 war. (Author)

performed heavy overhaul and modification work for the Air Force, though the service had resisted this political decision.

The IAF took on nonmilitary missions for the nation when necessary during those early years. Transports were given civil markings for flights beyond the border; especially in bringing Jews from predominantly Muslim countries. No fewer than 200,000 immigrants were brought to Israel via this means. Other missions included cloud seeding by the B-17s and C-47s, and insecticide spraying by C-64s and Dakotas. Bedouins who crossed into Israel to graze their flocks or smuggle goods, or Palestinians seeking to return to their former properties, were chased and occasionally fired upon from aircraft until they learned to respect the border.

Twenty Stearman Kaydets arrived near the end of the 1948 war but were only slowly assembled. They formed the core of the basic flight training fleet immediately after and many more were acquired in the coming years. A brace of these airplanes are shown in military colors, save for red training bands, because they would be expected to participate in any renewal of hostilities. (BIAF – Israel Aerospace Magazine)

In the years after the war, the Piper Cub grew in importance because of its ability to land in many areas inaccessible to heavier machines. It could also support Army small-unit operations with radio relay, some small arms fire, and light airdrop. This example (actually a later Super Cub) has a mount under the wing for a light machine gun or parachute-recovered loads to be dropped to forward-deployed squads. (BIAF – Israel Aerospace Magazine)

Fleet Shuffle

After the war, the IAF was eager to dispose of many of the 30-odd types it had collected, some of low military value, and create a more economically manageable force. It also needed to acquire a more solid core of combat aircraft, hoping to select the most suitable equipment for its circumstances, even if secondhand. However, budgets limited the options. Additionally, nations that could provide the equipment were either ambivalent about arming the new state or politics made this undesirable. In some cases, these governments actively impeded the Israeli efforts, seeking to deter an arms race and maintain some semblance of a regional military balance. The IAF had to look everywhere for any opportunity to obtain equipment by any means. It became a persistent and frustrating struggle to acquire and sustain suitable materiel, and the force suffered.

The potpourri of light-planes fell under 100 Squadron as the earlier units were consolidated. Between 1951 and 1959, the outfit was collocated with the IAF headquarters at Ramleh AB, but station flights were maintained at bases throughout the country. The unit sought to standardize on the Cub. Their primary duties remained liaison and scouting. The Pipers conducted some light bomb drops augmented with firing of light guns installed on the aircraft. They also served as the principal means of rescuing downed aircrew and other personnel given its ability to operate from some unprepared surfaces.

The service augmented 100 with two Hiller light helicopters in 1951. The 1948 experience reaching isolated settlements and troops was motivation to seek other means than airplanes risking operations from unprepared surfaces. Still, there were strenuous objectives to the expense of the helicopter purchase – the Ministry of Defence (MoD) pushing the idea, not the IAF. There was consideration of having the Army operate the Hillers.[26] That and the pilot rescue mission convinced the IAF to keep them, but the rotorcraft team struggled for years to be considered on equal footing with the other force elements. The helicopters served the usual liaison function, but also responded to some civilian emergencies.

The 141 medium transport/liaison unit was equipped with Second World War-vintage Avro Ansons plus Airspeed Consul and Oxford twins. Their principal role was training of navigators, radio operators, and multi-engine pilots. However, serviceability was atrocious. Lacking funds for replacements, it was 1956 before the last of these aged veterans were finally pushed aside.[27] The

A handful of Avro Ansons, and similar Airspeed Consuls and Oxfords, formed a squadron of twin-engine medium transports serving training and, secondarily, liaison duties during the 1950s. This Anson, in the company of S.11s, has two astro-domes supporting navigator training, but twin-engine instruction was also conducted on 141 Squadron machines. It was photographed at Kfar Sirkin AB on 27 December 1951 with the fuselage stripe denoting a training asset. (Shlomo Aloni Collection)

Hatzor AB hosts a lineup of 109 Squadron Mosquito FB.6 fighter-bombers in this image from July 1953. The war-surplus "Mossies" were acquired at low cost, but demanded considerable restoration effort and subsequent upkeep. (Shlomo Aloni Collection)

service sought more Harvards, eventually employed exclusively in training. In wartime, they were to take up light attack missions or serve as FACs and radio relay. Likewise, old Boeing Stearman trainers would serve liaison and observation duties in an emergency while primarily supporting flight training. In wartime such resources were to be flown by reservists, a few flight instructors not current with an operational unit for Emergency Posting (as staff officers also did), and some advanced students. This practice reflected a goal that all IAF aircraft and aircrew have a wartime mission. A handful of Harvards and Stearmans were scattered at bases across the country as proficiency mounts and liaison duties.

The heavy transport squadron standardized on Dakotas. More were acquired over the years to augment or replace earlier airframes. Many of its other "heavies" were transferred to the national airline, El Al, and inland carrier, Arkia, though to be mobilized in time of war. "Cargo bombing" persisted for only a short time while paratroop and cargo airdrop training continued. The C-47s were fitted with a shield ahead of the tail wheel strut after a paratrooper's chute became entangled there. This began a tradition, with the Israelis modifying foreign-built equipment to suit their specific needs, especially where safety or operational effectiveness were addressed. An effort to expand airdrop capacity was undertaken in 1954 by developing a pallet carried beneath the Dak that could be released for parachute recovery of up to 4,400 lb (1,996 kg) to include 20 bombs, a jeep, or two commando kayaks. Perhaps only one or two aircraft were modified for this mission.

The B-17Gs were properly fitted-out with the standard bomb racks, turrets, bombsights, and suitable ancillary equipment. Their capabilities did not lend themselves to close air support and so bomber training was meager and they were flown comparatively seldom. However, their range and windows made them suitable for the maritime patrol mission that helped to maintain flight proficiency. By early 1954 the cost of operating the old Boeings, plus their vulnerability in the jet age, became too much and they were placed into storage.

Major-General Laskov sought multi-role aircraft rather than specialized types in an effort to get the most from the investment. This policy would stand for the next generation. Dozens of used Mosquito fighter-bombers were purchased and those made airworthy were concentrated in 109 Squadron, stood-up at Hatzor AB (the former Qastina) in 1951. The unit was not operational until 1952 and not fully mission-capable until the next year.[28] There were initially too few pilots, and those on staff had to go to the UK for training. By 1953, sufficient aircrew had been trained locally to allow a second unit to be broken out as 110 Squadron, also at Hatzor.

Although the IAF had been looking forward to establishing a night-fighter capability, the few NF.30 Mosquitos were never fitted with intercept radar because that equipment was not released to Israel. The IAF mounted an AN/APS-4 search radar pod into the noses of a handful in hopes it would serve for intercept. This unit was poorly suited for night intercept, displaying only azimuth returns, lacking elevation. Although crews trained with the system, the means was so marginal that the night-fighter requirement remained essentially unfulfilled. The best that was achieved was aircrew in various aircraft vectored via ground control to a hopeful visual acquisition under lunar illumination.

The "Mossie" teams trained hard, even deploying to spartan forward bases to practice preparing for operations in the Sinai during wartime. The 110 Squadron focused on training for night fighting and were unique in the force at the time – ground attack under the illumination of parachute flares. The Israelis fitted rocket launch points under the wings to support such missions. However, the Ramat David AB fighter squadrons continued to receive the bulk of the accolades and promotions, leaving the Mosquito teams at run-down Hatzor feeling second-class. This made them prone to prove themselves with sometimes-reckless flying. That, the age of the wooden machines with prodigious maintenance demands, and the low-altitude mission, contributed to discouragingly high accident rates and some fatalities. Morale suffered and aircrew sought transfers.

A unique capability that helped improve spirits was PR that included missions beyond the borders. Even after jets began coming into the force, the range and payload of the Mossies were superior and the old aircraft was retained. This was challenging as the plywood airframes aged, but the IAF could afford little else. It became a common theme for decades to come as the service operated a high-end force of relatively current fighters and a low-end of aging, less capable warplanes.

The 101 Squadron, at Ramat David AB, standardized on Spitfires as the rest of the Czech birds were taken up. There was no great hurry in putting all these on the line as the IAF had only 25 fighter pilots in the first half of 1950, and most were performing flight instruction. The unit focused on operational training of Flying School graduates until, by the end of the year, the 105 stood up and assumed the training. More Spits were acquired through 1953 and the IAF planned for four fighter squadrons during this period. However, attrition matched with slow acquisition of "new" machines and pilots made this unachievable.

Surplus P-51Ds were also purchased through the mid-1950s. The range, payload, and reliability of the Mustang made it reasonable to acquire additional machines even as jets were being sought. The 101 initially operated both Spitfires and Mustangs. The latter

Despite the high maintenance demands, the twin-engine Mosquitos had respectable range and endurance, an admirable payload, and mission flexibility. This 110 Squadron FB.6, 06, is about to be boarded by its aircrew at Hatzor AB in late December 1953. (Israeli Air Force)

The plywood Mosquitos were obsolete when purchased. The Air Force then flew the old warhorse far beyond its useful service life. (The average life of such an airplane in the Second World War had normally been counted in months). As a consequence, the airplanes required considerable maintenance support and experienced low serviceability. This and numerous operational accidents earned the airplane a bad reputation. Then a spat of crashes spelled the demise of the type in Israel. These losses may have been due to warping and disbonding of the plywood structure in the dry climate of the Eastern Mediterranean, resulting in in-flight break-up. On October 26, 1953, Lieutenant Ovadya Nachman was flying Mosquito FB.6 2105 when, pulling out of a dive, the aircraft disintegrated. He found himself and his seat hanging in midair and so released himself and opened his parachute just in time to land safely. Although the cause was disputed, this accident was another source of grim speculation and falling morale. Flying such unreliable airplanes of questionable airworthiness on long-range reconnaissance (recce) missions over hostile territory earned 109 the nickname "Kamikaze Squadron." The fact that the IAF had to buy such machines and then operate them in such conditions for many years illustrates the neglected state of the service in the early 1950s.

This April 16, 1953, image of Ramat David AB shows lineups of 105 and 107 Squadron Spitfires of various finishes. This base was the principal home of the IAF fighters with Spitfires and Mustangs making up the force. The Mustangs continued to serve as a second-tier propeller-driven cadre even as jets were initially taken up. (Author's Collection)

The fighter squadrons chose to standardize on the P-51 and let go their Spitfires. Apart from meeting the combat mission of the fighter squadrons, the type had an important role to play in operational training of new fighter pilots even as jets were entering the force. These oil-streaked Mustangs were photographed in Athens while *en route* to Israel from Sweden in 1953. (Author's Collection)

focused on attack, rocket launch points being retrofitted, while Spits emphasized intercept. The 101 eventually standardized on Mustangs while passing its Spitfires to 107 Squadron, established in 1953 at Ramat David to conduct the fighter pilot Operational Conversion Course. However, this unit closed in 1954 as the last Spitfires were sold. The 105 took over the 51s as fighter pilot Operational Training Unit (OTU) in 1955.

Although sales of surplus Second World War aircraft were only marginally objectionable to foreign nations, Israel's inquiries about jets was met with stonewalling throughout the early 1950s. During this period, the major arms-producing nations of the West sought to maintain a balance of strength between Israel and Egypt. Usually ignoring Israel's other declared adversaries, these governments exercised restraint in arms sales to these two countries. Despite complaints of unfair treatment, an arms race was forestalled for five to six years.

Israel sought turbojet fighters to meet those already in opposition inventories, but also because they were then a prestige asset marking a modern and sophisticated nation. In late 1952, the UK agreed to sell Meteors, but only by providing a like number of jets to Egypt, Syria, Iraq, and Lebanon. This type was already growing obsolete, but the Israelis could ill-afford to turn down the offer.

The sale included 11 F.8 fighters and four T.7 trainers, plus spares, ammunition, and training. The novelty of new-built aircraft also provided the IAF its first experience with ejection seats. The Israelis began its practice of working with the manufacturer to tailor aircraft for their unique needs. This included integrating underwing rocket launchers and incorporating Israeli-manufactured 20-mm cannons. The new 117 Squadron at Ramat David AB started in 1953 with a core of two pilots and 13 maintainers trained in Britain and worked for a year to create a combat team. Initially only experience pilots went through 117's OTU course. Consequently, it was another year before new pilots began flowing to 117.

Efforts to acquire more jets continued to meet with resistance until 1955 when Britain sold seven used Meteor FR.9s and two T.7s. The IAF finally obtained a night-fighter capability when the

UK agreed in 1954 to sell six formerly owned NF.13s. Delivery was delayed until fall 1956 in reaction to the IDF's reprisal raids (*q.v.*). The need for night-fighters was becoming critical as the EAF prepared to introduce Il-28 jet bombers. As before, a like number of aircraft were provided to Egypt and Syria. Aircrew were trained in the UK and returned to form 119 Squadron at Ramat David AB.

Arms Race

Arab states sought an end of Western domination and explored their new nationalism while contemplating means of expelling the "Zionist entity." An Arab boycott of Israel was instituted and her shipping barred from the Suez Canal. Aircraft bound to and from Israel were forbidden to overfly Arab states. Border incidents were frequent, with loss of life on both sides. Arab states supported or were unable to restrain Palestinian refugee *Al Fatah* guerilla teams who crossed from their territory to conduct terror attacks on Israeli settlements and infrastructure. In 1955 alone, Israel claimed the attacks by Al Fatah's *Fedayeen* fighters killed 260 of her citizens. Palestinian militants soon coalesced into larger organizations. Israel contributed to ill will when she abruptly occupied the small al-Awja demilitarized zone on the Sinai border (the principal invasion point into Sinai), and increased intelligence gathering and espionage in surrounding countries.

In response to the growing threat, Israel adopted a policy of "active defense" with cross-border retaliation, usually out of proportion to the provocation to deter further aggression and encourage national authorities to reign in the Palestinians. The shelling and special forces reprisal raids typically targeted training camps and other military targets, but frequently these could not be separated from civilians and their property. These challenges emphasized the need for a competent army at a high state of readiness. However, except for the commandos, the IDF did not then generally reflect these qualities. Israel moved to improve the overall quality of its army and additional funding was allocated.

A Cub flying above attendees at the unveiling of a memorial to a paratrooper at Kibbutz Ma'agan, crashed into the crowd. The accident claimed 17 lives with 15 persons injured. An unofficial aerobatic team of flight instructors had practiced on Harvards before putting on a demonstration for high school students visiting Ramat David on August 18, 1954, flying Mustangs. Two of the aircraft collided before the horrified teenagers, with both pilots perishing. The aerobatic team was suspended for four years before another formal effort was sanctioned, though then with P-51s. Such mishaps plus operational accidents did not inspire deep respect for the IAF during this period.

The IAF was first committed to supporting the cross-border skirmishes only in 1951.[29] The international outcry was sometimes harsh and foreign arms deals would occasionally be suspended for a time in reaction to air action. Consequently, the Israeli government avoided employing airpower in retaliatory operations as it would appear to be overly aggressive. However, during this time the IAF began bold incursions into the Sinai and the Gaza Strip, testing Egyptian reaction time and seeking to engage REAF aircraft. The Israelis became known for aggressively defending their own airspace, with several unfortunate episodes against commercial air traffic in addition to opposition air forces. These defense policies earned her few international friends. Israel learned to be independent and resist outside pressures where it undermined security.

Egypt expanded its practice of brief penetrations by combat aircraft into Israeli territory, photographing installations, checking for gaps in radar coverage, and testing reaction time. A Quick Reaction Alert (QRA) was established with the IAF's new Meteors to promptly respond to the violations. It was not long before these air elements came into contact. The first aerial engagements since

With a slow start, the IAF's Meteor jet fleet grew to include the F.8 fighter. Though a dated type by the time the Israelis had equipped front-line units, the service made the most of the fighter. This Ramat David AB shot from October 27, 1953, pictures the leading jet pilots of the period with (kneeling left to right) Yosef 'Joe' Alon and Danny Shapira, and (standing left to right) Yaacov 'Yak' Nevo, Benjamin 'Beni' Peled, Aharon Yoeli, Menachem Bar (117 Squadron commander), and Abraham Yoffe. (Ra'anan Weiss Collection)

Until the mid-1950s there was little air action associated with the continuing border tensions. This changed when Syrian forces challenged Israeli sovereignty over the demilitarized zone and killed seven border guards. In retaliation, four Spitfires from 105 Squadron bombed the Syrian police fort at El Hama (Hammat Gadder) on April 5, 1951. The bombs seemed to fall everywhere, but on the target, and four 101 Squadron P-51s finally scored with rockets. The confrontation continued when Syrian troops occupied high ground on the Israeli side of the ceasefire line. After a few days of battle, it was decided to call for air support on May 6. No one at IAF headquarters would approve an armed attack, so four of 105's Spitfires, on a training flight, made 18 dry passes on the enemy until the Syrians withdrew. When one pilot fired on the troops, ground fire was returned and all four airplanes were slightly damaged. Despite the poor results, the negative international response to these actions led the government to consider airpower too provocative. It would be years before the Air Force was called on for such support again.

1949, and the region's first jet combat, occurred in fall 1955 with an EAF Vampire falling to a Meteor.

Until 1955, the Arab states were in no condition to wage war with Israel, but the sustained confrontation suited their ends. Israel desired cessation of the festering hostilities but did not have the political means to bring the Arabs to serious negotiation nor the international backing to force a decisive conclusion via war. Both sides had internal politics that made serious negotiations nearly impossible. The Arab's resentment of continued Western military presence in the Middle East, and the reluctance to sell arms in the region, led them into the Soviet camp. Consequently, in September 1955, Egypt purchased massive quantities of weapons from Czechoslovakia, with the approval of the Soviet Union. This included 86 MiG-15 and MiG-17 fighters, 39 Il-28 jet bombers, plus hundreds of tanks and artillery pieces. A similar deal was also made with Syria that included 100 MiG-15s.

The scale of the "Czech arms deal" was a shock to Israel as it dramatically tilted the quantitative and technological qualitative balance of power away from the small state. Israel was compelled to make sudden and sizable financial commitments to enlarge and better equip its armed forces. The West felt a need to restore the balance in the region and Israel soon found its requests for arms meeting with more success. Although several options were pursued, most were blocked by America or Britain who initially still urged compliance with the arms embargo. However, France ultimately agreed to sell warplanes and other armaments to Israel. Apart from the economic incentive and growing its arms industries, this also served as punishment to Egypt for its aid to the rebels in the French colony of Algeria. An agreement to purchase French jets had actually been signed prior the Czech arms deal, but it was quickly expanded.

Egypt may have sought the Czech weapons largely to help quell Israeli's border activity, but the West saw it as a decisive move into the Soviet sphere. The United States and Britain subsequently withdrew their promised financial assistance for building the Aswan High Dam, a project critical for ensuring Egypt's future economic viability. This had the effect of further driving Egyptian President Gamal Abdel Nasser into the arms of the USSR. The introduction of a Cold War dimension into the conflict shifted the strategic equation significantly for the next 40 years.

Within the span of a year, the IAF underwent a remarkable transformation in taking on two squadrons of current French fighters. The IAF chose to immediately acquire 24 Ouragans (standard squadron quantity) while awaiting production of the swept-wing and supersonic (in a dive) Mystère IVA that the Israelis would dub "MIVA." The straight-wing Ouragan was no match for the MiG-15, but was simple, had a good punch with its four 20-mm cannons, and could carry a reasonable assortment of air-to-ground ordnance. It also introduced the IAF to g-suits enabling 7-g maneuvering versus the Meteor's 4-g. The machines came from *Armée de l'Air* squadrons, though still fairly new. They went to 113 Squadron, formed in October 1955 and mission-ready in December. The 24 Mystères filled the re-established 101 beginning in April 1956 and operational in May. Its two heavy-hitting 30-mm weapons were much admired, with good rate-of-fire.

The French largess also included three Nord Noratlas "flying boxcars" bought as a concession for help in securing the first jet fighter order. The IAF had not wished to spend precious funds on transports while getting along well enough with Dakotas. However, the Nords presented a significant improvement in performance and payload with easy onload/offload through rear clamshell doors. The configuration also supported efficient airdrop.

The planned and actual acquisition of updated hardware allowed many of the older airplanes to go into reserve status or retirement. The Mosquitos were in particularly poor shape and so sent into inactive reserve with the aircraft stored. Meteors took over fighter pilot OTU and so many Mustangs were also stored. The reserve 116 Squadron would employ any reactivated 51s in an emergency, flown by School instructors.[30]

The Ouragan was a current type when the French agreed to sell them to Israel – a novelty for the up-to-then poorly equipped force. The small jet was relatively simple and had a good air-to-ground capability, all consistent with IAF philosophy of the period. This example wears 107 Squadron markings, a unit that took on the Ouragan in 1964. (BIAF – Israel Aerospace Magazine)

CHAPTER 4
SINAI CAMPAIGN

Israel's need to greatly set back the Fatah terror attacks from Egyptian territory, combined with British and French desire to retain control of the strategic Suez Canal, ran headlong into burgeoning Arab nationalism. This sparked a war few wanted, but from which only Israel benefitted – albeit briefly. Her Air Force performed well and extracted many valuable lessons.

Intensifying

The tit-for-tat routine of military skirmishes continued on the Egyptian-Israeli frontier into 1956. Aerial reconnaissance intrusions became more frequent and dogfights would occasionally develop. The IAF usually emerged victorious from such clashes. The Ouragans assumed the QRA role and brought down a Vampire in April. However, life for Israelis living near the border was becoming intolerable.

The need for revenue to fund the Aswan High Dam project prompted the Egyptian leader to nationalize of the Suez Canal in July. Great Britain and France both considered a Canal under international control essential to their commerce and national defense. They immediately began planning to neutralize Egyptian defenses and seize the waterway. When the Israelis learned of this, they saw an opportunity to use the emergency as a means of relieving the threat from Egypt's new arsenal and from Fedayeen attacks. The three countries also wished for a change to a more moderate government. The Allies welcomed Israeli participation and joint planning began in October. The French also saw benefits in operating from Israeli bases.

Israel hoped that a confrontation might also end Egypt's closure of the Straits of Tiran at the entrance to the Gulf of Aqaba and so controlling sea access to Israel's southern port of Eilat. Although an unacknowledged fact until September 1955, that month Nasser made it confrontational with guns commanding the passage. The Israelis had developed a plan to seize and open the blockaded straits. This was to include a paratroop assault on Sharm el-Sheikh at the southern tip of Sinai Peninsula, an armored force moving down the Sinai's almost trackless eastern shore to relieve them, and a preemptive airstrike to destroy the Egyptian Air Force's (EAF) offensive airpower that might intervene. Even if launched before the Egyptians fully integrated their new arms, the operation was risky given the IDF's readiness as it stood at that time and the difficult terrain for vehicles to cross. It was never approved.

Israel's principal role in the new planning was to create justification for Allied intervention. She would attack Egyptian forces in the Sinai, giving the appearance of another large-scale retaliatory raid. This incursion and Egyptian response would be held up as posing a threat to the Canal. The Allies would then demand that the combatants disengage and withdraw from proximity to the Canal, a demand Egypt would naturally reject. This would prompt the Allies to suppress the EAF and to land troops in order to secure the canal zone. Zahal would work to destroy enemy forces in the Sinai, greatly reducing Egyptian ability to seriously threaten Israeli security.

The agreement to work with France and Britain won Israel a promise of $80 million more arms. As part of this, another 37 Mystère IVA and six Ouragans arrived secretly in August, just weeks before the war. The IAF lacked sufficient trained pilots and maintainers to operate all these aircraft. Despite a frantic conversion effort, the 101 Squadron had just 21 pilots and so only 16 Mystère were operational on D-Day. Some pilots flew combat missions with just a few hours logged in the jet and never having fired the cannons. The 117 Squadron was undermanned and could not fill all its Meteor seats owing to personnel transferred to the new French jets. The 119 had just gotten its first night-fighters and was not ready for operations, so its pilots went to other mounts. The IAF's regular manpower strength was less than 3,000, with 133 pilots, but expanded to 12,000 personnel with 300 pilots upon mobilization.[31] France also responded to Israel's critical need for bombs, rockets and cannon shells, with shipments just days before hostilities commenced.

One of the IAF's new Mystère IVAs patrols above Sinai during the 1956 war with Egypt. Only 101 Squadron at Hatzor AB was operational on the type, although all its personnel were still just becoming familiar with the jet. It had insufficient aircrew to man all aircraft and so some were operated by French personnel. (Ra'anan Weiss Collection)

The IAF activated its reserve of piston-engine fighters. The 110 worked to restore Mosquitos to operational status. The 116 Squadron was activated at Tel Nof AB to operate P-51Ds pulled from storage while 105 operated from Ramat David. Two of the B-17Gs were made operational with a core of 69 Squadron mobilized. This pair was the only platform for delivering heavy bomb loads on distant targets, especially at night. Trainers and associated reserve units were prepared for their wartime missions of light ground attack or liaison. The Dakota numbers, key for airdrop, were augmented with 10 leased from France.

The MoD's concern that the IAF might be incapable of seizing and maintaining air superiority while supporting ground operations, especially given the better-equipped EAF, saw the airmen being assigned a supporting role in the coming war. There was fear of Egyptian bombs raining down on Israeli cities from Il-28s while the Air Force was off fighting in the Sinai and during the 36 hours before the Allies began neutralizing Egyptian airfields. This prompted Prime Minister and Defence Minister Ben Gurion to request that French squadrons be based in Israel to protect against a surprise attack. Despite some IAF dissension, the French subsequently established a command presence at Ramleh

AB and brought into the country two fighter squadrons plus a dozen pilots to operate Israeli Mystères. The French aircraft were given Israeli markings and the pilots issued IAF identification cards. France also operated eight Noratlases at Tel Nof, though with Israeli navigators. The anti-aircraft artillery (AAA) defenses were strengthened with the deployment of French batteries.

The ORBAT for the 1956 war:

Eilat	
100 Flight D	(4) Cub
Hatzor (Wing 4)	
101 First Fighter	49 Mystère IVA (1 photo-recce, only 28 operated, 12 by French crews)
113 Hornet	29 Ouragan (7 u/s)
Lod (Base 27)	
200*	(18) F-84F (French detachment)
Ramat David (Wing 1)	
69 The Hammers	2 B-17
100 Flight B	(2) Cub
105 Scorpion	13 P-51
110 Knights of the North	13 Mosquito FB.6 and TR.33
119 Bat	3 Meteor NF.13 (1 u/s), unit not initially considered operational
199*	(18) Mystère IVA (French detachment)
201*	(12) Mystère IVA (IAF assets flow by French pilots)
Ramleh	
100 Flying Camel	13 Cub (Flight A)[32], 1 Hiller 360
147	(25) Stearman (reserve, detached from the Flying School)
Sde Dov (Base 15)	
128	2 Pacer (mobilized Police assets)
Sde Teiman (emergency field near Beersheba)	
100 Flight C	(11) Cub
140	(22) Harvard (reserve, detached from Flying School)
Tel Nof (Wing 22)	
103 Flying Elephant	3 Noratlas (1 u/s), 18 C-47 (10 leased from France, 2 mobilized Arkia assets), 1 Constellation (mobilized El Al asset), 2 S-55 (not operated)
203*	(8) Noratlas (owned and operated by France)
115	3 Meteor T.7 (photo-recce), 2 Mosquito PR.16 (photo-recce)
116 Flying Wing	16 P-51
117 First Jets	11 Meteor F.8 and F.9 (deployed from Ramat David)
Flying School	25 Harvard, 38 Stearman, 3 Consul
* temporary identifications	247 total aircraft (minus French and mobilized assets)

(u/s = unserviceable)

Considering just the EAF, the IAF faced an enemy of greater number and, many thought, superior equipment. Egypt fielded about 60 MiG-15 and a handful of MiG-17 fighters along with about 75 older Meteor and Vampire jets. In the larger confrontation were hundreds of Arab aircraft of generally modern vintage, including the MiG-15 that had proven effective in North Korea against aircraft similar to the bulk of the IAF fleet. Egypt, Syria, and

This Mosquito PR.16, 115 Squadron's 2190, had an accident upon returning to Tel Nof after a reconnaissance mission over Syria during or soon after the war. The "photo-Mossies" were among the first long-range camera ships in the IAF and began the tradition of these hazardous missions over surrounding states. These were among the last of the Mosquitos in service at the time of the Suez Campaign. Note the "invasion stripes" on the starboard wing. (Shlomo Aloni Collection)

Commander

5th Commander – Dan Tolkowsky was the first pilot to be named IAF commander when, in May 1953, the IDF command staff felt that aviators had reached sufficient command experience to be considered to head their own organization. However, the General Staff hesitated over whether an officer with only a flying background was suitable. Hence, he remained a colonel for a year before promotion to general at just 32 years of age. Tolkowsky was a sabra but was educated in England as an engineer before joining the RAF where he was commissioned and flew Spitfires. After helping acquire aircraft in the UK, he flew as a B-17 crewman during the War of Independence while also serving in the Air HQ. He subsequently held senior staff posts before being appointed CO. He led at the beginning of the French Era of equipment and saw the force through the Sinai Campaign. Tolkowsky was also known for ensuring readiness during periods of relative calm with such measures as Quick Reaction Alert backed by central control with improved radar coverage employing new French gear. The first CO to be permitted to choose his successor, he retired after a MoD posting.

Still as a colonel, though Air Force commander, Dan Tolkowsky stands before a Spitfire he flew in 1955 as the type was being ushered out of 105 Squadron. (Ofer Zidon Collection)

Jordan joined their military structures under a joint command in late October and Egyptian air and army elements were transferred to Jordan. The IAF was prepared to strike at enemy airfields to establish air superiority, but the nation's leadership did not want to risk them in this manner, leaving the task to the Allies.

Tested

The IDF began mobilizing on October 25. The principal objectives were invasion of the Sinai to destroy the Fedayeen presence there and in the Gaza Strip, and seizing Sharm el-Sheikh to relieve the blockade of Eilat. This would begin with a large-scale paratroop assault deep in the Sinai to establish the "threat" to the canal. The IAF's role was then to provide transport and resupply for the advancing Zahal troops while flying air cover and supporting attack missions for the ground forces. The Air Force was to patrol no closer than 10 miles (16 km) east of the canal. This, it was hoped, would limit the Egyptians' initial response.

Operations began on the morning of the 28th. The Egyptian chief-of-staff (also commander-in-chief of the joint Arab command), with much of his staff, was flying to Damascus in an Il-14 and a C-47. The Israelis decided to shoot down the airplanes to sow confusion in the enemy's upper ranks. A pair of Mystères were sent out and vectored to the contacts, but they failed to intercept.[33] Another opportunity presented itself that night when the entourage returned to Egypt. This would be a night intercept by the new 119 Squadron and its NF.13 Meteors. The commander and his radar operator had never before conducted an actual intercept and the radar had to be calibrated in the hours before setting out. The target was the Il-14 and the mission was successful in secretly intercepting and destroying the transport over the Mediterranean. However, the intelligence was faulty. Although there were senior officers aboard, there were also journalists among the passengers. The chief-of-staff was aboard a C-47 delayed in Damascus. The operation remained secret for the next 33 years.

Reconnaissance sorties on the morning of the 29th found an Egyptian encampment on the western approaches to the Mitla Pass in western Sinai, objective of the paratroop drop, causing the drop zone to be shifted to the eastern entrance. In the afternoon, two pairs of P-51s cut telephone lines strung between poles in the Sinai to slow the Egyptian command's response time. Towed weighted cables had been devised for the task, but this failed to provide conclusive results – breaking away on initial contact. The pilots then improvised and cut the line with propellers and wingtips. Another pair of Mustangs repeated this the next morning.

What became known as the Sinai Campaign began in earnest with the late afternoon drop of a 395-man battalion by 16 C-47s – the largest airborne assault in the IDF's history. The low-level formation was escorted by a relay of fighters at higher altitude. Two other Dakotas were prepared to make a diversionary drop of dummy jumpers, but those sorties were cancelled after a Meteor flight along the Sinai coast elicited no reaction from the Egyptians. A navigational error placed the paratroops 2.5 miles

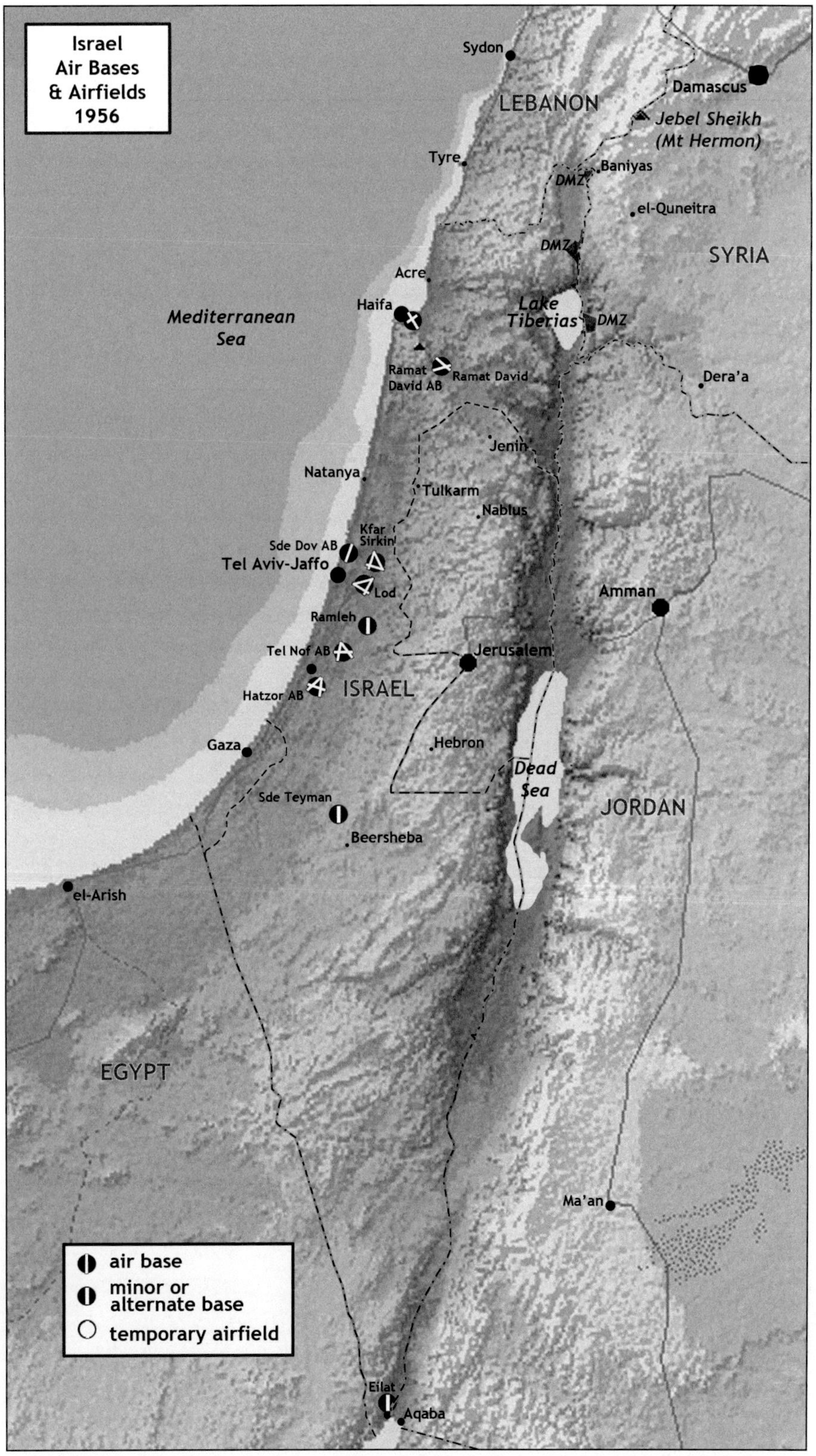

This map depicts the locations of the IAF air bases and other fields employed during the Sinai Campaign. (Author)

After struggling for its nearly decade-long existence to acquire a functional night-fighter capability, the IAF began operating dated Meteor NF.13s just as the 1956 war began. The one aircrew and airplane successfully downed an Egyptian transport just before the start of the outbreak, targeting high-level military personnel. The image from May 1957 shows 119 Squadron personnel beside one of their NF.13s at Ramat David. (Ra'anan Weiss Collection)

(4.0 km) east of the intended drop zone. The force marched to their objective, 25 miles (40 km) from the canal. After sunset, IAF and French airlifters made follow-up airdrops at Mitla that included ammunition and additional personnel. More replenishment airdrops followed the next night.

One of the principal objectives of the ground campaign was to rapidly reinforce the Mitla battalion, roughly 156 miles (251 km) beyond the border. Because of the poor roads and difficulty supplying the advancing force, airdrops were expanded to this and other IDF elements on the move. These were night operation as transport flights over the Sinai in daylight were not permitted until November 2. After that date, the transports and Cubs were also able to land at impromptu airlift centers, on hardpan, to bring in supplies and evacuate wounded. This included servicing the Mitla force that got itself into a significant battle. On the night of October 31, three Daks, their crews defying orders, landed on the small airstrip cleared by the paratroopers and lit by flares. They evacuated 100 critically wounded men, flying out over-gross. Egyptian airfields overrun in the Sinai were also quickly turned to use by IAF transports.

Having gotten wind of an imminent Anglo-French operation, Nasser pulled half of his Sinai forces back to the west bank just before the war began. Consequently, the major IDF thrusts crossing the border were numerically and qualitatively superior to the opposing Egyptian elements. Except for a standing Combat Air Patrol (CAP) over Mitla, though with a 30-minute gap between flights, a substantial portion of the IAF remained on standby during the first two days to deal with the potential of a strong response from the EAF. Apart from interdicting an Egyptian force heading for Mitla, Close Air Support (CAS) and other airstrikes were forbidden during this period to ensure that the IAF concentrated on air defense.

To Israel's dismay, the Anglo-French bombing and landings were delayed 13 hours until the evening of the 31st. However, it had become clear that attacks on Israel proper would not be forthcoming. Consequently, the whole of the IAF was released by noon on the 31st in response to the clamor for air support given attacks on Zahal troops by the EAF. Both combatants were making good airstrikes and engaging in counter-air missions, although the IAF was much more active and effective. Of note were Mosquitos making night strikes on Egyptian columns illuminated by flares, and a Meteor night attack on El Arish airfield. This was about the extent of IAF night ground-attack capabilities. Mosquito and Meteor reconnaissance was also vital in tracking enemy movements and checking whether other confrontation states were mobilizing. French air assets in Israel also contributed to the attacks in the canal area – the only known instance of foreign combat teams operating from Israeli soil.

On October 30, the Allies issued their ultimatum for Israel and Egypt to withdraw combat units from within 10 miles (16 km) of the Canal. When the Allies began their attacks on the air bases the next evening, the EAF dispersed its aircraft and its operations in the Sinai ceased. Facing a dual threat and the possibility that its elements on the peninsula might be cut off, that evening Nasser ordered all troops pulled back to the Suez. This was before the majority of the units had been engaged. The IAF and French air assets then focused on destroying these elements as they withdrew across the desert, but they escaped decisive defeat. This cost aircraft struck by ground fire. The first attack by 140 Squadron Harvards saw all aircraft hit, with the squadron commander killed outright and another aircraft making a crash landing. The strong IDF pressure had the Israelis in effective possession of the Sinai within approximately 100 hours of crossing the fence.

In advance of an IDF column struggling down the west coast to reach Sharm el-Sheikh, the IAF began attacking the defending

The Ouragan was slow and unsuited for combat against the MiGs the Egyptians had fielded. However, it had good air-to-ground capability and so performed effective interdiction and support attack missions. This example, presumably a 113 Squadron machine at Hatzor AB, is armed with rockets and napalm bombs. (Ra'anan Weiss Collection)

A forward logistics center was prepared at Sharm el-Sheikh after its capture. Here one of the IAF's first Noratlases and two Dakotas are shown at the location on November 6. The foreground C-47 carries a radar pod under the nose supporting maritime search and navigator training. All three aircraft wear the "invasion stripes" markings Allied aircraft wore during the 1956 war. (BIAF – Israel Aerospace Magazine)

Egyptian forces but suffered from effective AA fire. Preparing to assault the port, Dakotas collected 175 paratroopers from Mitla and took them to Tel Nof AB to make ready for another combat jump. That night, November 2, four C-47s dropped a company at El Tor airfield, about 60 miles (97 km) northwest of Sharm. In short order they secured the location and were ready to receive flights. Three aircraft bound for Sharm with another company diverted to El Tor after the port was determined to still be held by the enemy, making a jump too hazardous. They were reinforced that night by transport flights into the field deploying an infantry brigade and an airfield support team. Zahal then pressed an assault on Sharm from two directions. The seizure of Sharm el-Sheikh on November 4 opened the Straits of Tiran.

A ceasefire was declared on November 8, 1956, after 11 days of combat, although the last IAF attack mission was flown on the 5th.

All Told

The Israeli Air Force had conducted an effective and professional campaign despite its transitional state. It flew 1,846 sorties during the eight days of fighting, of which 831 were liaison (the Cubs seemed to be everywhere), 192 by large transports, 42 reconnaissance, 262 CAP, and 489 interdiction and CAS. Some 1,200 casualties were evacuated by air. The service managed an average daily sortie rate of 4.0 to 4.5 with the jets and 2.5 with the piston-powered combat aircraft. The two available NF.13s sat QRA and flew three unsuccessful night intercepts after October 28. The Mitla airdrop and seizure of Sharm el-Sheikh were partly or wholly made possible via airlift, and the IDF would surely have suffered more from enemy air attacks but for fighter cover. There were numerous instances where IAF strikes relieved pressure on hard-pressed friendly troops or turned back opposition reinforcements. Therefore, although the Air Force contribution was not considered decisive in the execution or outcome of the war, its performance earned it more respect than previously.

Much personal initiative was displayed on the part of IAF aircrew and commanders. Sound training underlay an ability to adapt. Pilots frequently flew into an area and only then received final target identification from a ground controller integrated with the troops. This permitted the most effective strikes with the very latest tactical information. Some attacks, especially with guns and rockets, were made within 100 feet (31 m) of friendly forces, but this was rare. The service chose to focus on interdiction as the most efficient use of airpower. Night activities were quite limited except for airdrops, though navigation was challenging to some of those crews and several failed to locate their drop points. Yet, such missions are notable as a rare capability for so small a service. Reconnaissance appeared to be timely, with missions generated fairly quickly and images available within a few hours of the flight's return. The liaison support was remarkable, with Stearmans delivering personnel all over Israel and Cubs all across the Sinai. Some physiological warfare was also undertaken, examples being a C-47 equipped with loudspeakers flying over Egyptian enclaves to undermine the messages from Cairo, and others dropping leaflets.

On the deficiency side, communications and control functions were sometimes overwhelmed, and radar coverage poor or unreliable. Air control radio traffic to aircraft over western Sinai had to pass through two Dakota relays.[34] The small number of frontline jet fighters and their relatively short endurance did not allow sufficient standing patrols. Many jets returned in critical fuel states. The Air Force was unable to prevent EAF fighters from executing effective sorties over the Sinai and a few penetrations of Israeli airspace by Il-28s that were, nonetheless, ineffectual. The Air Force was also unable to prevent the reinforcement of the Egyptian elements at Mitla and other troop movements, and there were several instances of attacks on own forces.

The Air Force's Super Cubs could land on much of the open pan of the Sinai, but most especially the roads that commanded the desert battlefield. This permitted ready communication with advancing elements of the IDF, the transportation of senior personnel, and evacuation of wounded. This aircraft, 53 photographed on November 2, 1956, appears to have had a tall antenna raised above it after landing. (Israeli Air Force via Lon Nordeen)

The EAF never made a concerted effort against the IDF campaign before essentially surrendering the sky when the Allies began to strike its bases. In 14 air-to-air engagements, the IAF reported destroyed two MiG-15s, a MiG-17, and four Vampires, plus a MiG-15 and MiG-17 damaged, with no loss to themselves. All the victories were by 101's Mystères. A MiG shot down one Piper and another was destroyed on the ground by MiG gunfire. Two Ouragans were damage in air combat, one making a belly landing with fuel exhaustion following the engagement.

The greatest threat to IAF operations was ground fire that cost the IAF eight P-51Ds, two Mosquitos, two Harvards, and a MIVA. The Dassault loss also occasioned the first IAF ejection from an airplane. Compared with the IDF's 171 men killed, four pilots were killed (including two squadron COs), two wounded, and one captured. The effective ground fire saw 28 other aircraft coming away damaged during ground attack missions, including over a quarter of the P-51 fleet. The B-17s executed only four missions after November 1 while others were aborted. The AT-6s only fought for two days, flying 24 sorties, before being withdrawn owing to attrition and low effectiveness.[35]

The Anglo-French airstrikes against equipment and installations accomplished much, with an estimated 230 to 260 EAF aircraft destroyed on the ground. Coming late, the delay allowed the international community time to rally and bring pressure to end the fighting before the Allies had achieved their objectives. The European forces were compelled to withdraw from the canal zone in December and the Israelis to quit the Sinai and Gaza Strip in March 1957. A commitment by the UN to station troops in the Sinai to act as a buffer between Israel and Egypt was instrumental in securing the pullout. Zahal left only after destroying any infrastructure of military value. Despite agreeing to allow Israeli shipping to transit the Suez Canal, the Egyptians again imposed their ban in 1959.

On the night of November 6/7, 1956, at the end of the Sinai Campaign, Sergeant Binyamin Gordon was flying 4X-AEQ (mobilized police Piper PA-20 Pacer) with the Southern Command CO, Brigadier General Assaf Simchoni and his aide, Lieutenant Colonel Asher Dromi. They were returning from Sharm el-Sheikh to the center of the country via a refueling stop in Eilat. The aircraft strayed into Jordanian airspace and was shot down with all aboard killed. The Israelis initially said that it had crashed into high terrain.

The Mustang performed invaluable close air support during the war but suffered greatly from returning ground fire. Several were left in the Sinai sands like this one. The October 31 crash landing of this 116 Squadron plane saw the pilot, Eldad Paz, become the only IAF prisoner of the Egyptians during the war. (Author's Collection)

Two of the three stored B-17s were made serviceable and flew a handful of bombing missions during the war. Their impact was hardly worth the effort and they were thereafter fully retired. Aircraft 1603/23 of 69 Squadron, at Ramat David AB, has bombs loaded under the inboard wing stations and still carries the APS-4 radar pod attached to permit sea patrol operations. (BIAF – Israel Aerospace Magazine)

CHAPTER 5
SEEKING AN EDGE

Following the Sinai Campaign, regional tensions persisted and the military threat to Israel grew anew. The IDF, and the Air Force in particular, had to become more professional and adopt increasingly complex and costly weapons in the event another round of war ensued. The IAF soon had a reputation for secretiveness and for boldness bordering on reckless, but also high morale with modest attention to military standards.

Sophistication and Identity

The Israeli Air Force's greatest concern continued to be the much greater number of opposition aircraft. It could only respond by working to train the highest caliber personnel operating modern equipment and by preparing to execute the strategy of preemption. Should surrounding states threaten Israel with imminent war, the IDF/AF would respond with an overwhelming first strike to destroy the enemy air forces on the ground. The hazard of bombing raids into Israel and airstrikes against her mechanized ground forces would thus be greatly reduced. The IAF could then provide the greatest attention to assisting the ground campaign designed to quickly overwhelm and destroy enemy forces with lightening armored blows.

Much needed to be done preparing to put such an ambitious plan into action, and the IAF received priority for continued modernization. This eventually consumed half of the expanding defense budget. However, the economy was growing robustly and so revenue became available. Still, Israel never bought as much as the Air Force sought. What they did get were protected as hardened aircraft shelters (HAS) began to be constructed and most ground-based air defenses were stationed at air bases. Base infrastructure began to be improved with hydrant fuel delivery systems and underground command centers. Air bases were also camouflaged, to include painting runways.

The 1956 war exposed the need to improve command, control, and communications (C^3). The radar network and other infrastructure for centralized control of air operations took some time to establish, but benefitted from French and American equipment.[36] The principal air traffic control center was established atop Mt. Meron in the north, the highest point in the country. In time, control was divided into three regional sectors, centered on Meron, Mitzpe Ramon in the south, and the center near Jerusalem.[37] A Central Command Unit controlled both intercept and ground attack assets enhancing all-weather fighting capabilities.[38] All operational elements soon adapted to the new measures.

Communications between ground units and air assets was improved to permit quick response to calls for support or respond to enemy airstrikes. However, calls from a FAC or other battlefield sources had to pass through central control and aircraft then vectored by sector.[39] The FAC could radio the aircraft once overhead.[40] To improve coordination with other elements of the IDF, the AHQ was relocated in 1959 to the Kiryah, the MoD compound in Tel Aviv. That same year, Sde Dov was reclaimed as a joint civilian/military airfield and 100 Squadron transferred there to support the staff in Tel Aviv.

The growth of the force required more pilots, and training expanded proportionally. Only 17 cadets entered the flight-training course in 1957, but the next year there were 80. Major-General Ezer Weizman, who took command of the IAF in 1958, improved the course's rigor and content. It came to be known as among the most selective anywhere, washout rates averaging 80 percent. Along these lines was ensuring high quality instructors. This included making instructor duty at the school more attractive and a requisite step for promotion. Instructors and staff officers continued flying with an operational squadron at least once a week – something practical in such a small country where all airfields were a few hours' drive or brief light-plane flight apart. In the event of hostilities, these officers would fight with that unit as an Emergency Posting. Reservists also flew about once per week to retain suitable proficiency.

Under Weizman's leadership, the Air Force also made great strides at improving its professionalism, the quality of its personnel, and slowing the drain of qualified aircrew. Adopting the slogan "The Best for Pilots," he sought to attract the cream of draftees for aircrew training, even though pilots had to serve five years beyond the end of training versus the normal three for servicemen. Weizman worked to ensure there was good potential for career advancement, despite the small force, and to improve living conditions. He struggled to give the Air Force its own identity within the IDF and to foster unit pride. In these ways, he helped to ensure retention of sufficient highly qualified personnel.

The experience gained by many young officers in the Sinai Campaign paid dividends in the growth of leaders and revision of training. Experience was still critically low and so some aircrew were seconded to French squadrons to gain operational exposure – but principally because Israel could not afford to keep the pilots current.[41] Officers also went to French senior service schools, French personnel contributed at Israeli academies, and there were some joint exercises. As part of Israel's cultural and military outreach to emerging countries in the post-colonial era, the IAF was called on to transport materiel far beyond the borders and to also train foreign air force personnel. Some training was

> Major-General Ezer Weizman's insistence on unwavering standards in selection during pilot training was notorious. He said that if wash-outs meant too few pilots, then that was the sacrifice for holding the line. This came true. The course completed in June 1959 passed out just a single pilot of 17 cadets who had begun. Instead of the usual public "wings" ceremony where the graduates were anointed and there was a fly-by of airplanes, Weizman shared champaign in his office with the new pilot. While noteworthy, such training attrition did not meet IAF manning needs. More was done to select the right candidates at the beginning of the course along with suitable adjustments to the curriculum.

Commander

6th Commander – Ezer Weizman took command in July 1958 at age 34. A sabra, he was a former non-commissioned officer fighter pilot in the RAF during the Second World War. He flew with the Air Service from its earliest days, commanding several small units, before flying fighters again with the new IAF. He commanded 101 Squadron after the war before being sent to the RAF Command and Staff College. Upon returning, Weizman organized a like course for the IDF and established the IAF Staff School. He went on to command the Ramat David wing and was put in charge of aircraft acquisitions from France. During the Sinai Campaign, he commanded the Hatzor wing. In December 1956, Weizman became head of the Air Department at the AHQ, effectively deputy to Tolkowsky. Hence, it was natural for him to take command two years later. As IAF Commander, he worked to instill greater esprit and professionalism. He also pushed for a growth in the IAF to answer the burgeoning Arab forces and counted as his greatest achievement ushering the Mirage IIICJ into Israeli service. He also began the intense planning and training that lead to the successful pre-emptive strikes that initiated the Six-Day War of 1967. After leaving the Air Force, he headed the IDF General Staff Division (Operations Branch) as IDF Deputy Chief-of-General-Staff but was not selected for the top post. His subsequent political career eventually led to Minister of Defence and then President.

Colonel Ezer Weizman was commander of the Ramat David Wing at the time he was photographed in 1955 escorting the Israeli President Yitzhak Ben Tzvi during a review of this Air Force honor guard. We was named IAF commander in 1958. (Ofer Zidon Collection)

performed at home and some in the distant lands, primarily in Africa. The experience usually benefitted both parties.

The IAF continued to seek a two-to-one ratio of pilots-to-warplanes and to generate sorties at a high rate by rapidly turning the aircraft for the next sortie. Reservists were fewer in the top-of-the-line squadrons to help ensure the greatest readiness and proficiency. Training and preparedness throughout the ranks were boosted to improve overall performance. Competitions were held to provide goals and foster an aggressive spirit. Despite the more central control that specified store loadings, routes, and timetables, aircrew and commanders were encouraged to lead by example, take the initiative, motivate their team, think creatively, and be bold if not aggressive.

Quick Reaction Alert was maintained for all missions including ground attack, reconnaissance, plus search and rescue (SAR).[42] The task rotated between squadrons and some flights were flown to forward locations to stand alert. Air bases were made further independent and the movement of personnel between assignments carried along successful practices. The IDF continued to be known as lax in dress and courtesies, to have an exceptionally young cadre of leaders, and for almost reckless behavior.

The preemptive airstrike became the focus of IAF training by 1963. The outline of a principal Egyptian airfield was made with black pitch in a remote area of the Negev where air-to-ground gunnery was practiced against dummy aircraft and facilities.[43] This was repeated until the pilots could hit their targets on one pass with a minimum of shells or bombs expended. The IAF adopted the four-ship as its basic ground attack formation vice the earlier two-ship, although the latter was retained for QRA and CAP. Support of ground forces also remained a major focus. The FAC practice was improved with better communication and cooperation via a coordination unit. Close Air Support was honed to an extent that aircraft could confidently hit enemy elements in contact with Zahal troops. Tanks began to be equipped with spotlights. Two or three of

The small size of Israel and its adjacent conflict zones permitted and demanded the Air Force maintain tight monitoring of all air operations. The IAF had a standard for decades of command over air combat from centers such as this one (image dating from the 1970s or 1980s). The IAF Commander himself would commonly be present to personally direct an engagement and to decide when it was to be broken off. (Author's Collection)

these illuminating a target from different angles could be enough for pilots to find and bomb the objective.

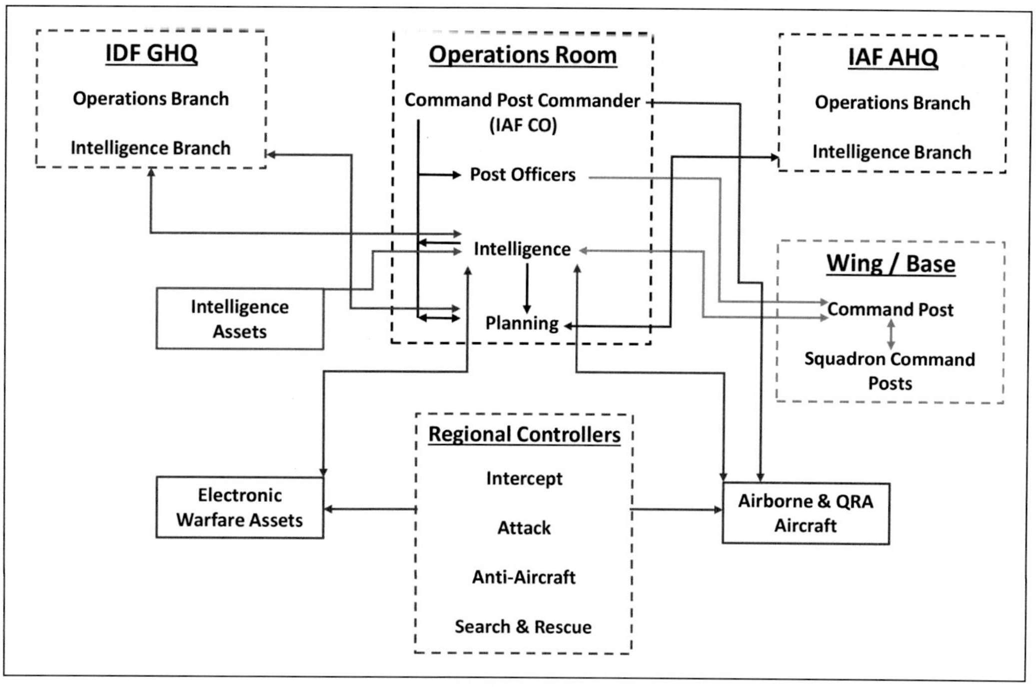

This is was the IAF operations command and control system circa 1960s and 1970s. Note the central role of Intelligence and the importance of electronic warfare, regional tasking of assets, and the IAF Commander's direct interaction with aircraft in action as Command Post Commander during an operation. (Author)

Rising Above

The 1956 war demonstrated the vulnerability of the piston-powered combat aircraft and plans to replace them were accelerated. France remained willing to provide factory new, up-to-date equipment to facilitate IAF modernization. Seeking an all-jet force, Meteors were turned to jet conversion and advanced training while Ouragans were employed in fighter pilot OTU. This firmly established the practice of second-tier warplanes and their units employed in training while retaining a combat mission.

Following the war, a second Mystère IVA squadron was created at Ramat David AB where the runway had to be extended to accommodate the aircraft. Flying with external tanks became common and teams began training for air-to-ground weapons delivery. Immediately after the war, Tolkowsky sought more MIVAs, but this was opposed by the MoD. Another war in the near future seemed unlikely and it was judged best to await newer types as combat aircraft technology was then advancing at a fast clip.

Acquisition of more advanced aircraft were slow due to budget constraints, but the French allowed the Israelis to evaluate their newest designs. The IAF was soon integrating a squadron of Super Mystère B2s ("SMB2"). Employing afterburner (new to the Israelis), it was capable of supersonic speed in level flight and could meet on equal terms the Soviet fighters being introduced by the opposition. Two 30-mm cannon were augmented with a 2,200-lb (998-kg) weapon load capacity matched with a fairly sophisticated bombsight. Therefore, although assuming the role of premier interceptor, the SMB2s were also to serve as multi-role machines once air superiority was gained. Consequently, air-to-ground tactics were among the training regimen. Also new was the braking parachute what was also added to the MIVA as it began to experience heavier take-off and landing weights with the greater assortment of tanks and bombs. Still, some runways had to be extended or airfield surfaces strengthen to accommodate the SMB2. A new advanced jet, it is not surprising that the Super Mystères had some "teething pains." The Israelis and the manufacturer worked through them.

Even with long-range fuel tanks, the French fighters could not carry a significant weapon load to distant airfields in Egypt or Iraq. A medium bomber – all Israel could afford – was needed and the French again offered a solution. The twin-engine Vautour had a

The Super Mystère B2 added a supersonic intercept capability along with a good air-to-ground loadout. However, anticipating the next newest French jet, only a single unit of the Super Mystères was purchased, equipping 105 Squadron at Hatzor AB. (Yoav Efrati Collection)

The French continued to sell the Israelis warplanes into the 1960s and so the fighter-bomber fleet was dominated by these types. Until 1962, these consisted of the trio shown with the Super Mystère IIB, Mystère IVA (aircraft 28 being a 101 Squadron machine) and the Ouragan. This French trio is on display at Hatzor AB during May 1960. (Ra'anan Weiss Collection)

1,900-mile (3,058 km) range on internal fuel with 4,000 lb (1,814 kg) of internal ordnance and 4,500 lb (2,041 kg) under-wing that allowed the IAF to place at risk very distant enemy bases. The Vautour would also provide a deterrent to Arab nations sending jet bombers over Israel via a creditable retaliatory capability – though Israel sought the Vautour before Il-28s were sold to Egypt. However, the aircraft were nearly $0.75 million each and so had to be procured at a slow pace and for a single squadron.

The Vautours' presence in Israel was kept secret for nearly a year, the aircraft not flown, principally to spare France from international recrimination and because of discord between French ministries. She also built unique Vautour IIA fighter-bombers and IIB reconnaissance variants for Israel. The IIBs were fitted with underwing racks to augment long-range attack capabilities. In service, the Vautour proved temperamental and challenging to fly, leading to mishaps that slowly eroded the fleet. The aircraft brought the IAF the first experience with braking parachutes and the engines deteriorated the asphalt cap on the runways such that the service had to transition to concrete.

The IAF acquired seven two-seat Vautour IIN models with night intercept radar. Even given the great expense, there was little hesitation in the purchase considering the need to answer the threat of nocturnal jet bombers. However, the range of Israeli early warning ground-based radar was still too short for sufficient warning allowing QRA night-fighters to intercept bombers at 40,000 feet (12,182 m) – as demonstrated on several occasions when opposition bombers performed photo-flash reconnaissance missions over Israeli facilities. The IIN's radar system was among the best of any operational combat aircraft at the time. Once the navigator locked the radar onto the target the pilot needed only to fly the blip to the center of his scope and the guns would fire automatically.

The 119, operating the Meteor NF.13s and the Vautour IINs, relocated to Tel Nof AB to react more quickly to EAF intrusions. For a few years, a IIN was on five-minute QRA every night. Given this mission, the aircraft's existence in Israel was classified. The 119 did succeed in intercepting several wayward airliners. One night engagement with gunfire against an intruding Il-28 failed to give positive results. The radar-controlled cannon fire of the IIN showed very poor accuracy during training.

Intending to develop expand Vautour IIN's utility with a night attack capability, bomb racks were installed on the aircraft. With the radar providing acceptable ground mapping images at up to 200-miles

Night fighters were boosted with the Vautour IIN operated by 119 Squadron at Tel Nof AB, as in this image from October 14, 1958. This was judged an essential dimension given Egypt's jet bombers flying nocturnal intrusions missions, but the Israelis never scored. This lineup has some Meteors in the background, operated for twin-engine proficiency. (BIAF – Israel Aerospace Magazine)

(322-km) range, it was possible to find and attack targets such as air bases. The Vautour could lead a formation of fighter-bombers. The IAF flew night reconnaissance missions over potential targets. Using a hand-held camera, the navigator photographed the radarscope image of the target and *en route* fixes. The photos were intended to help attack future crews identify their targets, especially air bases where harassment could disrupt preparations for the next day's operations. Alternatively, fighter-bombers could navigate to the target via dead-reckoning and – should it actually be found – identify the target in moonlight. The lead of a three-ship would drop parachute flares for the attack.[44] This method of attack, planned to be carried out at 5,000 feet (1,524 m), was abandoned as too hazardous after the Egyptians introduced Soviet SA-2 surface-to-air missiles (SAM) into the theater during 1963.[45]

The great concern about air defense of Israel, given the close proximity of adversary air forces equipped with fast jet bombers, was somewhat ameliorated when the Americans agreed to supply Hawk surface-to-air missiles. This was a major breakthrough in military equipment purchasing from the USA. Shown here in a 1965 image, the system was upgraded over the decades and served until about 2010. The SAM was active in all the wars with adjacent states and downed numerous enemy aircraft. (Israel GPO)

Looking at the enormous Arab arms buildup, with new air bases being built in the Sinai, Israel saw the potential for even more advanced Soviet warplanes being introduced like the Mach 2 MiG-21 fighter and the Tu-16 bomber. Any of those aircraft could dash across the borders and reach any point in Israel within 10 minutes. The IAF assessed it needed still more potent fighters. France was the only reasonable source and her developers were interested in IAF design input as Israel was the only nation employing French warplanes in a large way and in combat. Consequently, the IAF collaborated during development of the Mirage III, a delta-wing fighter with Mach 2 capability.

The Mirage IIIC appeared to depart from the IAF's dictum of multi-role fighters. However, the high-speed interceptor was modified as the IIICJ with additional fuel, weapons stations, and cannons. These Mirages were operated by 119 Squadron, likely deployed to Hatzerim AB for rapid response to Egyptian intrusions. (BIAF – Israel Aerospace Magazine)

The advantages of the Mirage, anticipated for years, meant that the SMB2 was always intended as a stopgap. Weizman dropped plans to expand the SM2B and Vautour fleets to focus available funds on the multi-mission Mirage and emphasize offense over defense. He wanted 100 Mirages to start with, and possibly a total of 200. The first quantity suggested $200 million, including spares and support equipment. Even voices in the IAF were questioning the wisdom of this move. The aircraft was conceived as a point defense interceptor, with an integral rocket booster to climb rapidly to the altitude of a bomber stream and engage with guided missiles. Suitably converting it to a fighter-bomber in line with IAF doctrine appeared questionable. Yet, the Israelis worked with Dassault towards this goal.

Coming soon after purchasing the SMB2s, the MoD would not consider buying any more warplanes immediately. The first order in 1960 was for 24 of the Mirage IIICJ variants. With favorable political winds and gifts of non-lethal aircraft from West Germany, the Mirage order was increased to 48 then 76. The Israeli J model differed in having simplified avionics, substituting a fuel tank for the rocket motor, two 30-mm cannon, plus external tanks and weapon stations. The cannon went against conventional wisdom that these were anachronisms. For the Israelis, it was a simple calculation of shells being much less expensive than missiles. Yet, the IAF hedged its bet and the Js had outboard hardpoints for air-to-air missile (AAM) rails.

As the Mirage was beginning to be introduced, the USSR provided MiG-21s to maintain the "balance." With persistent doubts that the IAF could adequately protect the country against the massed air forces of surrounding Arab states, the MoD also successfully sought Hawk surface-to-air missiles from the USA to augment defenses. Seeking to balance the capabilities of the adversaries, and with no foreign sources of SAMs to provide Israel, the USA agreed to the sale.

The Mirages began arriving in 1962 with 101 Squadron at Hatzor AB and 117 at Ramat David AB transitioning. Both units were combat ready by year-end, beginning a policy that new aircraft be operational in the shortest practical time. In 1964, the 119 took up Mirages at Tel Nof AB, placing a squadron of the premier fighter at the three geographic sectors of the country. It was not long before incidental engagements on the border allowed the Mirage to prove itself. Being a newly developed aircraft with unique features, the Mirage offered a number of growing pains that challenged the operators. The Israelis worked closely with Dassault to overcome these issues. The aircraft also brought with it the first UHF radios and so VHF sets in other aircraft and ground units had to be replaced over time.

The Israelis acquired a modest number of Matra R.530 radar-guided air-to-air missiles when buying the Mirage IIICJ. Uncertain of the effectiveness of conventional air combat techniques, they wanted to ensure they could destroy jet bombers beyond gunfire range. The Matra AAM was costly, heavy, and draggy, but it ensured the IAF kept up with current combat technology despite its comparatively small budget. One of the missiles is under 101 Squadron's aircraft 52. (Ra'anan Weiss Collection)

Several Soviet fighters fell into Israeli hands to provide opportunities for evaluation. A defecting Syrian pilot delivered a MiG-17 in 1965, allowing close examination and mock battles with IAF fighters. Much more valuable was a MiG-21 acquired in 1966 via the Israeli foreign intelligence agency, the Mossad, inducing an Iraqi pilot to defect with his aircraft and flight manual. The aircraft was used in mock engagements with all IAF fighter squadron leaders allowing the best way to defeat the jet to be identified. Likewise, a close examination located vulnerabilities to be exploited during engagements. The Mirage and MiG-21 were nearly evenly matched, so the knowledge from the captured jet combined with highly skilled pilots gave the IAF an advantage.

The all-weather Mirage was fitted with radar as standard equipment, and so the dedicated night-fighter became antiquated. The Vautour IINs' radar, although superior in some aspects, were removed and the aircraft became daylight attack jets (though lacking a true bomb bay). They joined the other Vautours in 110 Squadron. The second seat in the IIN and nose station in the IIB accommodated a navigator and so these aircraft led formations. Ultimately, however, the Mirage's Cyrano radar proved a disappointment and they were modified to provide just the simple ranging function. The Israelis attempted to develop an improved Cyrano, optimized for ground attack, but this was unsuccessful.

The IAF became familiar with air-to-air missiles that promised engagement at much greater range than cannon. They bought 40 early French missiles, the pilot-directed Nord 5103 (AA.20), for the SMB2, mostly just to become acquainted with the technology. The Mirage was equipped to fire a single Matra R.530 from the belly, equipped for semi-active radar homing. The IAF bought just 15 of these 429-lb (195-kg) missiles, at $50,000 each. It severely limited aircraft maneuverability, was complex and demanded very precise launch conditions, yet was largely ineffective. Although they got along well enough with gunfire at the time, Israel did begin developing a more practical and affordable AAM, similar to the infrared-guided (IR) AIM-9 Sidewinder that the Americans would not sell to the country.

The indigenous AAM was a product of Rafael, the acronym-derived name for the Armament Development Authority, subsidized by the MoD. At the time, only the Israelis thought they had any hope of developing a weapon at the leading edge of air combat technology. Work began in 1959 and the first in-flight firing was performed in 1962, including shots against maneuvering targets on a French test range. The IAF was so eager to obtain this Shafrir AAM that it placed an order for 200 in December 1962 even before testing had been completed. Flight trials produced mixed results and development continued. The missile was not available for service until late 1963 and, while intended for the fighters, also equipped Vautour IIB reconnaissance platforms. Even then, it was rushed into production before all of the "bugs" had been remedied. The full 200-unit order was never completed. Rounds may have been recalled one or more times for modifications, and refinement continued into 1964.

The Shafrir had a range of 1.9 to 2.5 miles (3.1 to 4.0 km) and its electronics were such that it could only be fired against a non-maneuvering target from an aft aspect. Throughout its service, the weapon suffered from low reliability, poor seeker head performance, and a too-small warhead. They began to be carried by Mirages in the latter half of 1963 and several were fired over the next few years without success. The follow-on Shafrir 2 began development in 1964.[46]

The Mirage represented the high-end fighter focused on intercept, though also equipped to take on attack missions once air superiority was achieved. It was matched with a large force of second-tier fighters focused on attack and operated where they were unlikely to meet opposition fighters. To bolster the ground attack force, the IAF bought an additional 40 inexpensive and rugged Ouragans for a second squadron as well as leasing six more Super Mystères.

In the 1960s, the Israelis conducted more extensive evaluation of aircraft for potential purchase and took on more modification of IAF machines as a means of stretching their capabilities. This last included expanded external fuel tank capacity, some developed and manufactured by Israel Military Industries (IMI) while some were licensed production of French designs. This answered the limited endurance experienced in 1956 and permitted strikes on distant enemy air bases. A wide assortment of bombs and rockets were also integrated on all the jets, some on revised mounts and racks also developed by IMI. The IAF also saw advantage in carrying a greater number of small bombs than a small number of large, and IMI developed suitable bomb racks.

The Israelis followed with interest development of small infrared-guided air-to-air missiles, but no one would sell them such weapons. They set out to develop their own and, to the surprise of all, succeeded in fielding the Shafrir in the mid-1960s (shown here under the wingtip of a Mirage IIICJ). It did not perform well but was the basis for more effective follow-on AAM. (Ra'anan Weiss Collection)

The new weapons and tanks required flight testing and clearance. An IAF Flight Test Unit had been formed in 1950 at Tel Nof AB for the usual maintenance flight activities. However, as the workload of aircraft modifications, weapons integration, and avionics improvements grew, their role expanded to experimental flight testing. Pilots began to be sent to foreign test pilot schools. Yet, operational units still undertook the preponderance of testing with fleet aircraft and line aircrew.

Airfield attack ambitions required reliable means of cratering runways to render them unusable. Normal 500-lb (227-kg) and 1,000-lb (454-kg) bombs could effectively do this if delivered in a high-speed dive, but that carried risk from ground fire. Efforts to introduce a more practical concrete penetrating bomb produced the Dibber. This was initially developed in France, but IMI bought the design and sought to perfect the weapon in cooperation with Matra. Initially 1,200 lb (544 kg), they worked to get the size down to one more practical for fighter-bomber employment. The resulting 154-lb (70-kg) Condib 70 was designed to be delivered at low-level and high-speed and was first tested in late 1966. Upon release during a 300-foot (91-m) pass, a parachute deployed to slow the bomb and cause it to pitch down. The chute was released and a rocket fired to drive the bomb into the concrete. A delayed-action fuse allowed it to penetrate below the slab before detonating to create damage very difficult to repair rapidly. A heavier version was also developed and entered production by June 1967. The Dibber generated more drag in carriage than most other ordnance.

Seeking an all-jet combat force also affected basic training. The French Fouga Magister was introduced in 1960 to replace the Harvard. Israel was again at the forefront as this was the world's first jet trainer. They again asked for alterations, the most significant being their choice of optional weapons to allow the aircraft to serve in light attack. A pair of .30-cal guns could be installed in the nose and two wing hardpoints per side were intended for rockets or light bombs. This continued the policy that all aircraft have some war role. As in the past, upon mobilization Emergency Posting personnel and senior School instructors, plus a few recent graduates augmented by reservists, would operate the Magisters. The 147 Squadron was at the time the only such emergency unit in the IAF.[47]

To allow indigenous industry to gather experience, Bedek (soon Israel Aircraft Industries, IAI) was licensed to produce the Magister airframe while France provided engines and many detailed parts. Fostering such skills might reduce Israel's dependence on foreign sources of armaments, which had proven capricious, plus employing skilled people to grow the economy. First delivery was in 1960, production was slow and this was adversely affecting training. The IAF had to lease aircraft from France while Germany provided 40. Just 36 were ultimately manufactured in Israel, a third or less of the total number employed over the coming decades.

Along with the new trainers came a new base when the School moved from Tel Nof to Hatzerim AB in 1966. This was the first major airfield built by Israel, allowing future basing of combat aircraft closer to the southern border and relieving aerial congestion over the center of the country.

Israel bought 100 Super Cubs between late 1956 and 1983.[48] It had a few-odd other types that included some with short take-off and landing (STOL) performance. The IAF was still willing to operate one-off types where they provided a unique capability. The greatest improvement in the light-plane fleet was acquisition of the single-engine Dornier Do.27s with its greater capacity and STOL performance. These were provided discretely by the Federal Republic of Germany, among other non-combat aircraft and light weapons, beginning in 1960 as a form of self-imposed war reparations to the Jewish people that greatly aided the struggling young state. This source dried up in 1965 when the secret dealings became public. More normal sales continued thereafter.

The Noratlases had proven exceptionally valuable and more were sought. Five came new from the factory and 16 lightly used from West Germany. The 103 Squadron became the envy of others in the service as its crews flew to distant lands and gathered more experience operating in inclement weather. Plans to displace all Dakotas with Nords could not be justified. The Douglas airplanes were inexpensive to operate and replacements were bought cheaply as required. However, the fleet reached a low of just four Daks in 1964.

The West Germans secretly assisted Israel by providing a more capable and uniform liaison fleet via the Do.27. The Dornier had good short-field performance and could operate on marginal surfaces. The wide doors permitted decent size freight to be loaded. The initial 10 Do.27Qs arrived in 1964 and were joined in later years by 14 additional that served for more than two decades. (Author's Collection)

Even as the IAF matured, it still operated small numbers of special types where they contributed important utility. The Pilatus Turbo-Porter was noteworthy in being represented by a single example from 1963, and when the first (shown) was wrecked another was acquired in 1968. Its STOL performance and easily accessible voluminous interior made it a much-respected resource. Note the Cub in the background. (BIAF – Israel Aerospace Magazine)

First acquired before the 1956 war, the fleet of Noratlas "flying boxcars" was greatly augmented in subsequent years. They offered a tremendous leap in capabilities allowing airdrop to be expanded and more practical flights to France for freight transport. Only the acquisition of sufficient numbers of Lockheed C-130s in the 1970s saw the hard-used Nords finally laid to rest. (Shlomo Aloni Collection)

The 103 considered airdrop its primary mission and trained hard for this role. Night drops were intended as the norm, with a standard three-ship formation flying as low as 1,000 feet (305 m) in the dark. During daylight missions, they flew as low as a wingspan height above the ground.

The Sinai Campaign had shown the value of airlifting heavy equipment into forward airfields during mobilization, or seized enemy bases, to meet the demands of fast mobile warfare for which the IDF was training. An airplane able to fly in heavy and wide equipment like bulldozers, trucks, command cars, and radars would be a significant plus. These aircraft would also make flights to Europe to bring back large quantities of materiel more practical. Required were transports of greater capacity and more practical onload/offload means. The IAF looked at the Lockheed C-130B, but at $3 million each and the USA consistently reluctant to sell armaments to Israel, this appeared beyond reach.

Israel Aircraft Industries proposed modifying retired Boeing B-377 Stratocruisers, the commercial spinoff of the United States Air Force (USAF) C-97 Stratofreighter, for the airlift mission. This plan ran counter to IAF modernization plans, the old prop aircraft likely to be maintenance-intensive, and it was uncertain IAI could deliver on their promises. Should the option be selected, the IAF requested substitution of turboprop engines, an added auxiliary power unit, fittings for rocket-assisted take-off bottles, larger flaps for shorter take-off and landings, and a braking parachute. They would need the C-97 cargo system of aft loading doors and wheel ramp with interior overhead freight winch to lift and position cargo, augmented by addition of a forward cargo door in the fuselage side, strengthened floor, and accommodations for paratroops and airdrop. Lastly, a swing-aside tail would permit especially wide cargo like armored cars and light tanks to be loaded. This list seems intended to make the program untenable compared with the C-130. Regardless, the economics of the IAI proposal, especially for Israeli employment and growing the aircraft modification capabilities, won the day.

Five stored B-377s were purchased cheaply and overhauled. The only changes practical in the available schedule and budget (1964 delivery and $0.5 million) were general militarization and the cargo modifications, sans airdrop. This was only possible by purchasing scrap C-97 aft fuselages,

Israel bought several commercial Boeing Stratocruisers with the intent to modify them as military freighters for the IAF. Israel Aircraft Industries added the cargo door in the forward fuselage and a swing-aside tail for aft loading via a wheel ramp. Aircraft 4X-FPV 10 "Arbel," wearing the 120 Squadron badge, was the first of what was eventually only two B-377Ms given that the full modification with swing-aside tail (inset) was not entirely successful. Three more B-377s were completed with C-97 aft fuselages and their integral cargo doors. (Military Aircraft Photographs and BIAF – Israel Aerospace Magazine)

which the Americans permitted. Only two of the aircraft received the swing-aside tail as the design was not entirely successful.

The C-47s and Boeings were combined to form 120 Squadron at Lod AB (the renamed Lydda) where they shared the same runway with the international airport. All the Lod machines were maintained by IAI under contract. Painted like commercial aircraft, the Boeings appeared less militaristic and could fly international mission while attracting less attention. These and 103's Nords were soon busy hauling military freight into Israel or other cargo into and out of Africa. One of the Boeings was given a temporary Very Important Person (VIP) interior and a special paint scheme to carry the head-of-state when traveling abroad. The Dakotas also began to take on specialized roles like airborne command post, extended radio relay, radio intercept and direction-finding, and some communications jamming. A Transport Command function was created in IAF headquarters to manage operations of all the airlifters.

With the USA relaxing its military equipment sales prohibition, Israel found its request for KC-97s meeting with some success. The Americans agreed to sell six decommissioned airframes, though requiring a two- to three-years overhaul before entering IAF service.

The IAF's small helicopter corps was eager to do more and the Army was willing to explore its air assault potential. Leadership had reluctantly agreed to buy two S-55 troop ships, and these were flying in the last days of the Sinai Campaign. They operated as a Helicopter Flight of 103 Squadron and offered first exposure to flying sling loads. However, the Sikorsky did not do so well in the hot Israeli climate. Yet, they got radio direction finding gear to locate downed aircrew equipped with British survival radios – the system called Sarah. Fitted with rescue hoists, the S-55s then displaced Cubs in the pilot rescue role. Most or all helicopters into the 1970s were equipped with Sarah as well as Daks and Noratlases.

The helicopter leaders' ambitions were reinforced when a delegation of Air Force and paratroop officers observed French heliborne operations in Algeria during 1957. They recommended the S-58 troop transport and the turbine-powered Alouette for liaison, casevac, and light transport. The usual budget angst caused a delay in the procurement, but training and experimentation continued with the S-55s, to include night operations. The IDF was then making night special operations forays into neighboring countries for reprisals, reconnaissance, or to tap communication nodes. An S-55 supported one such mission in Jordan during 1957, showing the practicality of night air assault, though the old Sikorsky was marginal as a combat asset.

Finally, seven S-58s started arriving from America between 1958 and 1960. Like the S-55s, these were commercial variants to reduce the appearance of military equipment sales. At twice the horsepower, they were a significant step above the 55 as they could carry a ton of payload to include 18 soldiers or eight litters, or 1,000-lb (454-kg) sling load. An optional external fuel tank could be installed to extend range. Training with these helicopters added another dimension to IDF airborne operations, especially more practical insertion and extracting of special forces at night.

With imminent arrival of the new Sikorskys, the 124 Squadron was inaugurated in 1958. However, the 58s arrived so slowly that the unit was not considered fully operational until 1962. The IAF leadership could mount little enthusiasm for a greater number of Sikorskys, so it was fortuitous when the USA saw to it that Israel received 24 helicopters (lower-capacity H-34s) in 1962 and 1963. These were new aircraft *en route* to Germany but transferred between German and Israeli ships. Additional machines were sent to German units who had no prior knowledge of the skullduggery.

Resources were then in hand for those advocating air assault tactics as part of the lightening attacks the IDF was preparing to implement. Given the environment of continuous low-level

During the 1960s the assault helicopter fleet was dominated by the Sikorsky S-58 in various models, some supplied by West Germany. This example has had German stenciling sprayed over. Airborne troops trained in rapid repositioning and resupply at critical locations via vertical lift, enhancing potential success of attacks. The numerous special forces operations during tensions on the border made good use of these assets. (BIAF – Israel Aerospace Magazine)

In its first 25 years, the IAF intercepted quite a few airliners or military transports that inadvertently crossed into Israeli airspace. Most were forced to land and then released after a short time. A more interesting event occurred on July 19, 1963, when Mirages IIICJs confronted an American RB-57A on a mission to photograph the nuclear research facility at Dimona, just as Egypt had been attempting to do. The fighters forced the USAF aircrew to land at Lod after firing warning shots. Having made their point and revealing that they operated Mirages, the Israelis released the Americans.

military actions at the time, the helicopters were in frequent use for such missions plus civilian emergencies. However, the sand and heat was hard on the 58s, with engines requiring overhauls at a quarter of the recommended interval.

Years of hard training came together in a demonstration of the IAF's new helicopter tactics during large-scale maneuvers in 1966. Hundreds of troops were airlifted into advantageous positions by the helicopters, day or night, and relocated when conditions required. Simulated wounded were rapidly evacuated and vital resupply was accomplished using vertical replenishment. The maneuvers proved convincingly the feasibility and practicality of such tactics on the battlefield. This also essentially ended parachute drops as the preferred means of entering battle by the paratroops.

Turbine-powered helicopters were introduced with the Alouette II executive transport from France. A small number made up 125 Squadron at Tel Nof AB, and later Sde Dov. They performed some typical battlefield liaison, light transport, and casevac duties. The VIP transport role expanded to include urgent movement of commanders to their mobilizing units. In 1966, France also began supplying Super Frelon helicopters with impressive performance via three turbine engines and rear cargo ramp for wheeled vehicles or weapons. As with the Sikorskys, the Frelons had winches above the personnel door to lift in survivors for rescue scenarios or allow troops to rappel down. The 114 heavy lift helicopter squadron was formed in 1966 at Tel Nof beside 124 and 125, possibly acting as a rotorcraft Wing.

Confrontation

Regional stability remained elusive following the 1956 war. President Nasser's ambition of leading the Arab world saw him forming military alliances in the region. Israel was emerging as possessing a role in the West's Middle East policies and was held forth as the principal adversary. All the nations expanded their militaries with mostly Soviet weapons. Egypt deployed forces into allied countries and fought in the Yemen civil war. Israel assisted the rebels in that conflict, including airdropping supplies via 14 Stratocruiser missions.[49]

Although the Egyptian border remained relatively peaceful for many years owing to the UN presence in the Sinai, Fedayeen raids from Gaza, Syria and Jordan continued. The shelling of Israeli settlements by Syrian batteries on the Golan Heights was growing intolerable. The first airstrikes since the 1956 war were flown in 1962 against the Heights, and more followed at an increasing pace. Egypt reacted in February 1960 with an armored division sent into Sinai as a show of strength. However, Israel's Army intelligence missed this and only an American warning prompted reconnaissance flights that located the force that far outnumbered the standing IDF strength in the Negev. The troops went on alert, but only the Air Force could have responded immediately if the Egyptians chose to attack while Zahal reserves were being mobilized. Although the immediate threat passed, it was a sobering lesson.

The Israeli project to divert some Jordan River water for its sole use brought vociferous protests, and the Arab League sought to thwart the project. The animosity grew from heated diplomatic exchanges to infantry firefights, shelling, and then tank battles. When Syria and Lebanon began an effort to divert the headwaters of the Jordan, it brought airstrikes. The Arab project eventually collapsed while Israel's was completed.

The Arab League also backed the growth of the Palestine Liberation Organization (PLO, successor to Al Fatah) and its armed struggle with Israel. The Israelis persisted with their policy of "active defense" using retaliatory raids across the border in answer to provocations. Only special forces and the Air Force were truly ready to react quickly enough, and they worked closely. Reconnaissance flights over all surrounding states continued, as well as sorties beyond the borders to calibrate Israeli radar, map enemy radar coverage, or as just a training challenge.[50] Daytime recce was rapidly growing excessively risky as the opposition gained

The Auster Air Observation Post was the most numerous light plane during most of the 1948 fighting. Performing liaison, casualty evacuation, bombing and gunfire, light transport, photography, and reconnaissance duties, their contribution far exceeded any expectation of the former RAF owners who sold them as scrap. This A.O.P.3 wears the common camouflage of the period with early A-13 code, the aleph letter denoting the Austers. Unit insignia and other markings were rare. The airplanes were hard used, and A-13 was destroyed in a crash on June 26, 1948 – the fate of three other Austers, while one was destroyed by anti-aircraft fire and another shot up on the ground by Egyptian Spitfires. All remaining were withdrawn in September 1949. (Artwork by Tom Cooper)

One of the earliest Avia S-199s, arriving in-country on 30 May 1948, D-107 is as it appeared during June 1948 while stationed at Aqir (the later Ekron then Tel Nof). It was likely the mount for two kills scored on June 3, but the machine was then wrecked on the 11th during a ground mishap – the end of many IAF S-199s. The dalet letter for the serial denoted the type and aft fuselage stripes were an added effort at identification to discourage own-force attacks. The aircraft paint color was the subject of debate for three-quarters of a century until resolved by researchers. It was a semi-gloss RAL 6013 Schilfgrün (reed green), though it commonly faded to a lighter shade in the Mediterranean sun – if the aircraft lasted that long. Squadron markings on the fighters were sporadic at this point. (Artwork by Tom Cooper)

The P-51D had a decade-long career with the Israeli Air Force, with aircraft coming from several sources over the years. Many remained unpainted while serving as training mounts, including this example from the mid-1950s. The red spinner was commonly associated with 101 Squadron, but close adherence to such things were not a priority at the time and aircraft transferred between units. During this period, aircraft types were denoted by the first two digits of the four-digit serial, the last two commonly used as the call-sign. All were camouflaged and displayed just two-digit serials by the time of the 1956 Suez Campaign. (Artwork by Tom Cooper)

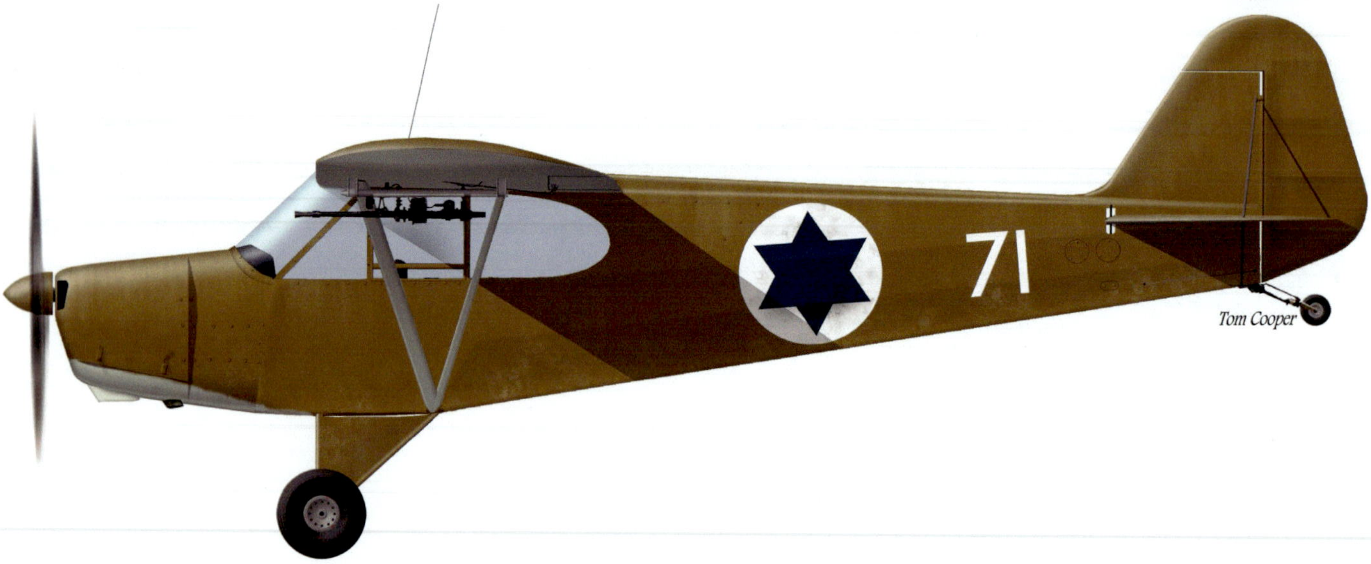

The Piper Cub also served for half a century with the IAF in many roles and in many paint schemes. This Super Cub had a rare but simple finish when seen in 1968, marking it as an Army cooperation craft. Unit markings were spurious given how frequently the Cubs moved around, especially as station hacks at various bases. The type most commonly performed patrol and liaison missions, but had also delivered small bombs, mounted light guns (shown), and dropped parachute-recovered packs. It was most noteworthy as picking up downed pilots, seemingly setting down almost anywhere, until the advent of helicopters. The Cub would eventually give up any combat role and so slowly assumed red and white training colors through the end of its service. (Artwork by Tom Cooper)

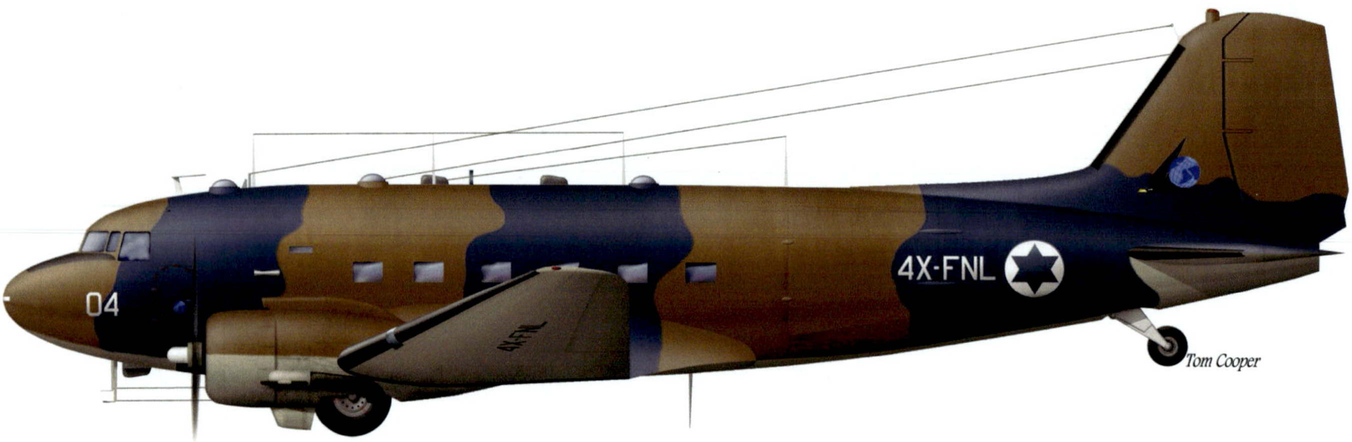

The C-47 Dakota had a decades long relationship with the Israeli Air Force and wore many paint schemes during that time. Through to the Six-Day War it commonly bore this 3-tone finish. Transports that had the potential to fly beyond the borders carried registration markings with 4X denoting Israel and the first two letters, FN, denoting Dakotas. This 120 Squadron machine was taken up in 1950. Employed as a navigator trainer, it had additional astrodomes and antennae on the spine. The extra-large red beacon atop the tail was an Israeli addition. (Artwork by Tom Cooper)

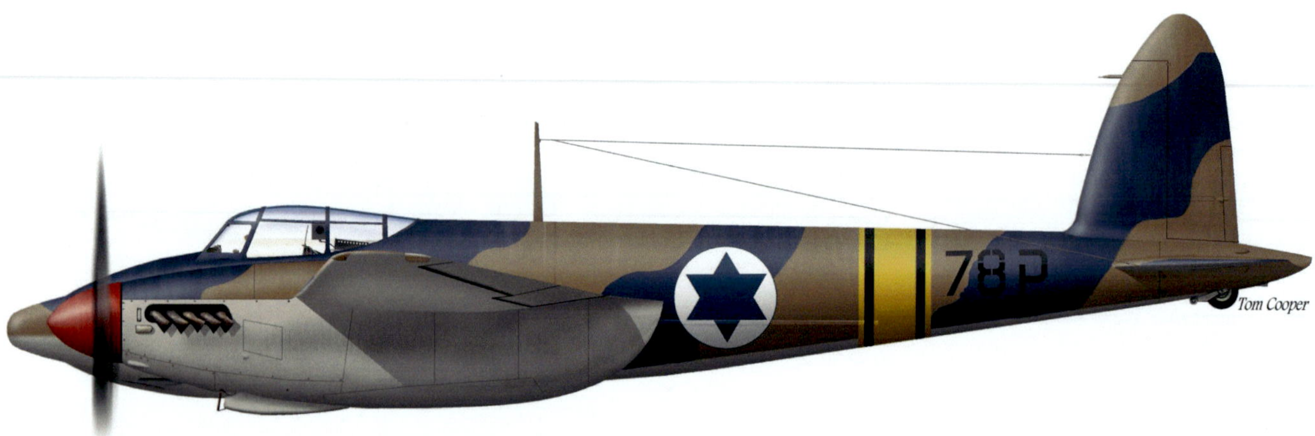

Liked by some but despised by many, the Mosquito had an important role in the IAF from 1948 through 1956. Serviceability was atrocious, but it had long endurance and could carry a respectable war load. Reconnaissance models were especially invaluable. This TR Mk.33 is as it appeared during the 1956 war, operated by 110 Squadron, with uncommon "invasion stripes" on the aft fuselage. The airplane was among 13 former Royal Navy machines acquired from Britain in 1954-1955. Being a dated type, stored until just prior to the war, it still bore the koof prefix to the code 78 (short for krav or "combat"). The red spinner was commonly associated with 109 Squadron. (Artwork by Tom Cooper)

Shown is a 117 Squadron Meteor F.Mk 8 in 1960 at Ramat David, lacking squadron markings. The practice then was that frontline fighters were unpainted natural metal while the lesser types, likely devoted to air-to-ground missions, were given camouflage – the once glorious Meteor so demoted by that time. The common colors of the period are displayed by 106. This was one of the earliest Meteor acquisitions and coded 06. The prefix digit (1, in this case) was sometimes added for further distinction or to confuse attempts to count the IAF fleet. The codes were as commonly obscured as were unit insignia, or spurious markings applied for disinformation. (Artwork by Tom Cooper)

At the end of its time as a frontline fighter type in 1965, 109 Squadron's Mystère IVA aircraft 32 (Ramat David style stencils) remains in natural metal, but with the unit's fuselage flash and yellow surround on the serial (though it quickly faded to invisibility). The French airplane would soon be camouflaged and take on air-to-ground roles, serving well in the Six-Day War and into the War of Attrition before retirement. Flight with the external tanks was common, and the type would get a drag chute container at the aft intersection of the vertical and horizontal tails as it took to carrying greater external weapon loads. This was among the earliest "MIVAs" to be acquired from France and survived to become a playground attraction. (Artwork by Tom Cooper)

The initial Sikorsky S-58s (H-34s) were supplied with the common IAF 3-tone camouflage scheme and worn throughout the years of service with 124 Squadron. Those from Germany were an overall forest green (RAL 6014) to which the sand fields were added, some as patches over German stenciling. Aircraft 07 carries fittings for the rare external tank that was probably only used for long-range special operations. The side nose antennae are for the Sarah direction finding gear to locate downed aircrew. A rescue hoist was common above the starboard side cabin door and smoke grenade mount routinely added to the gear strut on that side. (Artwork by Tom Cooper)

With the edict that all aircraft have a combat role during war, and because the Fouga CM.170 Magister was employed in the early stages of fighter pilot training, some of the light jets were armed. The two .30-cal guns in the nose were quite light, but the common rockets mounted beneath the wings could lend good support to ground forces. It was also camouflaged, but with either yellow training bands or with dayglow tape stripes that could be peeled off prior to combat. Aircraft 236 shows these attributes just prior to the 1967 war. Operated by the only reserve squadron in the air force, it fought hard and contributed much. However, the Magister was slow and lacked an ejection seat, and so the outfit suffered grave losses. (Artwork by Tom Cooper)

The IAF initially acquired ten Do 27Qs in 1964 from Germany as part of the undeclared war reparations that included non-lethal systems. Its capacious interior with generous door dimensions, plus short takeoff and landing performance off-field, was most welcome. As many as 24 additional machines were purchased in 1971-1972. Aircraft 037 of 100 Squadron is shown in the Do 27's second color scheme, acquired after 1967, and in which it completed its service in the mid-1980s. The only exceptions were a white and red scheme for a few machines employed by the Flying School. (Artwork by Tom Cooper)

The Vautour bombers were valuable enough to serve on into the War of Attrition despite the advent of Skyhawks and Phantoms. They were among the French airplanes that became increasingly difficult to maintain given the embargo. Their speed and systems were also not up to the battlefield of the 1970s. The machines were repainted in the 4-tone scheme and accumulated special marking such as a nose name and the 1967 campaign ribbon on the tail, and occasionally mission marks stenciled under the cockpit sill. Vautour IIA 421 of 110 Squadron, as seen in 1970, is named Cobra. It was withdrawn from use the following year. (Artwork by Tom Cooper)

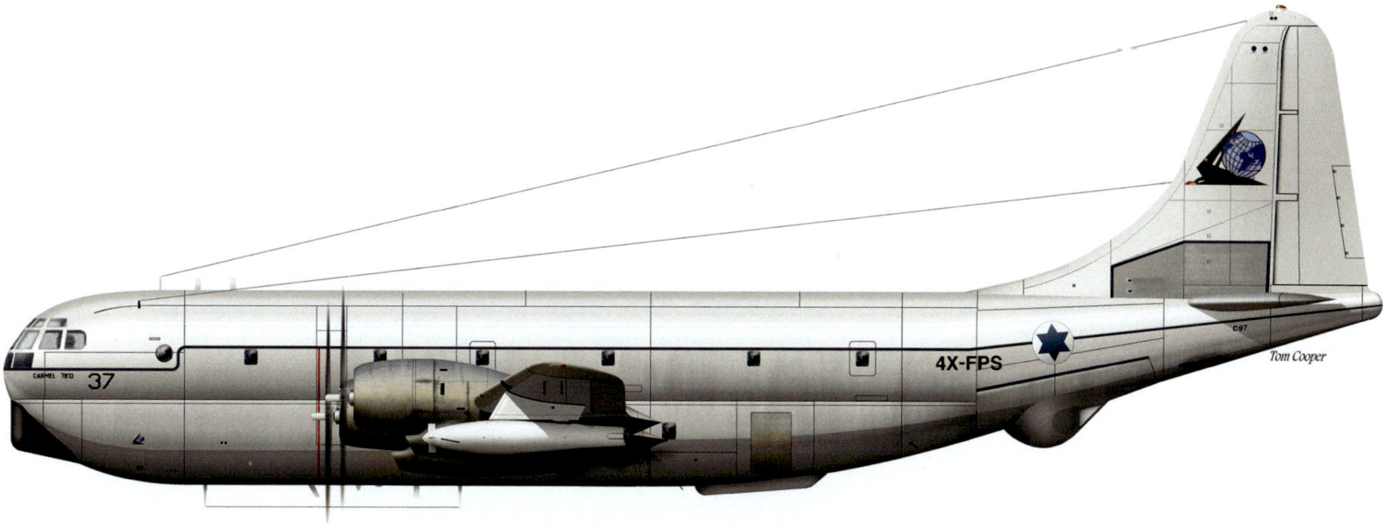

With the Americans delivering A-4s with aerial refueling probes and having trained IAF pilots in the task, plus permitting the Israelis to obtain refueling hose reel pods, the service lost no time in creating a suitable tanker. They initially adopted the Skyhawk "buddy refueling" pods to their KC-97s, sold without the flying boom. The boom operator pod was retained to monitor the operation. Among the first two such aircraft was KC-97G 4X-FPS/37 "Carmel." This had been operating with the IAF since June 1967 and converted to 2-point tanker soon after. It was destroyed at Lod International Airport on November 30, 1970 when, being towed across the runway without lights (practicing emergency dispersal), a Boeing 707 airliner collided with it. (Artwork by Tom Cooper)

An important expression of American support for Israel came with agreement to sell Skyhawk jets. However, the A-4Hs, first arriving in December 1967, had important equipment removed or downgraded. It was still a marked improvement in ground attack assets and they arrived during the challenging time of the War of Attrition. Aircraft 52 of 109 Squadron has the straight aerial refueling probe and drag chute housing that characterized the model. The common Mk 82 bombs with "Snakeye" fins are loaded, reflecting adoption of American ordnance. Shown in 1970, it retained the 20-mm cannon, yet to be swapped with 30-mm units the IAF preferred. (Artwork by Tom Cooper)

Three squadrons of F-4Es were operational by the time of the October 1973 Yom Kippur War. They executed vital heavy, deep strike missions that took a toll of machines and men falling to air defenses. These losses were central to the IAF commander's warning on the 10th that the force was approaching a "red line." Sending additional F-4Es was part of the urgent appeal to the US for immediate resupply. These began arriving on the 14th and were distributed to the squadrons. Aircraft 311 wears only the 69 Squadron badge and remains in US Air Force South East Asia colors – which the Israelis referred to as "toad." The prefix 3 denoted these airplanes, and some operated without repainting for many years. It carries cluster bombs and the usual load of air-to-air missiles. (Artwork by Tom Cooper)

The large, twin-engine Vautour gave a long-range, moderately heavy bombing dimension to the IAF, holding at risk distant adversary jet bomber bases. The IIA variant (this 110 Squadron trio photographed in January 1967) was a single-place machine with nose guns, a bomb bay, and external hardpoints under the wings. Expensive and complex, the Israelis fielded only a modest number of the Vautours. (Author's Collection)

The Israeli silver Mirage IIICJs were among the most identifiable symbols of the Six-Day War victory. In the hands of IAF crews, the type proved an outstanding air-to-air and air-to-ground platform. The three squadrons, including this 101 Squadron machine, contributed, as did all fighter-bombers, during the pre-emptive strikes against enemy air bases on June 5. Apart from showing wing-tip AAM launcher pylons, two choices of external tanks are displayed. (Author's Collection)

Seeking even heavy lift transports, the IAF was compelled by budget to buy retired four-engine Boeing B377 airliners militarized with elements of C-97s, and then mothballed KC-97s. This example was "dolled-up" as an executive transport to carry the Prime Minister on state visits to African nations in 1966 during a period in which Israel had a thriving exchange with these countries. (BIAF – Israel Aerospace Magazine)

The old "Dak" continued to be sustained and serve as low-cost transports. They were especially useful transporting personnel to and from Sinai bases during reserve duty and rotations. This 122 Squadron C-47B shows the beacon at the top of the vertical tail and the shield around the tail wheel that were introduced by the Israelis. The extra antennas seem to attest to an ancillary role of communications relay. (BIAF – Israel Aerospace Magazine)

The odd-looking Do.28 carried on the tradition of the Do.27 though with the advantage of twin engines and more capacious cabin. The purchase of the 25 airplanes in 1971 was less politically charged than prior acquisitions from West Germany. These machines would soldier on for more than thirty years. This 100 Squadron example is probably at Herzliya Airport awaiting servicing. (BIAF – Israel Aerospace Magazine)

For medium helicopter transport, the older Sikorskys were supplanted with Bell 205s. The "Hueys" were a mix of models, some commercial and some military. This 123 Squadron machine shows the skid steps the Israelis added, subject to rotation off the vertical. (Ed Okun Collection)

Unit Insignia, IDF/AF & IASF
1948-2020
(Part 1)

69 Squadron
The Hammers
(B-17, F-4, F-15I)

100 Squadron
Flying Camel
(Do.27, P.149, Islander, Do.28, Super King Air)

101 Squadron
First Fighter
(S-199, Spitfire, P-51D, Mystère IVA, Mirage, Nesher Kfir, F-16)

102 Squadron
Flying Tigers
(A-4, M-346)

103 Squadron
Flying Elephant/Elephants
(C-47, Noratlas, C-130)

105 Squadron
Scorpion
(Spitfire, Super Mystère, F-4, F-16)

106 Squadron
Spear's Point/Spearhead
(F-15)

107 Squadron
Lionhead/Knights of the Orange Tail
(Spitfire, Meteor, Ouragan, F-4, F-16I)

109 Squadron
Valley
(Mosquito, Mystère IVA, A-4, Kfir, F-16)

110 Squadron
Night Fighters/Knights of the North
(Mosquito, Meteor, Vautour, A-4, F-16)

113 Squadron
Hornet
(Ouragan, Nesher, Kfir, AH-64)

114 Squadron
Heavy Lift/Night Leaders
(Super Frelon, Sea Stallion)

115 Squadron
Flying Dragon
(A-4, F-16)

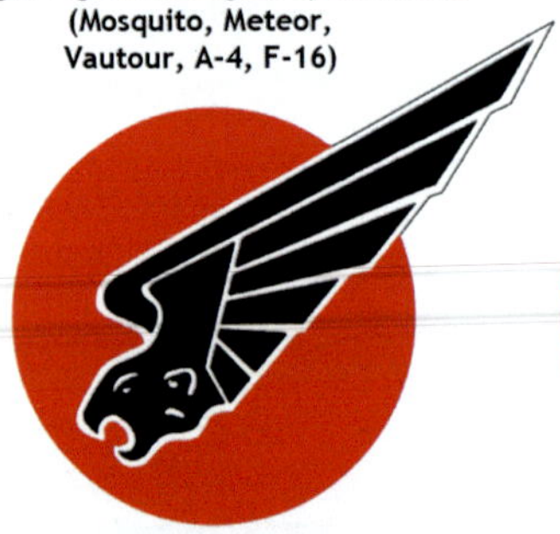

116 Squadron
Flying Wing/Defenders of the Negev/ Southern Lions
(Mystère IVA, A-4, F-16, F-35I)

117 Squadron
First Jets
(Meteor, Mirage, Nesher, F-16)

118 Squadron
Night Birds of Prey/ Night Predators
(Sea Stallion)

119 Squadron
Bat
(Meteor, Vautour, Mirage, F-4, F-16I)

120 Squadron
International/Desert Giants
(C-47, Stratocruiser/Stratofreighter, C-130, Boeing 707, Westwind, Sea Scan)

122 Squadron
Dakota/Pioneer
(C-47, Arava, OV-10, Gulfstream)

123 Squadron
Southern Helicopters/Southern Bells/ Desert Owls
(Bell 205, Bell 212)

Application of squadron insignia was not very common before the 1950s, and they were not universally applied until late in that decade. Many unit names and insignia evolved over time – usually as units transitioned between aircraft types. The review offered here shows the most frequently used insignia on types mentioned in the text: all are shown as oriented on the port side of the aircraft, where there was a unique orientation side-to-side.

Under the command of Ezer Weizman, the Air Force instituted various competitions between units to enhance *espirit* and skills. Among these were aircraft servicing competitions timing the arming and fueling of aircraft as if turning between combat sorties. Such is depicted here with 117 Squadron Mirage IIICJs at Ramat David AB in the mid-1960s. By 1967, the Air Force was well-equipped, skilled, confident, and enjoying very high morale. (Yoav Efrati Collection)

experience and scrambled more effectively against intruders. Night missions were then increased, areas illuminated by dropped flares. The Arabs performed similar nocturnal recce and IAF intercepts attempts were unsuccessful.

By the mid-1960s, the regional arms race was in full stride with both sides introducing more capable fighter-bombers, Mach 2 interceptors, AAM and SAM, and fast jet bombers. In this theater, with tensions and long-held animosities, it was felt certain war was coming. There had been few air-to-air engagements since 1960 and none successful. It was July 1966 when a Mirage destroyed a Syrian MiG-21 and this began a year of occasional air combat with IAF victories. Israeli intelligence collection and espionage activities also persisted. These humiliating demonstrations of Israeli prowess included a large-scale raid into the West Bank area with the November 1966 attack on Samoa.

The Arabs were feeling sufficiently confident to again take strong measures against what they saw as the last vestige of imperialism within their midst, and the source of vexing airspace violations, retaliatory raids, and espionage. Cross-border incursions soon became more serious and enemy aircraft began once more to probe the Israeli defenses. A very public confrontation with Israel would go a long way in solidifying Nasser's self-assumed role as the leader of the Arab people. The steady campaign of anti-Semitic rhetoric threatening Israel's destruction was taken seriously by a nation who had suffered millions of family members murdered by the Nazis. War was probably not Nasser's intent, and his armed forces were in no condition to execute successfully a large-scale campaign, but events escalated beyond his control.

CHAPTER 6
SIX-DAY WAR

Years of dedicated military preparation paid astonishing dividends for Israel when the Middle East again erupted into war. From the gloom of inevitable destruction to heady lightening victory and territorial gain, Israel emerged from the brief 1967 war in what appeared an enviable strategic position. The IAF was so central to the success that it was suddenly seen as perhaps the best air combat team in the world.

March to War

The road to war in 1967 was paved with misjudgments built upon the tensions and political maneuvering sown in the previous year. There were suspicions that the Israelis were planning a major military action following significant border clashes. Amongst these clashes was a massive Israeli air attack on Syrian positions on April 7, 1967, following a long simmering dispute over the demilitarized area and repeated Syrian shelling. When the Syrian Arab Air Force (SyAAF) challenged the IAF, six MiG-21s were lost and survivors were chased all the way to Damascus where the Mirages laid triumphant sonic booms across the city. These incidents were coupled with an erroneous Soviet warning that the Israelis were massing troops on her northern border. The six-month old mutual defense pact between Egypt and Syria compelled some measure of response.

On May 15, Nasser placed his armed forces on alert and deployed 100,000 troops and over 900 tanks into the Sinai. He called up reserves the following day. The gravest event was the removal on the 19th of the UN peacekeepers from the Sinai at Egypt's insistence. This was followed on the night of May 22-23 by the overt blockade of the Straits of Tiran to Israeli shipping. The Israelis had made clear this would be construed as an act of war. The major powers, who had guaranteed Israel's free transit through the waterway, took no action.

The IDF began mobilizing on May 22 and the IAF eventually approached its full 11,000 mobilized personnel strength.[51] Jordan joined the Egyptian-Syrian mutual defense pact on the 30th and welcomed Egyptian troops on its soil. Iraq joined the pact on June 4 and some of her combat units moved into Jordan. The combined forces came under Egyptian command. Saudi Arabian, Kuwaiti, and Algerian elements were also deployed to the war zone, while Libya pledged support. These moves, along with vociferous rhetoric of destroying the Jewish state, may have been intended to solidifying Nasser's political leadership, but the threat exceeded the Israelis' tolerance.

During the prolonged crisis, the Israeli cabinet and military leadership appeared to lack resolve. They were not fully confident of the Air Force's ability to execute the decisive preemptive airstrikes and still protect the country from enemy bombers. International diplomacy had brought nothing but another arms embargo. Even France's President Charles de Gaulle refused Israeli requests to borrow combat aircraft, though the French Defense Ministry did provide some items such as R.530 missiles and Mirage external tanks, plus turned a blind eye to use of French assets already in the country for maintenance activities.[52]

The threat to Israel's existence had not appeared so dire since 1948. Many respected voices in world military affairs spoke of the nation's coming demise. Even within the country, there was pessimism about the government's decisiveness and the ability of the IDF to respond effectively. The government underwent a change and the mood improved. With the cost of the mobilization mounting and the economy suffering, an Arab attack appearing imminent, the new government chose to execute its preemptive strike plans on the morning of June 5.

Israel's objectives in the war were reopening the Straits of Tiran and elimination of the immediate threat posed by the massed armies facing her. The Air Force's plans followed classic airpower theory: first gain air superiority, second interdict and destroy the enemy lines of supply, and lastly support ground forces operations. The IAF nominally possessed approximately 250 combat aircraft, with some 70 percent operational at any given time. The nearly month-long run-up to war permitted serviceability to reach 97 percent. Additional work included installing door guns on the S-58s and external fuel cells on a few.[53] Several French aircraft under depot maintenance at IAI were mobilized. Despite the IAF long-held objective of two pilots for every airplane, it possessed a ratio of just 1.4:1 (including reservists).[54] There were also HAS for only about half the fighter-bombers.

When the war began, the ORBAT was (some data best estimates):

Fighter-Bombers
65 Mirage IIICJ (1 u/s)
3 Mirage IIIBJ (two-seat, used as combat assets)
11 Vautour IIA
6 Vautour IIN (1 u/s)
30 Super Mystère B2
(8) Super Mystère B2 seized French assets[55]
33 Mystère IVA (1 u/s)
51 Ouragan (3 u/s)
44 Magister (armed trainers)[56]
1 MiG-21 (captured and deployed)
Photo Reconnaissance (also employed for attack)
2 Mirage IIICJ(R)
2 Vautour IIB (modified to BR standard)
camera packages for Noratlas and C-47, photographers in other aircraft
Transports
5 B-377M modified (2 u/s)
2 C-97
23 Noratlas (3 u/s)
10 C-47 (2 u/s)
(6) C-47 seized French assets
(2) Boeing 720 (mobilized El Al assets)
(5) Boeing 707 (mobilized El Al assets)
(5) Dart-Herald (mobilized Arkia assets)
1 Turbo-Porter
10 Do.27
32 Super Cub (7 u/s, or conglomerate of 100 Squadron fleet)
2 C-180
1 Rallye
Helicopters
4 Super Frelon
28 S-58
2 Alouette II
Training
23 Super Cub
16 Magister (unarmed)
2 Meteor T.7
3 Meteor T.7/8
13 Bell 47 (1 u/s)
425 total aircraft (excluding leased, loaned, and mobilized assets)

The IAF mobilized just about every aircraft in the country to support the 1967 war effort, though mostly commercial transports. The two Cessna 180s were actually transferred from the police at the end of 1966. This example has had the seats removed for accessibility during maintenance. The 100 Squadron operated the light-planes from Sde Dov AB during the war. (BIAF – Israel Aerospace Magazine)

Hatzerim (Wing 6)	
147 (reserve, detached from Flying School)	Magister
Flying School (some elements still at Tel Nof)	Cub, Magister, Bell 47
Hatzor (Wing 4)	
101 First Fighter	Mirage IIICJ
105 Scorpion	Super Mystère B2
113 Hornet	Ouragan
(124) deployed from Tel Nof for SAR	S-58
Kfar Sirkin	
(100) dispersal flight	Cub
(103) dispersal flight	Noratlas
(120) dispersal flight	C-47
Lod (Base 27)	
120 International	B-377M, C-97, C-47
(107) deployed from Ramat David	Ouragan
(145) all or mostly Arkia personnel	Dart Herald [57]
Meggido	
(100) Flight B	Cub
Mitzpe Ramon	
(124) deployed from Tel Nof for SAR	S-58
Ramat David (Wing 1)	
107 Lionhead	Ouragan
109 Valley	Mystère IVA
110 Knights of the North	Vautour, Meteor
117 First Jets	Mirage IIICJ
Tel Nof (Base 8)	
103 Flying Elephant	Noratlas
(109) deployment for initial strikes	Mystère IVA
(110) deployment for initial strikes	Vautour
114 Heavy Lift	Super Frelon
116 Flying Wing	Mystère IVA
119 Bat	Mirage IIICJ
123 Southern Bells	Bell 47
124 Rotor and Sword	S-58
Sde Dov (Base 15)	
100 Flying Camel (Cub Station Flights throughout country)	Cub, Do.27, C-180, Turbo Porter, Rallye
125 Light Helicopters	Alouette, Bell 47
Sde Teiman	
(100) Flight C	Cub
(124) deployed from Tel Nof for SAR	S-58

The primary and secondary Israeli airfields that contributed to the Six-Day war are shown on this chart. (Author)

The confrontation states' 5.3:1 superiority in bombers and 2.8:1 in fighters (strictly counting airframes and not considering serviceability, sortie generation rate, or operator skill) was ominous when contemplating an Israeli ground campaign supported by airpower plus defense of the tiny country. The pre-emptive attack was the only solution to address this significant numerical disparity. However, confronting only Egypt, intelligence reports suggested the EAF could put up only 156 fighters and 55 bombers against the IAF's 208 front-line combat types. This was a significant finding leading to a decision to attack. Spying and many years of aerial photo reconnaissance had provided detailed flight approach information, airfield layout and organizational routines, and even biographies of EAF commanders. Combined with meticulous planning and exhaustive training, all this gave the IAF confidence it could execute this crucial role.

During the two weeks before June 5, the IAF executed dozens of reconnaissance flights across the Egyptian frontier. Both sides flew probes and high-speed runs towards the border to test reaction time and to keep radar operators on edge. There were a number of IAF helicopter and reconnaissance flights in the southern portion of the front and over the Gulf of Aqaba. This activity led the Egyptians to expect an attack from this quarter, and they transferred MiG interceptors to the Sinai. Although this meant that the fighters were not at the bases initially targeted for

This Mirage IIICJ(R) camera ship was operated by 119 Squadron when photographed at Tel Nof AB, the long-time high-speed photo reconnaissance unit in the IAF. (The camouflage marks this as an image from 1970.) It is not a standard recce Mirage as the nose was specially constructed; this one called Universal and mounting American cameras, could be interchanged with other noses. (Israel Ministry of Defence)

destruction in the Nile Valley, it tended to reduce the air threat to an attacking IAF force and placed more of the EAF force within ready range of Israeli fighter-bombers.

Flying was much reduced in the two weeks preceding the war to help ensure a maximum in-service rate, but also to lend to the appearance of a lowering level of alert. In the last few days, the IAF appears to have intentionally reduced all provocative activity in an effort to lull the Egyptians into believing that the crisis had receded. Israel even announced that some of the mobilized reservists would be sent home.

Preemption

Aircrew were briefed that their preemptive strike missions were a national "all-out, do-or-die" priority. Surprise and mission accomplishment was paramount, even over safety. They had to do everything to conceal the inbound attack formations and could not execute an immediate return to base if they had an emergency during the launch period so as not to disrupt sortie generation. If the aircraft could make it to the target, they were to attack even if the machine could not return home, or they could eject at low (and unsafe) altitude. The IAF expected a 25 percent loss rate. The three Mirage squadrons each contributed a quartet to QRA (5 percent of the fighter-bomber force) to respond to enemy aircraft penetrating Israeli airspace. Two more 117 Mirages escorted a pair of Vautours devoted to jamming. A Vautour and two 119 Mirage recce aircraft flew photography missions. All other attack aircraft were committed.

The air base attacks were to be executed in successive waves as aircraft returned and were turned for follow-on sorties, pilots briefed, and targets selected based on combat reports or post-strike photography. Each jet typically carried external tanks and two 550-lb (250-kg) bombs, except for the Vautour IIAs and Ns that had eight 150-lb (70-kg) bombs on racks under the wings while long-range fuel cells occupied the bays. The Ouragans carried eight rockets in some strikes. Targets were hit by a formation of four aircraft acting in pairs, and off the target before the next formation arrived. The pairs attacked from different directions to complicate the AA gunners' task. Bombs were dropped at runway

Commander

7th Commander – Mordechai 'Modi' Hod took command in April 1966 at age 40. A sabra, he had fought with the British during the Second World War and then in the Palmach in the days leading to independence. He trained as a pilot during the war and graduated soon after as a fighter pilot. Flying with 101 Squadron, he transitioned to the first jets entering IAF service. Hod went on to command 101 and, after completing the Command and Staff Course, lead a support squadron at Ramat David AB. He was then selected to command the first Ouragan squadron and fought with that unit during the Sinai Campaign. Hod went on to command the Hatzor wing and then lead the IAF Operations Branch. As head of the Air Department of the GHQ, he spent a long term as Weizman's deputy before moving up. As CO, he continued honing the force to a fine edge for the pre-emptive air base strike mission and led the force in the 1967 war. Hod followed Weizman's example and held the post for seven years, through the tough War of Attrition period and ushering in the American era of equipment. He also supported efforts to build a fighter jet in Israel. After handing over the reins in May 1973, Hod served additional distinctive roles in the IDF and MoD, to include seeing the Kfir into production.

Major-General Moti Hod is shown before a Mirage during a meeting with the press following the resounding success of the Six-Day War. (Author's Collection)

Israel's sole MiG-21 had proven invaluable in revealing the weaknesses of the fighter to be exploited by IAF combat pilots. However, performance of the "captive" was so good that it was not left idle during the June 1967 emergency. It was fitted with a pair of Shafrir 2 missiles and was prepared to intercept MiG-21R photo-recce flights over the Negev. The nation's premier test pilot, Danny Shapira, awaited his opportunity, but it never came. He also sat QRA on June 5 with 101 Squadron to intercept any retaliatory strikes from the nations being pounded by the IAF, but this was also fruitless. The aircraft was given high-visibility red markings to hopefully inform Mirage pilots that this was a "friendly." Reflecting the covert nature of its acquisition, the aircraft was coded "007" after the fictitious British secret agent. Like many other enemy assets falling into Israeli hands, it spent time in America undergoing evaluation.

The IAF had acquired a MiG-21F-13 in 1966 via an Iraqi defection (with Israeli instigation). This aircraft proved invaluable in air combat training and the jet was put to use as war loomed in 1967. It was fitted with the new Shafrir 2 AAM and was prepared to intercept Egyptian reconnaissance missions over the Negev, then sat alert during the preemptive strikes on June 6. The colorful markings were to help prevent overzealous Israeli fighter pilots from engaging the MiG. (Aerofax Collection)

intersections and at other points such as taxiways to provide insufficient clear take-off length for combat aircraft. The 154-lb (70-kg) Dibber runway cratering bombs were still in short supply, and the heavier version even more so. Consequently, many common 550 to 1,100-lb (250 and 500-kg) "iron" bombs were employed but fitted with hardened steel noses and tail fuses. The fuses could be set for impact detonation to destroy surface targets, or seven to 15 second delay for cratering. Three strafing passes were then executed to destroy aircraft on the field. Fighter bases were prime targets for the first wave in order to cripple the enemy's air-to-air capability before turning to bombers. As the primary combat bases were neutralized, other fields were added or secondary targets hit such as radar, SA-2 batteries, and AAA sites. Airborne interceptors were to be ignored until the primary mission had been executed.

Enemy personnel monitoring Israeli radio traffic and watching via radar might have detected the disruption in routine. The IAF sought to deceive listeners by having Magisters fly daily missions mimicking routine training and liaison flights and make appropriate radio calls. A pair of Mirages and some Cubs also flew seemingly routine morning missions. Each air base also transmitted recordings of radio traffic. Part of the IAF training had included a two-year routine in which a flight of jets launched each morning, flew out to the Mediterranean, and then descending for low-altitude flight below the Egyptian radar horizon before returning home. When this same routine occurred on June 5, the radar operators took no special notice.

Several special missions were flown in the morning of the 5th in support of the preemptive strikes, particularly electronic warfare (EW) tasks. An S-58 was perhaps the first IAF aircraft to execute a war mission when it flew into Sinai early in the morning to monitor Egyptian radio traffic, probably to detect if they had been alerted to Israeli plans.

The 255 or so aircraft of the 10 fighter-bomber squadrons were matched to targets as a function of range and defenses. The Israeli formations attempted to fly very low-altitude routes permitting final approach from unexpected directions and avoiding densely populated areas. The low-level ingress and egress from the target areas, to around 150 feet (46 m), was also well below the effective altitude of the SA-2. All navigation was by dead reckoning.

The first air base attack wave was 45 formations of 174 aircraft (several aborting) launched from just four airfields beginning at 0714 and continuing for approximately 90 minutes. The first formations off were returning as the last were dispatched. By 0740 Israel time (one hour ahead of Cairo), at the 17 EAF airfields in the Sinai and eastern Egypt, the dawn patrols had returned and alert state was relaxed. The crews were having breakfast and, in Cairo, commanders and Defence Ministry officials were on their way to work in the dense morning traffic. The Egyptians' ability to respond quickly was at its lowest level. The early morning mist was just lifting in the Nile delta. The air was relatively calm and provided the best visibility of the day. The attackers in the Sinai also benefited from having the sun at their backs.

At 0745-0750 the IAF aircraft began their attack on eight airfields, three in Sinai and four across the Canal. A ninth base deeper inside Egypt was initially hit at 0810. Cairo International was hit by mistake and another field was shot up by a departing formation. In the first 90-minute wave, each of these fields were struck two to seven times, but typically five. A few key radar stations in the north-eastern Sinai were also hit in the first wave by four formations of Magisters. Some Mirages bombed their targets and then assumed CAP over the Sinai. After the first strikes and loss of surprise, radio silence was abandoned and attackers flew direct routes to Egypt over the Mediterranean or Sinai at more fuel-economical altitudes. Low-level ingress/egress to the target was still employed until the enemy radar network had been neutralized and the potential for intercept was further eroded. The last formations still contributed to runway cratering, but found few airplanes remaining for strafing. So, radar, SA-2, and AAA were targeted in some cases.

Virtually no Egyptian aircraft were kept in HAS in 1967, and few in revetments, so they were ready targets. Pilots were told to

Some of the Israeli Magister jet trainers were equipped to mount twin .30-cal guns in the nose and carry light bombs or rockets under the wings. They were camouflaged, but with dayglo tape striping on the nose, tails, and wingtips for training that could be peeled off before entering combat. A squadron of reservists, flight instructors, and advanced students flew these light attack jets during the war. (Yoav Efrati Collection)

prioritize their selection, with the Tu-16s having top priority for destruction, and then moving down through MiG-21s and other fighters, to ground attack jets, and so on. However, they were to reserve some rounds in the event that they were challenged on the flight home. Marksmanship appeared almost unbelievably precise, attesting to the high standard of IAF training.

An Il-14 airborne command post with the Egyptian chief-of-staff, the Air Force commanding general, and many other senior officers, was aloft at the time of the initial attack. They eventually managed to land and evacuate the airplane just before it was strafed and set ablaze. In the two hours they were out of touch, these men could not counter the chaos being wrought around them. Many of the commanders of Sinai forces were at Bir Thamada airfield awaiting the VIPs when the war broke out and they took many hours getting back to their units. With the generals airborne over the area, most air defense units in the Sinai had been ordered to a "guns tight" state between 0800 and 0900. Jordanian radar detected the unusual IAF activity, but a message of warning to their ally went unread because the Egyptians had changed their transmission codes the previous day and were tardy informing the Jordanians.[58] All of this was a stroke of luck for the Israelis.

The first wave suffered eight aircraft shot down, perhaps one or two by Egyptian fighters and the rest to AAA. Five pilots were killed, two taken captive, and one recovered. Three aircraft returned to base badly damaged and with injured pilots. Several enemy aircraft in the air at the time of the initial attacks were downed. More important were the many dozens of aircraft destroyed on the ground and runways rendered inoperable. The EAF was badly mauled and the Israelis had in a stroke gained air superiority. The results were much better than anticipated, but the pressure had to be maintained to destroy the opposition force.

Mirage and Vautour recce aircraft overflew the most critical bases to assess damage and prepare for the second wave, participating in the strikes and taking post-strike photography. Other Vautours employed cameras during their bombing and fighters also brought back gun camera film of some assessment value. Most images were surely hours in being processed and evaluated for bomb damage assessment (BDA). Mission debriefs helped in making the selection of targets for the second wave, but retasking was possible with aircraft *en route* to their targets.

Aircraft were turned in 60 to 90 minutes and pilots ready in a comparable period. Mid-morning, 31 formations of 164 aircraft total began to depart. The QRA Mirages were released to contribute to attacks or fly CAP over key points traversed by the formations. Flying at altitudes for better range, some more distant targets were struck. Eight bases from the first wave were worked-over again as well as six additional. Missions were finding the air bases out of action and no suitable targets other than the engineering equipment attempting to repair runways. Some formations were diverted to more fruitful targets in-flight as these reports came in. More radar, AAA sites, and air base assets were attacked. No additional Israeli aircraft were lost, though some were damaged. Although encountering several airborne EAF fighters, and shooting down a few, no attempts to intercept the Israeli formations were observed. Many SA-2 missiles were fired, but none guided successfully.

Nasser did not confess the virtual annihilation of his air force when he encouraged Jordan and Syria to join the war. Shells began falling from these quarters, some hitting airfields and threatening the vital air campaign. Some enemy jets executed minor incursions into Israel and caused insignificant damage apart from destroying a Noratlas and a Super Cub dispersed to Kfar Sirkin. Although a few of the attackers were shot down, Israel had to respond.

Many third wave formations beginning to take-off just after noon were retasked to attack bases in Jordan and Syria. The aircrew were sufficiently familiar with the targets and the routes, during a clear day in a small theater, such that this airborne redirection was successful. Some 25 formations of 95 aircraft total were included in this wave, roughly defined, with only two formations continuing to Egyptian fields while the rest were diverted. As these were smaller air forces, neutralizing four Syrian and two Jordanian bases plus radar sites was sufficient to achieve air superiority in those quarters. Syria moved aircraft to far distant airfields to reduce loses. Jordan did not do the same and its small force was effectively destroyed. Losses were comparable to the first wave with seven jets downed (two air-to-air and one to friendly fire) with four pilots killed, two made prisoner-of-war (POW), and one recovered. Three Israeli air-to-air kills were recorded.

Early afternoon missions, roughly considered a fourth wave, were 10 formations of 33 aircraft total. This further worked-over three Syrian and Jordanian bases while adding another Syrian field and the distant Iraqi air base of H-3. Hitting H-3 was to forestall expected Iraqi bombing of Israel and reinforcement of Jordanian airpower. Many of these formations were less than

The 110 Squadron Vautours performed their intended function in attacking distant air bases, especially those housing jet bombers. Four of the 19 aircraft were lost during the war. This IIA, 29 "Pogrom," was actually a used French aircraft taken up shortly after the war and is shown in summer 1969 after being freshly painted by IAI. (BIAF – Israel Aerospace Magazine)

full four-ships due to lost or damaged aircraft and injured pilots. Turnaround time was also lengthening. Three aircraft were lost and others damaged.

A fifth and final wave of preemptive air base strikes was in late afternoon with 15 formations of 63 jets total. Strafing was discouraged to avoid exposure to AAA and because most aircraft targets had been destroyed. All returned, albeit some with damage. They revisited a dozen EAF and Syrian fields to disrupt reorganization efforts and runway repair work, especially by dropping delayed-fuzing bombs. The targets included Cairo International where combat aircraft had been dispersed. Ras Banas was the most distant target of the war, requiring Vautour flight time of an hour each way at cruise altitude to bomb the runways, but found no aircraft. Such missions were led by two-seat N-models.

Over the day, the IAF devoted 132 formations of 474 warplanes to hit 26 airfields while suffering 18 aircraft destroyed. It conducted 20 more airfield strikes over the next two days to slow runway repair or hit reinforcements from other nations, losing three additional machines. Pilots typically flew three sorties during the 5th. Things did not all go perfectly. Several aircraft aborted on the ground or inflight. Some had mechanical problems and could not drop their ordnance or fire their cannons. Some bombs did not detonate and some aim points were missed. Many ships returned in a critical fuel state, some diverting as necessary. Mechanics returned many damaged jets to flying status in a day or two. Enemy interceptors partially disrupted several attacks. A few formations found themselves mixed up over a target and some got lost. Some dummy aircraft were hit and some real, previously hit, were shot up again. Regardless, the results were stupendous. In the order of 300 enemy aircraft were destroyed on the ground and about two dozen claimed downed air-to-air.

> In one of the more bizarre incidents of the Six-Day War, an Israeli Hawk SAM shot down an Ouragan. The aircraft had been attacking a Jordanian air base when hit and the pilot injured. Unresponsive, he apparently flew by chance towards the no-fly zone around the Dimona nuclear research complex in the Negev. His mates tried to arouse him, but with no luck. The air defense team acted under orders to protect the high-value facility.

Sinai Days

Difficult ground combat in the Sinai remained to be fought to relieve the threat from the Egyptian Army and lift the blockade of Eilat. With Israeli dominance in the sky, the advantage lay with the IDF. Zahal crossed the border at 0745 on June 5 with only Magisters available to offer air support. Under Southern Command direct control, these were active from the first hours attacking Egyptian artillery emplacements on the northern axis of the Sinai assault. The Magisters, with their light weaponry, were fairly ineffective against these fortified targets. More success was had in striking convoys, troop concentrations, and sowing general confusion. Jets with heavier armament became available as the day wore on.

The Air Force also provided the usual liaison, airlift, and airdrop resources. Some Cubs had a cramped third seat or carried a radio for relay or C^2 communications. The helicopter equivalent was the Bell 47 of which each division and corps commander theoretically had one on call.

The key to defeating the Egyptian army in Sinai was Abu Agheila and its fortified defenses with massed artillery. The IDF chose to silence the artillery with a night heliborne assault from the rear. Two choppers first flew in fading daylight on June 5 to locate the landing zone, 2 miles (3 km) from the objective. Teams positioned light beacons, marker panels, and electronic navigation aids to guide the troop ships. Some of 124 Squadron helicopters were tasked with other priority missions, and so the lift was slower than hoped. For several hours S-58s flew three relays to the landing zone (LZ). Some crews became lost in the dark and the LZ had to be relocated after shells began falling in the area. When that site also came under fire, the lift was suspended. However, the assault proceeded with 200 of the planned 300 men and successfully disrupted supporting artillery fire. The night armor attack then broke through the weakened defenses.

After this one major ground battle, and facing disaster, the Egyptian Army leadership issued orders on the morning of June 6 for its forces in Sinai to pull back across the Suez Canal. Since the IDF's mission was to destroy the army, the enemy was pursued to the waterway. The Air Force worked to slow the retreating columns so that ground forces had a chance of catching up. The airdrop of fuel to some fast-moving Zahal elements sustained the pace. The IAF quickly became the principal bane of Egyptian soldiers as hundreds of vehicles and other equipment was destroyed via interdiction attacks. One of the most telling images of the war is the Mitla Pass choked with scores of burned-out vehicles hit with rockets, napalm, and gunfire. Zahal continued to press the enemy from the ground and the air as it retreated until the Egyptian forces disintegrated.

Attacks by Ouragans had left the El Arish runway lightly damaged so that it could be quickly repaired and employed by the IAF for casualty evacuation and resupply flights, or forward deployment of the Magister squadron.[59] Transport Command prepared to drop a brigade of paratroops at El Arish on the night of June 5/6 in coordination with a Navy landing of light tanks, to seize the airfield. A Boeing and 15 Noratlases were on standby for the lift. However, the ground campaign advanced so quickly that El Arish was overrun on the morning of the 6th and the IAF was using the airfield by that evening. The 7,000-foot (2,133-m) runway at Jebel Libni was bombed so that 3,500-feet (1,067-m) remained undamaged – insufficient for EAF fighter operations, but enough for IAF transports. Another airstrike just before sunset on the 6th dropped anti-personnel ordnance over the base to delay repair operations until the IDF could take possession of the field the following day. It, too, was turned into an airlift center. Once Bir Gifgafa was secured, Noratlases and Dakotas began flying in supplies, probably operating from intact taxiways. Operations from other Sinai bases were conducted as necessary to evacuate wounded. There appears to have been none of the off-field operations executed in 1956.

A daylight drop of 350-400 paratroops and gear was planned for Sharm el Sheikh at dawn on June 7. This was to have been 20 transports with fighter escorts. However, a Navy landing party found the post deserted. Consequently, a dozen S-58s and three Super Frelons lifted a force of 150 paratroopers followed by three Nords with more soldiers. Several command cars were airdropped, but high winds ensured all were damaged on touchdown. Later, some of the troopers were flown to El Tor to effectively block the Gulf of Suez. Ras Sudr, on the west coast, followed on the 8th with elements of the same force helicoptered to the site. By June 8, the IDF was on the Canal and mopping up remaining enemy elements in the peninsula.

Operations were not entirely free of EAF action, but their efforts were small in scale and frequently disrupted by IAF interceptors. The Israelis claimed 11 EAF airplanes downed air-to-air on the 6th and nine on the 8th. The SA-2s continued to be a menace and at least one Mirage and a Super Mystére was lost to the threat.[60] The IAF attacked many of the SAM sites on the 7th and 8th. Some 23 sites were destroyed plus 16 radar installations.[61]

The Bell 47 was purchased to increase the helicopter pilot training capacity in the early 1960s but served for only a few years. As with all IAF aircraft of the period, it had wartime roles that included scouting, liaison, and senior personnel transport to forward locations. (Author's Collection)

The Cub participated in its third and last Arab-Israeli war during 1967 before being devoted solely to training. This example, in solid olive drab finish, is shown in the company of three Stratocruisers, one with 120 Squadron markings. The Boeings conducted many logistics flights plus some electronic warfare missions. (Military Aircraft Photographs)

By the time of the Six-Day War, the IAF had a large fleet of S-58 piston-powered helicopters and a modest number of turbine Super Frelons. These supported assaults in large-force actions, but also small-unit insertion and extraction. The Frelon had a drop-down loading ramp for wheeled cargo and a greater troop capacity, offering more options of assaults with heavy equipment. Note the flare tube beneath the pilot side window and the nose antennas for pilot Sarah survival radio signal reception. (Author's Collection)

Other Fronts

Attacking Egypt alone had not limited the war to one county. Syrian and Jordanian harassing fire, and Jordanian armored forces movements on the West Bank threatening Israel's narrow waist, could not go unanswered.

Zahal troops crossed into the West Bank on June 5 and the Jordanian army fought back hard. As in Sinai, Magisters dominated during the first half of day one, but more IAF airstrikes were directed to supporting IDF troops over the next two days, some hitting quite close to friendly forces. This included night airstrikes under the illumination of parachute flares. Hitting artillery positions and interdicting enemy armored columns were especially helpful. After two and a half days of heavy fighting the remains of the Jordanian forces pulled back across the Jordan River. On the 9th, the Israelis blew the bridges, the IAF dropping two of the spans. The whole of Jerusalem and the West Bank was in Israeli hands. King Hussein credited incessant air attacks, night and day, as the principal source of his forces' defeat.

In the early hours of June 9, Egypt accepted the UN-sponsored ceasefire. Although Syria also welcomed a ceasefire, the Israelis would have none of it. The IDF was not going to miss an opportunity to end two decades of Syrian harassment shelling of civilian targets. The enemy had launched a weak offensive on the 6th, but local militias and the IAF had stalled the effort. The next day the Air Force made repeated and heavy attacks on the Syrian emplacements and personnel on the Golan. So well-constructed were the defenses that the intense aerial bombardment had little effect. The IAF also hit Syrian air bases again.

The assault on the Golan Heights beginning on the morning of the 9th was aided by the decision of the Syrian command, facing the prospect of battling the Israelis alone, to pull back from the escarpment. The Air Force assisted the ground assault with many attack sorties. Troops were also rapidly repositioned by S-58s into blocking positions in the rear of the Syrian lines. The Super Frelon's ability to lift in jeeps mounting recoilless rifles aided this effort. These IDF forces, at strategic crossroads and other positions, established the extent of captured territory for postwar negotiations. When the ceasefire finally held on the evening of June 10, under threats of Soviet intervention, Zahal had overrun the Golan and pushed the enemy back beyond artillery range of Galilee.

This 116 Squadron Mystères IVA is serviced in a hardened shelter between sorties during the first few days of the 1967 war. The aircraft was struck by ground fire on June 7 and abandoned by the pilot. Such aircraft and aircrew flew several missions per day during the war. (Ra'anan Weiss Collection)

The C-47 was still a vital element of Israeli "heavy" airlift capability. Augmented with French airframes, it provided airland resupply throughout the campaign and prepared for paratroop airdrop – all capabilities unusual for such a small and relatively impoverished air force. By 1967, the use of C-47s by a world-class air force was considered "quaint." (BIAF – Israel Aerospace Magazine)

The Air Force supported the fast moving armored thrust across the Sinai with airdrop of vital supplies as well as landing at evacuated Egyptian air bases. These 103 Squadron Noratlases are conducting heavy airdrop. Operating from Tel Nof AB, the two dozen Nord's were the most numerous transports. (BIAF – Israel Aerospace Magazine)

Accounting

The IAF destruction of the Egyptian air force in strikes against its air bases on the morning of June 5, 1967, is among the most successful surprise aerial attacks ever executed, ranking with such events as the German destruction of the Soviet air arms in summer 1941 and the Japanese December 1941 attack on Pearl Harbor. The event, combined with the momentous IDF victories in the following days, were astonishing. The IAF's tremendous contribution to these successes propelled it to prominence among airpower teams. Israel had been a novelty in its creation and growth, its evolving culture, and its continuing security challenges. Now it also appeared to possess one of the most capable militaries backed by a bold intelligence service and determined leadership. Many wanted to know more, yet the Israelis revealed little and made intentional misstatements to enhance its appearance of invincibility and to conceal actual capabilities.

Numbers offered by the Israelis at the time were surely manipulated, but the fact of the greatly unbalanced results is indisputable. They estimated the IAF had destroyed about 60 percent of the enemy's aircraft, the majority on the ground. American spy satellite imagery counted 246 Egyptian, 26 Syrian, and 18 Jordanian aircraft destroyed at airfields.[62] Having established air superiority early on, enemy fighters that made it aloft were usually met by superior numbers of Israeli interceptors.

The IAF flew 2,591 ground attack sorties, only 268 on the 5th, while suffering 22 aircraft lost. Intercept and CAP sorties numbered 637 sorties and they prosecuted some 60 air-to-air engagements downing 58 enemy airplanes while losing 12 to 19 in the bargain for a rough 4:1 exchange ratio. Israel got its first "ace" out of the war, and 42 more IAF pilots would gain that distinction over the coming 15 years.[63]

Twenty-five IAF aircrew were killed or approximately one in 11 of the fighter pilot cadre participating. Five were wounded, seven were captured, and 15 rescued. At least one pilot who safely ejected from his aircraft was murdered by locals once on the ground – a crime that would be repeated several times over the coming decades. A total 47 aircraft were lost outright or written-off (all but two a fighter-bomber or 23 percent of that force), with a further 23 requiring extensive repair. Approximately three-quarters of the losses were in air-to-ground missions.[64] With a total 3,318 fighter-bomber sorties, this amounted to a loss rate of just 1.4 percent. Although appearing light, this constituted 17 percent of attack assets that would be difficult to replace.

Losses broke down to 10 Ouragans, nine Mirages, nine SMB2s, seven MIVA, six Magisters, four Vautours, a Noratlas, and a Super Cub. The Ouragans and Magisters were comparatively slow and so more vulnerable to ground fire. The Fouga's lack of armor and ejection seat or jettisonable canopy was especially felt, and the .30-cal guns of little value. The pilots of all six of the downed machines were killed (though one murdered after reaching the ground), unlike losses of other types. The Magisters also flew more frequently in the first three days and the pilots averaged about four sorties per day. Once the full weight of the fighter-bombers were brought to bear in ground support missions, 147 Squadron stood down on the 8th. However, they were committed again on the Golan, deploying a dozen airplanes to Ramat David. The first strike saw the squadron CO killed and this brought home the vulnerability of the light jet. No further missions were launched.

A 107 Squadron ground crew swarms a returning Ouragan at Lod, preparing it for another sortie. The ability to quickly refuel, rearm, and turn jets to sustain a high sortie rate assisted the IAF in making the most from its comparatively small fleet and short of their goal of two pilots per aircraft. The slow Ouragan, devoted to ground attack, suffered more losses than any other type at 10 machines. (Ra'anan Weiss Collection)

The Super Mystère B2s were among the highest performing of the fighter-bombers, and the 105 Squadron worked hard during the war (aircraft 12 with 250 kg bombs and 1,300-l drop tanks). They flew the greatest number of sorties (504), but also suffered the most losses as a proportion of their numbers with nine aircraft destroyed and six pilots killed. (Ofer Zidon Collection)

There is no denying that the IAF made impressive use of its fighter-bombers for all manner of combat missions. This spoke well for their ability to adapt the airplanes, the skills of maintainers and armorers, and efficacy of pilot training. Aircraft averaged several (albeit brief) sorties per day. Pilots typically flew three missions per day during the first four days, about half this for the final two, for an average 13 total. The pilots were aggressive yet disciplined and pressed home attacks with unusual determination.

The IDF was generally dissatisfied with the coordination, communication, and responsiveness of the Air Force. The IAF liaison officers were few, concentrated at command elements not necessarily at the forward edge of the battle, and lacked resources to perform the coordination required. Most strikes were initiated by the IAF on its own.[65] The division of attention between Sinai and the West Bank on the 6th overwhelmed their resources, and many requests for air support went unanswered. The fighting in Syria was so fierce that, again, the requests for air support overwhelmed the IAF's system and air assets were not tasked efficiently.

The IAF did well interdicting reinforcements and executing strikes on enemy positions. It was less effective at CAS for which fast jets are ill suited. At the time, the IAF had been training to attack 655 to 820 feet (200 to 250 m) ahead of its advancing forces. There were a few instances of hitting friendlies. Air support of troops in built-up areas were few, but civilians were still casualties of airstrikes. Effectiveness against armored vehicles appears to have been quite marginal. However, even airstrikes that left few vehicles actually destroyed was often enough to cause the enemy to pause or withdraw.

The IAF appears to have become a bit over-confident after June 5, as exemplified by repeated attacks on H-3. The effectiveness of the hasty Vautour strike on the first day was difficult to judge and so missions were flown on the next two days. Each was supported by more Mirages but, coming from the same direction, were detected *en route* and met by increasing numbers of enemy aircraft. This cost Israel jets and lives, with H-3 likely not knocked out of action for long. However, the Iraqis did cease contributing to the war.

One of the lessons other air forces drew from the war was the great success of cannon fire in bringing down so many adversaries and destroying ground targets. Although firing 26 Shafrirs and four R.530s, cannons accounted for all air combat victories. The Arab adversaries fired missiles as well with little success. This contributed to a rethinking worldwide of deleting cannon from fighters. The vulnerability of air bases and the need to protect all combat aircraft in hardened shelters was also noted. At least in the limited scope of the Arab-Israeli conflict, multi-role fighters were suitably effective where more-limited weapons like heavy bombers were too costly. The SAMs had a disappointing score, but a multi-level anti-aircraft defense was clearly needed to suitably deter preemptive airstrikes.

Transports flew 757 sorties and light-planes 258. The combat helicopter force flew 840 hours and proved its worth in lifting troops into advantageous positions to affect battles dramatically. They were also of great value in extracting wounded with 563 flown to rear aid stations compared with 240 for fixed-wing aircraft. The Israeli national airlines flew support missions throughout the war. The El Al Boeing 707s and 720s were particularly helpful collecting critical supplies from overseas suppliers, such as gas masks from the USA. The Arkia fleet of Handley Page Dart-Herald turboprops was also mobilized and flew 70 hours during the conflict. They lifted water in and wounded out of Sinai airfields.

The war illustrated the lengths the Air Force would go to recover downed aircrew. Although Cubs still picked up a few men, helicopters assumed more and more of the SAR role, counting 13 saves and beginning the IAF practice of carrying medical corpsmen or doctors. Some helicopters flew into dangerous areas to retrieve the airman while attack aircraft would keep enemy heads down. Several men were recovery at sea and a difficult Super Frelon mission across the Canal sought to retrieve two pilots shot down on the morning of the 5th.

Most important for the IAF was that their expensive warplanes helped Israel win such a resounding victory, silencing many MoD protests and questioning of earlier fiscal decisions. The Air Force would continue winning the lion's share of the security budget as it assumed more defense responsibilities.

CHAPTER 7
WAR OF ATTRITION

Tensions on the borders soon flared anew following the 1967 war. Egypt, especially, kept up the pressure, but the northern and central fronts also saw persistent engagements. The IDF remained very active with more consistent military action than ever before. As this situation grew in scope, the cost escalated in lives, materiel, and treasure. The geopolitical stakes rose and Israel found itself fighting the Soviets indirectly and, in some cases, directly, while dependence on American supply deepened. Responding to need, the IAF grew in size, adopted more complex systems, and trained for new tactics – all in the tumult of combat action of escalating intensity.

Fallout

Israel's success in the Six-Day War brought her many new challenges. She became the occupier of vast stretches of captured territory three times the area of Israel. The Sinai and Gaza Strip offered previously unavailable strategic depth and a comfortable buffer to military adventure by the Egyptians. However, continued hostile exchanges on the Suez front meant extended lines of communication. Likewise, the Golan Heights served as a buffer, but continued tensions required a sizable military deployment there. The West Bank, however, was viewed as Judea and Samaria – historical elements of ancient Israel. Here, especially, the territory made Israel's borders more defensible and Israeli settlements began to be established immediately. The liberation of the whole of Jerusalem, with its holy sites, held particular emotional rewards. These lands also came with approximately one million Arab inhabitants.

The conquered territories and outcome of the war lent fresh fuel to the terrorism waged by the Palestinians and other groups, supported by surrounding states. This brought IDF crackdowns followed by international condemnation. The occupation became a troubling military, civil, and legal issue for Israel.

The government declared that the country would remain in the occupied territories until "a just and lasting peace within secure borders" could be negotiated. Since it was clear that Israel could never achieve a military victory capable of imposing an end to the conflict, the Territories represented a new political element in offering to exchange land for peace. However, the occupation of their land taken by force and the humiliation of the Six-Day War were not motivations for Arab reconciliation.

The Arab states became more intransigent than ever and made ready for continued confrontation. Egypt blocked the Suez Canal and, with no evidence the strategic waterway would be reopened in the near future, the Middle East conflict became of concern to the entire world. The Arab League expanded the long-standing Arab Boycott and compelled many emergent nations who had welcomed Israeli assistance in the past to distance themselves from the country. Members covertly sponsored and trained Palestinian terrorists who began to act against Israeli personnel, assets, and general Jewish interest throughout the world. Israel found itself engaged on all sides and isolated as never before. With the perception as an international pariah and its persistent struggle to obtain arms, Israel was compelled to adopt more clandestine methods. She became known for bold if borderline illegal intelligence gathering operations and daring self-defense actions. Their attitude became that the world community did not treat Israel fairly and so Israel did not need to play fair. Although Israel insisted it should be held to a higher standard than surrounding states, it as often expressed resentment of the double standard. Additionally, along with her heroes, Israel has long lionized those who broke laws in the interest of state security and the protection of Jews worldwide, making such actions less likely to be rejected. Such attitudes persisted for decades.

With the aid of oil-rich Arab nations, Israel's opponents were rearmed within months with more advanced Soviet weapons. These were in greater quantities than ever before and accompanied by hundreds of "advisors." More airfields and HAS were constructed. Emboldened, Egypt and Syria kept the borders hot with artillery barrages, commando raids, and airstrikes.

Israel responded in kind while also answering terrorist attacks from Jordan and Lebanon. The requirement to respond quickly to combat on the Suez drove the IAF to adopt former Egyptian fields in the Sinai. Bir Gifgafa (renamed Refidim) and Ras Nasrani (renamed Ophir) were substantially expanded, with fuel systems, command centers, and HAS. El Arish became a training base to take advantage of Sinai airspace, students flown back and forth from Hatzerim.[66] Others were kept as emergency landing strips. An entirely new base, Etzion, was constructed opposite Eilat. Squadrons rotated forward-deployed aircraft and personnel through these facilities.

The continuing conflict made it imperative that the IDF, and the Air Force in particular, replace lost equipment. Israel also had to progressively upgrade systems to meet the expanding threats. With the Algerian issue resolved, France under de Gaulle was seeking to increase its influence on the 'Arab Street' and had less interest in Israel as a potential base for military operations. It began to moderate its accommodations to Israel. However, individual ministries executed policies of their ministers that were not always in concert with central direction. Consequently, the French embargo of arms to Israel was stricter in appearance than reality. Some deliveries and support continued for a time, occasionally transshipped through third parties, until even this largely ceased after 1968. The Israelis were forced to take extraordinary measures to continue operating their French equipment, including neglecting to return six Super Mystères undergoing overhaul.[67] This included surreptitious deals with South Africa, the other famously pariah nation. The Israeli defense industry took on more work to manufacture parts, remanufacture aging aircraft, and install upgraded systems. The Air Force was also compelled to turn its attention to developing its nascent EW capability for jamming, information gathering, and suppression of enemy air defenses (SEAD). These were all costly efforts that the Israelis partially offset by selling such products and services internationally. Owing to the frequent operational uses of the equipment and the Israeli reputation for combat success, it became a selling point that the gear was employed by the IAF.

Fortunately, the Americans had begun to sell Israel weapons with increasing volume. They sought to "balance" arms being provided to Arab states and at first sold only "defensive" warplanes. However, sales expanded almost exponentially in step with Soviet support for Israel's adversaries.

All this came at a heavy price. The size of Israel's standing armed forces grew over 40 percent to 130,000 personnel. By October 1973, the defense budget was consuming 30 percent of the Gross National Product, with the IAF accounting for over 50 percent of that budget.

The Vautours became difficult to sustain given the French embargo following the Six-Day War. Advent of the F-4 Phantom made their service increasingly redundant. The aircraft were turned to electronic warfare until retired in 1970 and 1971. This 110 Squadron Vautour IIN "Dragon," shown in January 1969, has various ground kill and mission markings on the tail. (BIAF – Israel Aerospace Magazine)

Re-equipping

The Ouragans, Mystère IVAs, and Vautours were slowly withdrawn as American equipment was taken on. All had been flown well beyond their design service lives and were ill suited for the battlefield of growing lethality. However, fearing the Americans' willingness to sell warplanes might prove capricious, Israel worked to prolong the service of the remaining French aircraft. Pilots took extra risks to bring ailing airplanes home and damaged aircraft that would normally have been written off were repaired. The Super Mystères were given upgraded American and Israeli avionics and modified to take more external weapons. An extensive rework fitted the American engine from the A-4H the IAF was acquiring. This increased thrust without afterburner, and so improved fuel economy while sacrificing air-to-air combat potency, making these 27 *Sa'ar* more practical attack jets.[68] (Israel devised Hebrew names for her aircraft and weapons as motivation and concealment.) Upgrading the Mirages included adding Radar Warning Receivers (RWR) and uprated engines. They adopted the name *Shahak* for the reworked fighter. The fleet grew more diverse and seldom were two aircraft of a type identical – something that would characterize the IAF throughout its existence. This complicated maintenance and operations. However, the presence of long-serving reserve cadre with deep knowledge and experience eased adverse consequences.

The extraordinary relationship between France and Israel – through always a tacit alliance short of a mutual defense pact – especially in military aviation, had previously experienced close cooperation on warplane development. The last expression of this saw Israel working with Dassault to develop a variant of the Mirage more suited to its needs. The Mirage 5J saw avionics simplified including substituting a rangefinder for the radar and giving up the little-used night and all-weather features, volume freed-up for additional internal fuel, and addition of two more external store stations. It would be easier to maintain and faster to turn between sorties. Israel ordered 52, but the French embargoed the jets following the Six-Day War. Although Israel paid the full $62 million, de Gaulle was steadfast in refusing delivery and the money was refunded.

The Mirage III remained the premier IAF interceptor, yet numbers shrank via attrition. Consequently, Israel's desire for the Mirage 5 was unshaken, yet there seemed no way to induce delivery. She could not simply spirit them away as the IN had done with five embargoed missile boats. Israel's indigenous aviation industry, which had worked so closely on the Mirage 5 development, convinced the government it could manufacture the jet locally, though some equipment would have to come from abroad. There were stories of the intelligence services acquiring design and production details in Europe. However, much of this appears to have been subterfuge to conceal an ongoing and extensive collaboration with French industry. Since the portions of the contract regarding "parts and accessories" remained in force, aircraft components were built in France. Third parties in the transaction ensured that there were no direct French sales to Israel. Components were flown to Israel in IAF Stratocruisers and Noratlases, and assembled by IAI with French-supplied tooling. The jets began rolling out as the *Nesher* in 1971, but their existence remained classified until 1982.[69] Heavier than Mirages, they were felt to be slightly inferior in air-to-air combat.

The interceptor force came to carry IR-guided AAMs routinely after 1967. The Shafrir scored its first kill soon after and was credit with two total. However, it and Russian Atolls adopted from captured stock were considered so marginally effective that some pilots were firing them well outside engagement envelopes simply to clean-up the jet before closing to gunfire range.[70] The Shafrir 2 began supplanting the original round in 1969 and was immediately successful.[71] However, the IAF also began buying AIM-9D Sidewinder missiles from the USA for the new American warplanes being acquired. It was more reliable and effective than the Shafrir 2 and could be acquired more rapidly. Integration onto the Mirages was at the instigation of a squadron commander after

The sunset on the French era of IAF equipment is suggested by this image as a 113 Squadron Ouragan lands in front of two Phantoms waiting to take the runway. The 113 was the last squadron to operate the type, setting its last aside at the end of 1972. By then the slow jet was just too dated for the evolving Middle East battlefield. (Ra'anan Weiss Collection)

The dwindling Mirage fleet was bolstered by the similar Nesher. Essentially Mirage 5s constructed in France but assembled in Israel, delivery began in 1971. However, their existence was not publicly acknowledged for a decade and the black nose was meant to deceptively suggest a Mirage IIICJ even though there was no radome or radar. This 113 Squadron Nesher took flight with tanks for an extended-endurance patrol and a pair of Shafrir 2 missiles. (Ra'anan Weiss Collection)

he encountered reluctance at headquarters. The AAMs were also integrated onto reconnaissance Vautours to given them a defensive capability such that a fighter escort would not be essential.

The IAF needed heavy and light attack aircraft with air-to-air capability. Still seeking an answer to the enemy's distant bomber bases, in Israel sought to buy F-4s from the USA. A top speed greater than Mach 2, typical combat range of 800 miles (1.288 km), a true multi-role and all-weather fighter-bomber with 16,000-lb (7,258-kg) weapons load, and the safety of twin engines, all made the Phantom the leading combat jet of its time. The proven radar and AIM-7 Sparrow missile system gave a beyond-visual-range (BVR) air-to-air dimension. This would clearly have upset the military balance in the region and was rejected. However, the Americans did agree to sell A-4 Skyhawks for light attack to balance other arms sales in the region and with the appearance of a more defensive system.

The 1966 agreement was to supply 48 new A-4Hs. These were A-4Fs with much of the "offensive" weapons delivery capability (RWR, AAM) removed and with a fixed gunsight. This left it essentially a pure attack machine and so inconsistent with IAF policy of operating multi-mission warplanes. However, it was relatively inexpensive, rugged and simple, and could carry 8,200 lb (3,720 kg) of ordnance compared with the Mirage's 4,000 lb (1,814 kg) while possessing twice the endurance. The Israelis asked that a braking parachute be added, as they were concerned its warplanes might have to operate from bombed runways reducing serviceable length.

The first Skyhawks arrived in December 1967 and saw its first action in February 1968. As the fronts heated-up, the little jet was employed more and more frequently. Consequently, 52 more Hs were ordered, set for delivery beginning in fall 1969. The need was growing rapidly and the USA, seeking to restrain Israel during intense diplomatic efforts, provided more than 50 refurbished former US Navy A-4Es and some TA-4Js that started arriving in 1971. The Es retained much of the systems deleted from the original Hs. The two-seaters were armed and an observer could occupy the second seat such that the machine might serve as an airborne FAC.

The A-4 became a real workhorse, seen almost daily over the battlefields. With the Air Force taking on the dominant role in the bitter struggle, making airstrikes in response to almost every provocation, attrition took its toll. They lost eight A-4s through August 1970.[72] Although the United States briefly held up approving further Skyhawk sales in an effort to bring Israeli agreement on a ceasefire, the losses were soon being replaced on a one-for-one basis. As a result, the IAF began to acquire some of the defensive avionics systems the USA had developed during the Vietnam War for their A-4Fs.

A large and persistent role for the A-4 appeared certain, and the service continually sought ways to improve the jet and form it to their particular needs. Working closely with McDonnell Douglas, they requested more power from an uprated engine matched to larger intakes, a stronger combat punch with Israeli-manufactured 30-mm cannons, and greater weapons delivery accuracy with improved navigation from an Israeli-developed nav-attack computer and Head-Up Display (HUD), plus reintroduction of

The USA agreed to sell the Israelis A-4 Skyhawks before the Six-Day War following long negotiation. With delivery beginning in December 1967, these machines began to contribute almost immediately to the ongoing low-level combat operations. This A-4H of 109 Squadron is one of the earliest Skyhawks to enter IAF service, photographed in 1970. (Author's Collection)

AAM capability. The added dorsal "hump" contained much of the new avionics with hopes it would someday also enclose defensive avionics.[73] The IAF showed their conviction that this A-4N Skyhawk II was a winning combination by ordering 80 in 1971 and another 36 in summer 1973. Some aspects of the N, such as the 30-mm, combat avionics with hump, braking parachute, and engine, began to be retrofitted to earlier jets. With three principal models and upgrades being applied as resources permitted, the Skyhawk fleet grew diverse.

Israel had persisted in efforts to obtain the Phantom, the Premier making a personal appeal to the American president in January 1968. Given Arab intransigence regarding peace negotiations, growing Soviet presence in the region, the French embargo, plus American election-year politics, the USA agreed by the end of that year to supply 50 new F-4Es. Delivery would not begin for another year. Unlike the just-under $1 million a copy Skyhawk, the Phantom ran $4.5 million – an enormous expense for the little state, eased a bit with fund drives at home and abroad. This saw Jewish children raising money to buy warplanes for Israel.

A large IAF cadre returned from training in the USA to form the first Phantom squadron by the time of initial deliveries on September 5, 1969. They also brought back knowledge of American combat tactics employed in Vietnam and how they dealt with SAMs. Aircraft arrived at a rate of four per month. The new 201 Squadron then had to assimilate the complex aircraft while training more personnel and also becoming operational – flying their first strike mission on October 22. The squadron put together a two-month course for new aircrew, but the students were being sent on missions before completing the training. Through the next 11 months of intensive fighting until a ceasefire, 20 additional aircrew supplemented the original five. The second outfit was the 69 Squadron reformed in November.

Follow-on F-4 orders of 80 aircraft, delivered through October 1973, included 62 former USAF machines. Some of these were one-for-one replacements for losses. The IAF began modifying its jets with the new wing leading-edge slats to enhance maneuverability. They explored substituting the favored 30-mm cannon for the standard 20-mm Gatling gun, but this was eventually dropped. The Phantom did well with the 20-mm, and the Skyhawks eventually found they seldom used the 30-mm introduced with much effort.

As the F-4 and A-4 were introduced into the force mix the Mirages and later Neshers became devoted almost exclusively to the counter-air mission. Further efforts at enhancing their air-to-ground capacity were dismissed.

The Magisters were restricted to training and its attack role eliminated. However, training still demanded that the Fouga be sustained and even grown as the size of the Air Force expanded to meet combat demands. Fifty more were acquired, half from France and half from Germany, flown to Israel disassembled in Stratocruisers during low-profile night missions. Accidents in all manner of training during this period was summing to an average of more than 10 airplanes destroyed per year, owing principally to undisciplined flying.[74]

The desire for the Hercules finally bore fruit in 1971. However, with so much being spent on Skyhawks and Phantoms, only two new C-130Hs were procured. With addition of the C-130s to 120 Squadron, the Dakotas were broken out into the new 122 Squadron at Lod in 1971. The new airlifter greatly expanded paratroop and cargo airdrop plus off-field assault landing capabilities. They and the Noratlases began training for such specialized missions as low-altitude parachute extraction system (LAPES) delivery of vehicles and guns.[75]

The old Stratocruisers soldiered on and more KC-97s were acquired. They remained a troublesome lot and some were retired when they simply became too cantankerous. The Stratos began to take on more missions like EW and aerial refueling (AR), though these were just one or two airframes each. The nose-and-drogue AR capability allowed strike formations of the A-4 fighter-bombers to be refueled to extend their endurance and reach to distant targets.

Light transport was beefed-up with the arrival of 36 Cessna U206 Stationairs. With a powerful engine and wide doors for the generous cabin, it had high utility in the liaison and light cargo

The Phantom increased the IAF's bomb delivery tonnage, range, and accuracy by an order of magnitude. During the War of Attrition the complex airplane, requiring two aircrew, was integrated into the force and pressed into combat in a period of increasing enemy air defense lethality. The Phantom teams were greatly challenged. (Author's Collection)

One of the IAF's two new 120 Squadron C-130Hs (4X-FBA 102) shows the paucity of markings common on the heavy transports given their low-profile missions beyond the border. The Hercules represented a tremendous increase in tactical airlift capacity, to include cargo and paratroop airdrop, but funding constraints during the War of Attrition continually delayed initial purchase and then expansion of the fleet. (Author's Collection)

The B-377s were slowly supplemented with C-97s as they emerged from Israel Aircraft Industries overhaul and equipping. Ship 4X-FPX 98 "Zipori" of 120 Squadron is a B-377 with cargo loading doors under the tail. It was photographed at Gatwick in 1969. (Military Aircraft Photographs)

In 1968, the IAF began refreshing its liaison fleet with U206 Stationairs. The Cessna airplanes had performance suitable to high gross weights and hot days, with wide doors accommodating transport of critical supplies. Some were fitted with a belly cargo pack. The U206s served for nearly 30 years. (Amos Dor Collection)

The heavy lift Super Frelons were joined and soon outnumbered by Sikorsky S-65s at Tel Nof AB beginning in 1969. The 118 Squadron was immediately at work during the height of the War of Attrition, especially in supporting special operation raids in all the surrounding confrontation states. As with all Israeli medium and heavy lift helicopters, this Sikorsky has a winch above the crew door. (Ofer Zidon Collection)

delivery roles. Two litters could be accommodated as well and simple airdrop by shoving packages out the door. Seeking to increase capacity of the STOL liaison types like the Do.27, the IAF bought 15 of the twin-engine Do.28. All 100 Squadron Cubs were sent to training in 1972.

Eight additional Super Frelons were delivered before supply was cut off. Parts were acquired from the French for a time longer before Israel sought sources wherever they could be found. The heavy lift helicopters had proven their value in the Six-Day War and the continuing conflict, with extensive special forces operations. Additional such resources became a priority. Of the available American equipment, the Sikorsky CH-53 Sea Stallion became the choice and upped capacity to 55 troops or 24 litters or 1.5-tons internally, loaded across the rear ramp, and a substantial sling load. Perhaps 17 were supplied, but as commercial S-65Cs.

Moving to an all turbine rotorcraft fleet, the Bell 47s were retired as additional Alouettes were purchased. However, they were growing obsolete and so confined to training while Bell 206 JetRangers were acquired beginning in 1971 for liaison and light transport. Their wartime job remained ferrying commanders to forward-deployed units.

For medium transport "choppers," the American "Huey" was sought. Again, the USA supplied a commercial model, the Bell 205, although this was essentially a UH-1D. The 51 helicopters were delivered starting at the end of 1967 and the S-58s

A number of enemy aircraft fell into Israeli hands over the decades. These were captured as forces overran airfields, were provided by defectors, or mistakenly landed on Israeli soil. This last was not always by way of blunder, but also Arabic-speaking IDF ground controllers on enemy mission frequencies giving misleading directions to land where they could be seized. (Such deception was also employed in combat to lure enemy pilots into positions advantageous for intercept.) The pilots could then be used to bargain for release of IDF personnel. In an apparent case of simply getting lost and possessing old charts, two Syrian student pilots landed their MiG-17s at the Bezet emergency strip on the Israel-Lebanon border on August 12, 1968. A crowd of locals gathered and snapped pictures before service personnel arrived. The two machines were soon given Israeli markings and flown on evaluation or air combat practice against IAF fighters. At least one was provided to the Americans for their assessment and the pilots eventually returned in a prisoner swap.

were gone within a year. The Israelis ensured the 205s got rescue winches and soon added a step to each landing skid to ease entry and exit. In this period, the troop helicopters began to adopt flare grenade launch tubes attached to the fuselage. The Bell 205s also got machine guns mounted to be fired from the cabin doors to provide suppressing fire onto "hot" LZs.

Expansion

The USSR poured weapons into the Middle East at an alarming rate and so Israel worked incessantly to obtain as much of her own as she could afford and the USA would provide. In the face of continuing belligerency of her neighbors, Israel was seeking an unquestioned military superiority. In just the few years following the Six-Day War, the Israeli Air Force expanded roughly 50 percent from 250 or so combat aircraft to about 350, from nine to 14 combat squadrons, and from four to seven principal air bases. Just as importantly, Israeli pilots logged about 200 hours annually compared with an average 70 hours for Egyptian combat pilots. Despite repeated protestations of being the underdog, in resources and capabilities, the IAF became one of the top air forces in the world.

By the end of 1971, the IAF had increased its weapons payload capacity four-fold from that existing before June 1967. By October 1973 another doubling of payload had occurred – from 570 tons in 1967 to 2,000 by 1973, or a 350 percent increase. Lethality against ground targets also increased 12.5 times above that in 1967. This was due largely to the navigation and attack electronic systems that increased bombing accuracy by a factor of 3.5 over the earlier generation aircraft. All this left the Arab adversaries far behind as the USSR delivered no comparable warplanes.

With the new nav/attack systems came new tactics. Bomb-toss delivery supplemented the familiar dive-bombing method. The Skyhawks became known for the "Indian circle" attack pattern with a pair of jets circling the target and alternately diving in to attack. One aircraft was always opposite the attacker looking for threats. In attacking SAMs, many tactics were tried by the Phantoms until settling on an extremely low-level ingress followed by a pop-up scissors. The IAF also adopted American bombs, slowly displacing the locally produced weapons. Napalm began to be replaced by cluster bombs. Rockets continued to be used by the Sa'ars and Skyhawks.

Although the A-4 was a fairly simple warplane, it possessed more electronic systems than the IAF had previously experienced. The Phantom was another large step of increasing electronic and maintenance complexity. It was one of the most complex combat aircraft ever produced, difficult to effectively maintain and operate. Its logistical demands were prodigious. Maintenance specialists were so short for a time that American technicians had to fill in. The American maintenance concept required some adaptation. The F-4's two-man cockpit was a new operational concept that also required adjustment. Dealing with new and sophisticated equipment, engaging in continuous combat on three fronts, developing new tactics to deal with the SAM threat, the challenge to maintain personnel quality given rapid expansion, training, and advancement, plus the slow, but steady drain of experienced manpower due to losses, made this the most turbulent period in IAF history.

Many air arms were interested in the IAF's experience meeting Soviet systems in combat. Yet, the Air Force remained an enigma to most outsiders as Israelis were extremely security-conscious and gave few insights into the workings of its MoD. They felt a collective sense of isolation and holding against outside threats given the continuing military conflict and guarded support from distant allies. Unit identifications and location were all suppressed, and personnel kept anonymous. Air bases were not marked on maps and were screened by stands of eucalyptus trees. Aircraft markings were obliterated from photographs or covered during public viewing, and a third digit added to displayed two-digit serials. Even when dealing officially with friendly nations, Israel aggressively sought assets and information it desired while giving little in return or delivered grudgingly.

The new USA aircraft and systems brought a closer relationship between American military and aviation industry. The Israelis were almost fanatical about learning all they could about their weapons from the manufacturer and other operators before and after purchase – even to the point of stealing the information. They were then able to establish the true limits of performance and push the machines beyond operating manual redlines when the need arose. The information also provided data for later modification or upgrade, often without the need to employ the expensive services of the foreign supplier. This attitude originated with the periodic embargo on arms imposed during much of Israel's existence, but continued after. Unlike the French, the Americans were initially more restrained in the arms relationship and placed conditions on sale plus use of the weapons supplied. The Israelis felt unfairly treated and imposed few restraints in doing whatever was necessary in meeting their security needs.

Low-Level War

The first action on the Suez Canal occurred on July 1, 1967. After heavy artillery attacks the IDF responded by shelling the cities on the west bank of the canal, killing and wounding hundreds of people. After the Egyptians sank the Israeli Navy flagship in October, the destroyer *Eilat*, Israel shelled and set fire to oil refineries and chemical plants near the canal, and destroyed port facilities in Suez City. Nasser was compelled to evacuate the 400,000-450,000 inhabitants of the canal cities.

The canal limited the IDF's traditional mobile doctrine, with any armored incursion on the west bank implying a major military operation with significant international repercussions. The government decided that the least costly and most politically acceptable option was to hold a line on the waterway, remaining defensive and maintaining the *status quo* in hopes of a political settlement. A series of static emplacements, the Bar-Lev Line, were constructed, backed by artillery and armor units moved along new roads.

Continued provocations on the Suez and Golan brought predictable Zahal responses. Artillery exchanges, commando raids, and airstrikes became weekly events. With the IAF intruding into neighboring airspace at will, Egyptian and Syrian jets occasionally rose in challenge. They fell to Israeli interceptors and anti-aircraft systems at a steady pace. While all this demonstrated Israeli daring and technical prowess, it did not deter her enemies. Seeking a respite to allow the Bar-Lev Line to be completed, Israel notched up the violence in the south to send a message of vulnerability in hopes of compelling military restraint. Operations began focusing on civil infrastructure.

The most noteworthy strike was on the night of October 31/ November 1, 1968 when 114 Squadron flew special operations (specops) teams to attack a bridge and a hydroelectric plant with dam deep inside Egypt. Only the Super Frelons could then perform the mission of about a 435-mile (700-km) round trip, though with reserve fuel cells installed and requiring all seven helicopters then on-hand. The electrical station and bridge were heavily damaged, but the dam less so. Portions of Cairo were left without electricity for a time. The guns on the canal fell silent until March while the Egyptians improved their early warning network.

Jordan and an Iraqi force within its territory also engaged in shelling. However, Israel's greatest activity was countering persistent incursions by Palestinian irregulars across the borders, especially in the Jordan River Valley. Jordan, struggling to deal with the new influx of Palestinian refugees, tried to avoid giving Israel cause to strike. Syria also trained Palestinian military groups that usually operated from Lebanon. The terrorist forays brought Israeli reprisals in an effort to change internal policies and rein-in the militants.

After several Palestinian outrages that included hijacking an El Al airliner and attacks on several others at European airports, the Israelis chose similar targets in an effort to compel Arab governments to change course. On December 28, 1968, IAF Frelons and Hueys landed commandos at Beirut International Airport where they blew up 13 Arab-owned airliners. This attack on international air traffic at a civilian facility brought vociferous condemnation.

In March 1970, the Syrian-backed Palestinian guerrillas had begun a coordinated effort to infiltrate Israel and carry out terror attacks. Israeli strikes on targets beyond the Golan only emboldened the Syrians, and the cycle of violence escalated. As in Egypt, Israel then moved to hitting civil infrastructure to compel Syrian reconsideration. On March 16, 1970, Frelons were again in action flying teams to destroy electrical lines along the Damascus-Homs road. On June 17 the target was a bridge on the Damascus-Suida road.

Palestinian forces were already shifting their bases to southern Lebanon, although still with strong Syrian backing, and continued to hit Israel. In an effort to prompt the Lebanese government to act against the guerillas, Zahal executed many attacks inside the country. On May 12, 1970, the IDF launched a large operation into the area of southeastern Lebanon adjacent to the border that became known as "Fatahland." The objective was to encircle and destroy a force of 1,500 guerrillas. The SyAAF interfered with IAF airstrikes supporting the operation and air battles ensued. Israel then began to build a security fence across the full length of the Israel-Lebanon border backed up with continuous patrols and, later, sophisticated sensors.

Near the end of June 1970, tensions flared anew on the Golan and the adversaries exchanged artillery and tank volleys, plus brief penetrations of the ceasefire line. A major series of attacks on Syria followed in early August in what became known as the Three-Day War.

Palestinian forces were especially active launching terror missions from Jordan. Once evidence was found that a squad had crossed the river, infantry teams were airlifted into the vicinity to track and block the force. The helicopter remained in the area to perform airborne searches, to reposition the team, or bring in reinforcements. Many times the door gun was used to pin down the insurgents until the infantrymen could arrive. In July 1968 alone, the IDF fought 98 engagements against guerrillas inside the

The Alouette was early identified as a desirable light helicopter for combat support, but, when acquired, served principally for training as the IAF began to field turbine-powered assault helicopters. Yet, the few that the Israelis purchased did possess a wartime mission of liaison to include transporting commanders to forward-deployed units. This machine carries side litter supports and a medical airlift marking, though armed men are boarding the helicopter. (Israel Ministry of Defence)

On May 12, 1970, a pair of 109 Squadron A-4Hs were flying air support for Zahal forces operating in "Fatahland," southern Lebanon. Leading was squadron CO Lieutenant Colonel Ezra 'Babban' Dotan in ship 03. His wingman spied a pair of Syrian MiG-17s below and the Skyhawks dived on them, though their aircraft were not equipped for air-to-air combat. His wingman fired the 20-mm cannon but missed (the Skyhawks then with only a fixed bombing sight). Dotan fired two pods of 2.75-inch rockets (38 projectiles) at one of the enemy aircraft, but also missed. The Syrians took no evasive action and so the lead tried again, closer in. With his remaining rockets impacting, the target disintegrated. The IAF jets then became the attention of a brace of other MiG-17s, but Dotan managed to latch onto one and fired his cannons (the only A-4 then with 30-mm). A wing separated from the target. The IAF jets then broke away. These were the only air-to-air kills for the Skyhawk in IAF service.

occupied territories. About 1,000 Palestinian fighters were killed in this bloody period with many more captured and imprisoned.

Israel constructed an electrified fence along much of the Jordanian border, supported by outposts and patrols. However, continued attacks brought swift and harsh Israeli retribution. The largest came on March 21, 1968, following a series of bloody outrages. The targets were terrorist bases at Karameh, across the river from Jericho, and three other towns near Sodom. The 15-hour operation involved perhaps thousands of troops supported by 150 tanks, helicopters, fighter-bombers, and leaflet drops. However, several problems delayed the operation, with many terrorists escaping. The Jordanian army intervened and a battle developed until the IDF withdrew. Results did not seem to justify the loss of life and equipment.

Shifting to attacking Jordanian infrastructure, on the night of December 1, 1968, the IAF's force of Bell 205s positioned troops to seize two highway and railroad bridges. Once traffic was halted with the aid of door guns, the choppers positioned bombs on the spans that demolished the structures.

The Israeli intrusions and general lawlessness of the Palestinian "state-within-a-state" finally compelled King Hussein to take decisive action. On September 16, 1970, his army began the suppression of armed Palestinian forces. The action, dubbed Black September by the Palestinians, quickly became a bloody civil war with as many as 25,000 deaths and many civilian casualties. Israel allowed Jordanian tanks to pass through its territory to surround Palestinian fighters. When Syria made a move to intervene, both the Americans and Israelis were poised to make airstrikes in support of Hussein's comparatively moderate regime. A force of Syrian tanks advancing on Jordan was encouraged to turn back by a four-ship overflight of IAF Phantoms and confrontation with Jordanian armor.[76]

Over most of the following year, Jordan continued the suppression and expulsion of Palestinian fighters. Most of these groups moved their base of operations to Lebanon where the factional government could not effectively contravene. More arms caches and training bases were established among the refugee camps. Each new rocket attack against Israeli settlements in Galilee or terrorist outrage abroad brought an IDF commando raid or, more commonly, a bombing mission. When terrorists seized and murdered Israeli athletes at the Munich Olympic Games on September 6, 1972, the IAF responded with the heaviest series of airstrikes mounted since 1967. As many as 75 warplanes hit eight Palestinian bases in Syria and Lebanon on the 8th. In Lebanon, these strikes also targeted supporting infrastructure and the county's economy suffered.

The policy of setting back Palestinian terror preparations or executing retaliatory strikes prompted a February 1973 raid on

The Mystère IVAs fought on as the region continued to simmer following the Six-Day War. These 116 Squadron jets at Tel Nof AB prepare to support the Karameh raid in Jordan on March 21, 1968, with 250-kg bombs. The type was withdrawn three years later. (Ra'anan Weiss Collection)

The Israelis acquired a goodly number of two-seat Skyhawks when they began acquiring the type. These served for training within squadrons as well as observation platforms during attacks. They eventually came to serve as advanced trainers. This TA-4J bears the badge of the Advanced Training Squadron within the Flying School where Skyhawks came to serve beginning in 1972 (this image is from after 1974). (BIAF – Israel Aerospace Magazine)

The period of the War of Attrition was the halcyon days for the Mirage squadrons as they became devoted to intercept and scored many victories over particularly the Egyptians. They began to employ missiles more and more, with the Shafrir 2, American AIM-9, and even captured Soviet rounds. This example (253 Squadron, forming in 1976), preparing for a static engine run, carries several kill markings and has the uprated Atar 09C engine. (Yoav Efrati Collection)

two camps just north of Tripoli, Lebanon, some 110 miles (177 km) north of the frontier. The Army force was brought in by the Navy, but extracted by the Air Force using Frelons and S-65s. Skyhawks were overhead to respond if the situation grew out-of-hand.[77] The operation was the first such employing all three services under a single, joint command – a harbinger of things to come.

Escalation

In March 1969, President Nasser abrogated the ceasefire agreement and declared a War of Attrition to weaken the manpower- and materiel-constrained IDF. This, it was planned, would force Israel to withdraw from the canal, accept a settlement on Arab terms or, at worse, be preparatory to an invasion of Sinai. The extended conflict suited Egypt's ability to absorb casualties and leveraged her almost limitless materiel support from the Soviet Union.

A pattern of attack, reprisal, and counter-reprisal quickly developed, with shelling, commando raids, airstrikes, and some fairly large cross-canal operations by ground forces. IDF casualties reached a high of 31 killed and 81 injured during the month of July 1969 alone. The manpower demands of the static strategy and the almost constant state of alert put great strain on the IDF's reserve structure. Conscript service was extended from 30 to 36 months and some reservists were called back for regular duty.

The Israeli leadership reluctantly agreed to greatly expand the Air Force's role. Because it could deliver devastating ordnance on a target while exposing the fewest IDF personnel to harm, the IAF became a quick response strike force. The fighter-bombers came to be called "flying artillery," reflecting the IDF's deficiency in number of batteries. This was not necessarily the best use of airpower. Because the government chose not to say the conflict was a war, Air Force reservists were not called up (save for those on their usual rotation) and squadrons fought with just the core of regular personnel (commonly 10 pilots, 20 aircrew for Phantoms) who soon felt the stress of the increasing operations tempo.

Israel was determined to demonstrate that the EAF could not protect a large-scale canal crossing. In summer 1969, the IAF began employing a strategy of "planned air combat" to draw the EAF into battle and destroy them. A common tactic was to fly a high altitude formation or other decoy near the Egyptian fighter bases to entice them to come up, and then engage with another flight that had been flying below the radar horizon. Jamming of enemy communications was frequently employed. Scores of Egyptian aircraft were downed in these dogfights. The War of Attrition became the heyday of the Mirage/Nesher teams as they racked-up victories. The potential to claim kills was so great that squadrons appealed to the CO for QRA postings in the south for their opportunities. Soon after the F-4E came into the force, it began contributing to aerial kills. Its effective radar and missiles made it the choice for night alerts.[78]

The IAF became the only quick-response offensive arm of the IDF in the static battle on the canal. They seized the initiative with 500 strike sorties in a weeklong operation, commencing on July 20, 1969, targeting Egyptian artillery batteries and the anti-aircraft network. An Israeli armored expedition made an amphibious landing on the Gulf of Suez shore on September 9 to wage a "Ten Hour War," destroying everything within reach before being extricated. The IAF provided continuous aerial cover, with at least 30 aircraft overhead at any moment. This was followed later in September and early October by a six-week series of heavy air attacks that systematically destroyed the Egyptian air defense elements.

The Egyptians were equally determined to exact a high toll for Israel's strategy. Soviet resupply saw SAM batteries and AAA grow in numbers and density while aircraft were replaced almost as quickly as the Israelis could shoot them down. As the Egyptian air defense complex expanded, the Israelis had to shift more and more forces to destroying this network and ensure freedom of air operations. The increasingly complex struggle saw the Egyptian defenses again in a shambles by December 1969. The IAF had complete air supremacy.

The Egyptians continued to fight as best they could with artillery fire and air attacks into the Sinai. Israel was eager to begin deep strikes into the enemy heartland. These would serve as a means of moving to the offense, relieve pressure on the canal defenses, and potentially alter the enemy's strategy. Still awaiting the F-4s, the alternative was to employ formations of Noratlas transports to drop bombs on high-value assets with explosives rolled out the back of the cargo compartment – a return to the cargo-bomber concept of the War of Independence. Two night missions, in April and October 1969, targeted bridges beyond the reach of fighter-bombers. The first had mixed results while the second was aborted after two airplanes were badly damaged by AAA. This tactic was set aside.

Commando raids continued at a steady pace. Some requiring Air Force support that was greatly aided by addition of the S-65s. A noteworthy raid on January 22, 1970, required all of 114 Squadron's helicopters. The goal was the capture of Shadwan Island commanding the entrance to the Gulf of Suez. After a seven-hour battle, the IDF blew up all the military facilities and took vital elements of a sea radar. Skyhawks sank two torpedo boats that attempted to intervene.

In the summer of 1969, the Israelis began a practice of laying sonic booms across adversary cities to frighten residents and make clear the costly air defenses could be penetrated. Cairo was boomed repeatedly as well as Nasser's personal residence. The Arabs responded in kind, Syrian MiG-21s twice booming Haifa and escaping. This tactic was not entirely without harm as glass from thousands of broken windows and heart attacks claimed victims, and buildings were weakened.

On January 7 the deep penetration bombing missions commenced, the vital need for which the F-4s were adopted. Targets were hit up to 100 miles (161 km) from the canal including early warning radar, military depots, and supply infrastructure in

The Skyhawk also added considerably to bomb delivery capacity when compared with the early French aircraft. This would play significantly in the growing contest with the Egyptian air defense network on the Suez. This 115 Squadron A-4H also shows the 20-mm cannon at the wing roots that the Israelis slowly replaced via modification with 30-mm weapons. (BIAF – Israel Aerospace Magazine)

the Nile delta. Some objectives lay within just 5 miles (8 km) of Cairo's city-center. With Israeli air attacks now within full view of the Egyptian public, it was expected that pressure to seek a ceasefire would mount. However, the bombing only brought the citizenry together against a national foe with willingness to make staggering sacrifices.

On January 24, the cascading list of Israeli successes prompted an angry President Nasser to appear in Moscow seeking immediate assistance. The Soviet leadership continued to refuse delivery of "offensive" weapons but felt that it had to support its ally. Within a month, an entire Red Army Air Defense Division was setting up in northeastern Egypt. By mid-March 1970, battalions of the latest model SA-2 and 32 battalions of SA-3 SAMs were in place around the principal cities of the Nile delta and other vital areas. These placed at risk even aircraft flying at low altitude and were largely impervious to existing Israeli EW gear.

While the IAF prepared to destroy the new additions, the Soviets introduced 150 of their latest MiG-21Js operated by 200 of their own pilots. The Egyptian MiG-21C/Ds had been no match for the Israeli jets, but these more advanced models were a concern. A regiment and an independent squadron of the MiG-21s, and two squadrons of Su-15s, entirely took over five EAF airfields beginning in March and April.[79] The EAF also became more active, bolstered by 200 pilots returning from a year of training in the USSR.

During the Soviet build-up, the Israeli pressure continued, and some of these foreign personnel were killed. Israel declared the 13th Meridian (about 20 miles/32 km west of the canal) as the line east of which Egyptian forces could expect to be attacked in retaliation for any provocation. In the first four months of 1970, the IAF flew 3,300 sorties and delivered 8,000 tons of ordnance while admitting to the loss of six aircraft.[80] A Russian source reported that on the night of May 31 alone the Israelis flew 400 sorties and delivered 2,000 tons of ordnance. However, the consequences of killing any of the 15,000-20,000 Soviet personnel caused the Israeli government to reconsider their strategy.

The 21 deep penetration Phantom raids (120 sorties) were terminated in April 1970 as the potential for meeting Soviet-manned fighters rose.[81] Several errors had caused civilian casualties and international outcry. The Americans placed a temporary hold on sales of additional Phantoms and Skyhawks to encourage moves towards peace. This was the first time the USA suspended arms deliveries to induce a political decision, and it would not be the last. The IAF turned its full attention to hitting anti-aircraft defenses. These strikes were often made with six to eight aircraft armed with general-purpose and cluster bombs. They were immediately successful, claiming to have destroyed about 80 percent of the network in a short time with high enemy casualties. However, the defenses were rebuilt as fast as the IAF could tear them down and a grinding contest developed. Other targets included an Egyptian destroyer and other vessels at Ras Banas, hit in retaliation for enemy attacks in Eilat harbor. Eight Phantoms flew a 1,300-mile (2,092-km) roundtrip to deliver 50 tons of bombs.

With the added defenses provided by the USSR and operated by Soviet personnel, the Egyptians, again, notched-up their attacks in the canal area and Israeli casualties began to mount. The EAF flew a massive series of strikes on April 21-23. The Egyptians and Soviets began in May to move their SAM and AAA batteries toward the waterway in a mutually supportive "belt" protecting friendly ground forces from Israeli air attacks. The IAF worked to counter this, claiming to have destroyed 38 missile "sites" in April, 80 in May, and more than 100 in June. Egyptian casualties during May alone were 1,000 to 2,000 and morale was flagging. Although the Israelis let it be known that they would restrict their operations to the canal zone as long as the Soviets did not challenge them, the USSR proved unwilling to accept a *status quo*. By June, the Soviets extended their aerial operations over the canal defenses.

As the Israelis reacted, they found the environment to be much more hazardous than previously. The latest Soviet equipment was notably more effective and the Israelis did not possess the proper EW assets. Only the Phantoms came close and they soon assumed full responsibility for the attacks. Skyhawks, SMB2, and Vautours were kept farther back while the Mirages/Neshers continued their intercept domination. Still, the Israelis persisted in relying primarily on airmanship and determination while avoiding sophisticated and costly solutions. Losses mounted, but with only mixed success as a reward.

The Boeing 377s and C-97s provided generous interior volume and power generation accommodating EW gear, with some modification performed in country and others in the United States. This modified KC-97G of 120 Squadron was probably lent from the USAF (likely 52-2639) as it has features common to American EW variants of the Stratofreighters, though the number 032 was shared with another IAF "Strato." (BIAF – Israel Aerospace Magazine)

The Egyptians and Soviets did impressive work rebuilding and extending their network and moving batteries in a "shell game." On the night of June 29-30, thousands of personnel worked feverishly to build the emplacements to facilitate moving the missile systems. Fifteen new batteries, including improved SA-2s and three SA-3 units, were emplaced along with AAA in a 50-mile (81-km) long and 17-mile (27-km) wide "SAM box" 19 miles (31 km) from the canal. This would eventually contain up to 103 SA-2 batteries, each with six or more launchers. Soviet-piloted MiGs patrolled its northern and southern flanks.

The Israelis felt they had to have relative freedom of operations over the canal in responding to threats against IDF forces. They fought hard during July to bomb the batteries as fast as they were built in a "Rolling Missile Campaign." However, two weeks of intensive effort left little appreciable degradation in the defenses. Losses were sapping the strength and spirit of the IAF squadrons. They flew their last cross-Canal heliborne commando raid on June 29.[82]

The F-4E units executed many of these hazardous attacks, initially at a rate of one or two a week and rising to as many as five to ten. Missions became more complicated when defenders began firing missiles in volleys. The maneuver then being used to evade SAMs was to wait until the missile was seen at its normal size and then to abruptly reverse direction. This was prior to warhead detonation, but late enough that the missile could not maneuver abruptly to follow its target. With several missiles fired at a single airplane, this tactic was not always effective. Phantoms and precious aircrew began to be lost at an increasing rate and mission effectiveness was substantially degraded.

A major raid was mounted on July 18 with an all-out attack on the entire missile network. Electronic countermeasure (ECM) pods provided by the Americans were hastily adopted without thoroughly understanding or even testing them.[83] While the pods seemed to be effective in countering the SA-2s, a SA-3 battery that had escaped detection was unaffected and found its targets. One aircraft was destroyed, 201's CO was killed and his navigator captured, and another flown by 69's commander returned badly damaged. Another F-4 was downed by SA-3s during an August mission while a Phantom barely returned to base riddled with shrapnel and the pilot wounded. The Phantoms had been flying the most difficult missions of the war without respite since they entered combat almost a year before. Eight of the aircraft had been destroyed during 11 months of operations, five in SEAD missions, with at least two crewmen killed, five captured, and others injured.[84] The two squadrons were depleted, tired, and demoralized.

The IAF may have lost as many as 14 aircraft during the last six weeks of the battle to destroy the missile belt, termed the "Electronic Summer." Between June 30 and August 7 alone seven IAF jets fell in combat. Soviet pilots had begun engaging Israeli aircraft. The conflict was entering a more dangerous phase with the Egyptians having finally found an answer to the IAF. On July 23, his county's honor restored, Nasser agreed to a ceasefire and to peace talks.

Despite the looming ceasefire, the IAF decided to demonstrate Israeli airpower superiority for the USSR via another "planned air combat." On July 30, Soviets pilots were lured up with apparent reconnaissance "bait" and the trap sprung with 12 Mirages and four Phantoms engaging 16 MiG-21s. The IAF then jammed the enemy radar intercept network and it put up some of its best pilots to ensure results. The largest air battle yet experienced in the Middle East saw five MiGs downed and one pilot killed while a Mirage suffered minor damage. All the kills were scored with missiles, signaling another combat shift.

The August 7 ceasefire in the north and south endured for three years. There were still clashes, but on the scale of what had become normal of the Arab-Israeli conflict.

Although the terms of the ceasefire required the Egyptians to freeze the SAM belt in numbers and locations, they were immediately expanded, augmented with more AAA, and pushed closer to the canal. This became the most concentrated air defense network in the world. The missiles could hit aircraft flying over the Sinai within approximately 20 miles (32 km) of the canal. Although the Israelis protested and withdrew from the peace talks, no action was taken. They could not afford resuming the costly battle against the missiles, nor risk the adverse responses of the United States and Soviet Union.

The USA helped to ensure Israeli restraint by agreeing to provide more fighter-bombers and defense suppression equipment to "balance" the situation. The IAF received Shrike Anti-Radiation Missiles (ARM) for a standoff kill capability against anti-aircraft radars. A dozen were fired in September 1971 in retaliation for Egypt shooting down a reconnaissance aircraft well to the east of the canal.[85] This was an ineffective gesture given the range at which they were fired and because the Egyptians simply ceased emitting or employed countermeasures.

On September 17, 1971, KC-97G 4X-FPR, number 033 "Arad," was shot down about 15 miles (24 km) east of the Suez Canal, north of Ismailiya, at 28,000 feet (8,534 m). Two SA-2 missiles hit the airplane, modified for oblique photography, in an apparent planned action. The Stratofreighter crashed 22 miles (35 km) east of the waterway. Of the eight-man crew, only the flight engineer managed to bail out and survived. Thereafter, only fighter-type reconnaissance aircraft were used for photography missions.

The continuing tensions between IDF forces on the Suez and Egypt into the 1970s resulted in an unexpected tragedy. When a Libyan 727 accidentally crossed into the Sinai on February 21, 1973, the IAF scrambled F-4 fighters to intercept the intruder. Fearing a terrorist act, the fighters attempted to force the airliner pilot to land at a Sinai airfield. When this proved fruitless, the fighter pilots fired warning shots and then shot into the wing. The Boeing caught fire and crashed when the pilots attempted a forced landing. Of the 110 persons aboard, only nine survived. The Israeli government later paid $3 million in compensation and apologized.

Summing Up

Israel adopted the name War of Attrition for the roughly 1,000-day struggle following the Six-Day War. Through October 1973, 738 Israeli servicemen were killed with 375 falling on the southern front. Egypt suffered perhaps 10,000 casualties, with 2,000 deaths from 1967 through August 1970. In the air, thousands of IAF ground attack sorties were flown delivering many thousands of tons of munitions. A total 10,520 combat sorties were flown.[86] The service reported the loss of 28 aircraft and 33 aircrew (30 more captured) on all fronts, yet also reported losing 25 aircraft in the SEAD missions alone.[87] Other summaries enumerated seven aircraft lost to SAMs, eight to AAA, and perhaps nine to 19 in accidents. Clearly, the numbers conflict, but offer some insight.

Credible sources report that the Israelis had engaged in 97 air battles and shot down 113 enemy aircraft through August 1970 and 141 through October 1973, with another 37 downed by surface-to-air systems.[88] Five IAF aircraft were lost to enemy fighters, for an exchange ratio of 25:1 air-to-air. Although 1967 saw great success with cannon, once reliable and effective AAM became available, the Israelis slowly warmed to them. Approximately 30 percent of the kills were made with missiles. The IAF's experience with the Phantom's radar-guided AIM-7D Sparrows was mixed, with four kills for 17 fired. The IR-guided missiles were much more successful.

Nasser had been unable to move to the next stages of the armed conflict. The Israelis considered this tacit acknowledgement that the IDF remained superior. Likewise, the Syrians had engaged in periodic "battle days" to keep the Israelis on edge but appeared unwilling to expand the scale of the confrontation. Airpower was felt to have been central to both of these perceived outcomes. The great disparity in air-to-air combat was another blinding factor. These near-sighted conclusions engendered over-confidence and a deeply rooted belief that the Arabs would not risk a war for years to come given particularly the IAF's superiority. Yet, the deeper lessons were more troubling.

The IAF had failed to deter the Egyptians. Israeli escalations to induce Egyptian restraint had only caused the enormous expansion of opposition assets and introduction of Soviet combat units into the theater. Targets were then restricted fearing political repercussions. The ceasefire came without Israel having found a solution to the SAM threat. With the missile screen covering the canal, the Air Force's ability to assist ground forces was greatly impacted and the IAF lost much of its offensive ability. Yet, it failed to fully appreciate this. In the short-term, they recognized their failures at the point the government chose to accept the ceasefire. Because of the extent that the nation had come to depend on the Air Force's ability to serve as an "equalizer" and deliver devastating blows on enemy ground forces, the implications of the new battlefield equation were profound. However, this was downplayed as the IAF prepared for a next round. They remained confident that, should war come, they could degrade the air defenses and carry on as before.

The IAF began introducing features of the A-4N into their earlier Skyhawks as the Ns were being delivered. Externally this included the 30-mm cannon at the wing roots and drag chute housing under the exhaust visible in this image of a 109 Squadron A-4H (tail badge partially obscured by the censor). The spine "hump" would come next. (Israeli Air Force via Lon Nordeen)

This 107 Squadron F-4E carries an electronic countermeasures pod mixed with a heavy bomb load and Sidewinder air-to-air missiles. The IAF began adopting ECM equipment in greater numbers during the War of Attrition, but with mixed feelings. They continued to rely more on bold offensive action and airmanship to counter enemy air defenses. (Author's Collection)

The Ryan Firebee drone provided a critical high-speed, unmanned, reconnaissance asset in the face of the deadly adversary anti-aircraft systems. It was launched as shown via rocket motor and recovered under parachute, snatched in midair by a passing S-65 helicopter. The 200 Squadron was formed at Palmachim to operate the remotely pilot vehicles, where this image was probably captured. (BIAF – Israel Aerospace Magazine)

The IAF had expanded and adopted new weapons to meet the escalating violence on three fronts. The A-4 proved rugged and an upgrade program was initiated to make them more suited to IAF needs. Through August 1970, Skyhawk squadrons had flown almost 6,000 sorties and lost aircraft, with one pilot killed and two captured, including 102 Squadron's CO.[89] The multi-role F-4 provided an order-of-magnitude increase in capability, but demanded adoption of a crew cockpit. "Navigators" for the back-seat weapons system officer stations were critically few for the early operational debut of the jet. Yet, in 10 months, two squadrons stood up to operate the new jet while executing combat missions of increasing complexity. They lost seven aircraft in combat and one in an accident. Of the initial cadre of 10 crewman trained in America, one was dead and three POW. Although occasionally restrained, American willingness to equip the Israelis became vital as the conflict ticked up and the combat challenges expanded. Additional Skyhawks and Phantoms were acquired in the years after the ceasefire.

In those few years after the Electronic Summer, the IAF integrated additional equipment to counter anti-aircraft defenses. The Americans were generous in an effort to restrain the Israelis from renewing the shooting war. It continued supplying ECM jammer pods for the Phantoms and ARM weapons like the Shrike for A-4s and F-4s. Jammers were also placed on a number of other platforms, including helicopters, which could fly slowly across the approach path of a strike force to disrupt air defenses. The service began to deploy Precision-Guided Munitions (PGM), with television (TV) contrast trackers, such as the GBU-8 HOBOS freefall bombs. The A-4Es from the US Navy included the ability to launch Walleye TV-guided glide bombs.

Reconnaissance over the expanding SAM threat grew so hazardous that the IAF sought another solution. In 1969, the Army Intelligence Corps (*A'man*) adapted small remotely controlled hobbyist airplanes to carry cameras aloft to look "over the hill" at enemy preparations. The IAF refused to take up the capability and so it withered within a year. Instead, they adopted American Firebee jet-powered Remotely Pilot Vehicles (RPVs). These were operated by the new 200 Squadron established at Palmachim in August 1971. This location had been used since 1963 for missile tests but was not considered a functional air base.

Also in 1971, the IAF looked at inexpensive decoys that would "soak-up" ready missiles and so briefly open a gap in the SAM belt for fighter-bombers to penetrate, or to cause radars to be activated and then struck by ARM. It bought the Chukar I jet-powered target drone for this role and worked with Northrop to create a ground-launch capability (it had normally been air-launched). Since it would be flying low and beyond line-of-sight, a fully pre-programmed flight was devised along with parachute recovery. The 200 Squadron prepared to launch these from Dalton airport in northern Israel and two sites in the Sinai. After a brief demonstration flight, the decoys were stored and no flight training took place. This helped ensure the capability remained secret.[90]

The Israelis trained to destroy anti-aircraft concentrations in complex, carefully orchestrated operations. These were to include the decoys causing radar to begin emitting and ready missiles fired, ARM attacks on the emitters, other standoff weapons employed to destroy key elements of the air defense network, artillery shells delivering chaff ahead of a strike, jamming from aircraft out of range, and then penetration by fighter-bombers to strike the rest. Among the standoff weapons was an Israeli ground-fired rocket, the *Ivry*. This would permit support of Zahal mobile elements while also opening holes to permit attacks in the enemy rear. But, it was opposed by the IAF and so starved for funds such that only 18 were deployed by October 1973.[91] Air base attack would use large strike packages of separate formations hitting defenses, runways and HAS, and another as CAP. Attacks on Egyptian canal crossing bridging equipment and bridgeheads was planned to have fighter-bombers executing bomb-toss attacks outside the effective range of remaining missiles. The need to maneuver at low altitude just to the east of the canal before popping up for an attack, over largely featureless desert, led the IAF to erect numbered marker towers of stacked barrels to help orient the aviators.[92]

All the new weapons and tactics added complexity to IAF operations and greater cost for the nation. It remained for the future to determine the effectiveness of these preparations. Failure of the IAF to defeat decisively the SAMs lent the Arab opponents a sense that they had an answer to their enemy's superiority. This was a vital factor in the decision to take on the Israelis anew.

The Northrop Chukar I target was acquired to serve as a decoy to cause the enemy to launch their ready SAMs and so ease the ingress of a strike force of fighter-bombers. The drone was revised to permit ground launch. This example is seen near during the Yom Kippur War ready to launch on a decoy mission. (Ra'anan Weiss Collection)

CHAPTER 8
YOM KIPPUR WAR

From the heady days of the Six-Day War through the tough slog of the War of Attrition, the Israelis remained assured they could consistently deter and defeat the Arab militaries. The Air Force was central to that belief, with considerable treasure expended on its equipment and training. When Egypt and Syria succeeded in launching a combined assault of unprecedented ferocity in October 1973, the IAF was tested as never before.

Run-up

Despite the ceasefire, Egyptian forces remained at a high state of readiness. Their new President, Anwar Sadat, repeated the late Gamal Abdel Nasser's promises of war against the Jews to liberate national territory. The entire country was mobilized in preparation for the coming clash. Sadat continued to press the USSR for arms tipping the balance in Egypt's favor. The Syrians also remained on alert, maintaining a large standing army, expanding its air arm, and building an air defense network similar to Egypt's. Realizing the potential for a Middle East war leading to dangerous confrontation with the West during an era of *détente*, the USSR steadfastly refused to provide Egypt and Syria with potent offensive weapons. Although the Soviets provided three battalions of mobile FROG-7 ballistic missiles, these were short range and of poor accuracy. They finally sent Egypt a few mobile Scud medium-range ballistic missiles capable of hitting Tel Aviv, a small number of bombers with AS-5 Kelt standoff missiles, and a squadron of Su-20 fighter-bomber with a more respectful air-to-ground weapons load. Soviet personnel continued to play an active role in support and employment of some systems.

With no serious new proposals to break the impasse and resolve the conflict, Sadat began to despair. His country could not long endure the expense of mobilization and he was compelled to consider war. By recapturing at least some of the Sinai and inflicting great losses on the IDF, he hoped to force the major powers to influence the Israelis to consider some formula for settlement. The simultaneous surprise attacks on two widely separated fronts by powerful forces would divide and dilute the immediate Israeli reaction. Both offensives would be covered by the dense anti-aircraft defenses to neutralize the IAF.

Although there was much evidence that the Arabs were determined to take on Zahal once again, the Israeli leadership was certain that they would not launch a war in the foreseeable future. So sure were they of this assessment that the readiness of the armed forces was allowed to slip. Occasional air combat continued to see the Israelis come out on top, presumably demonstrating military superiority. Egypt and Syria enforced the Israeli delusions with a deception campaign that allowed the Arabs to remain one step away from a major offensive without arousing suspicions. The IDF was put on alert at great cost for several weeks in the spring of 1973, but eventually stood down. This only worked to further desensitize the Israeli leadership to enemy preparedness.

Despite its tremendous expansion, the IAF still faced a numerically superior foe. The Air Force possessed about 380 combat aircraft against about 490 Egyptian and 265 Syrian, discounting those from other Arab nations that might be brought to bear. The surprise attack in October 1973 also caught the IAF with 22 percent of its fleet unserviceable and still training sufficient Phantom crews. The raw numbers concealed the personnel qualitative advantage of the IAF, its superior tonnages and accuracy for weapons delivery, and its EW systems. On October 6, 1973, the IAF stood at (some data best estimates):

> A significant action just prior to the Yom Kippur War developed as the Syrians reacted to a photo reconnaissance effort on September 13, 1973, in which the IAF sent four RF-4Es over their country simultaneously. The protecting interceptors engaged and nine SyAAF fighters were destroyed for one Mirage hit by an Atoll missiles. The Israeli pilot ejected and was floating in the Mediterranean when the Syrians appeared again to disrupt the helicopter rescue. They lost four more fighters.

Fighter-Bombers
103 F-4E (15 u/s)
162 A-4E/H/N (38 u/s)
19 TA-4F/H/J employed as attack assets
30 Shahak (modified Mirage IIICJ)
4 Mirage IIIBJ employed as attack assets (likely excluding one permanent flight test machine)
40 Nesher (19 u/s) Israeli-assembled Mirage 5MJ
25 Sa'ar (8 u/s) re-engined Super Mystère B2
Photo Reconnaissance
6 RF-4E
1 Mirage IIIC(R) and 2 IIICJ modified for camera noses
8 124I Firebee RPV
(2) C-97 modified with camera packages
Electronic Warfare
-- C-97
-- C-47
-- Katef payload optionally installed in assault helicopters
Aerial Refueling
(2) KC-97 with wingtip hose reel pods, developmental
-- a few A-4 buddy refueling pods
Transports
2 C-130H (1 u/s)
3 B-377M
8 C-97 (4 u/s) includes one tanker, several EW
22 Noratlas (8 u/s)
12 C-47 (2 u/s) several EW
14 Do.28 (5 u/s)
30 Do.27 (6 u/s)
30 U206 (4 u/s)
2 Cessna 172
2 Cessna 180
1 Rallye

(1) Piper Navajo (mobilized Chemavir asset)
(11) Islander (mobilized Kanaf-Arkia and Shachaf assets)
(3) Arava (mobilized IAI assets)
(3) C-47 (mobilized Netivei Nepht assets)
(4) Dart-Herald (mobilized Arkia assets)
(3) Vickers Viscount (mobilized Arkia assets)
(2) Westwind (mobilized IAI assets)
(10) Boeing 707 (mobilized IAI and El Al assets)
(2) Boeing 720 (mobilized El Al and leased assets)
(2) Boeing 747 (mobilized El Al assets)
Helicopters
16 S-65 (2 u/s)
11 Super Frelon (4 u/s)
47 Bell 205 (12 u/s)
12 Bell 206 (3 u/s)
11 Alouette II (3 u/s)
Decoy
30 Chukar drone[93]
Training
-- A-4, TA-4 (to operational squadrons for war)
90 Magister (some possibly stored)
40 Super Cub
783 total aircraft (excluding mobilized assets)

Etzion (Wing 10)	
140 Golden Eagle	A-4E (not operational, aircraft to 110 and 116 for war, aircrew likewise dispersed)
144 Guards of the Arava	Nesher
Hatzerim (Base 6)	
102 Flying Tiger	A-4H
107 Knights of the Orange Tail	F-4E
123 Southern Bells	Bell 205 (operated mostly from Refidim, Ramat David, and Mahanayim)[94]
Flying School	Magister, Cub
Advanced Training Squadron	TA-4 (aircraft to 102, 109, and 110 for war)[95]
Hatzor (Wing 4)	
101 First Fighter	Shahak and Nesher
105 Scorpion	Sa'ar (detachment of four aircraft at Ophir)
113 Hornet	Nesher
201 One	F-4E
Lod (Base 27)	
120 International	B377M, C-97, C-130H
122 Dakota	C-47, Arava, Westwind
(145)	reservists flying mobilized and leased jet transports[96]
Ophir (Base 29)	
--	detachments from fighter and helicopter squadrons
Palmachim (Base 30)	
200	Firebee, Chukar
Ramat David (Wing 1)	
69 The Hammers	F-4E, RF-4E
109 Valley	A-4H
110 Knights of the North	A-4E
117 First Jets	Shahak
Refidim (Base 3)	
(200)	detachment, Firebee and Chukar
--	detachments from fighter and helicopter squadrons

Sde Dov (Base 15)	
100 Flying Camel	Cub, Do.27, Do.28, U206, C-172, C-180, Rallye (relocated to Ramat David for war, flights at fields in Israel and Sinai) 151 Flight – Islander, Navajo
125 Light Helicopters	Bell 206, Alouette
Tel Nof (Base 8)	
103 Flying Elephant	Noratlas
114 Heavy Lift	Frelon
115 Flying Dragon	A-4N
116 Flying Wing	A-4E/N (N's operated by 115 during the war)[97]
118 Night Birds of Prey	S-65
119 Bat	F-4E, RF-4E
124 Rotor and Sword	Bell 205

The Suez front featured in excess of 150-160 SAM batteries, with fully one quarter of the Egyptian armed forces devoted to air defense. Over 60 SA-2 batteries (with six launchers each) and 30 SA-3 batteries held at risk aircraft up to 50,000 feet (15,240 m). Some 40 mobile SA-6s covered up to 18,000 feet (5,486 m). Filling the low-altitude zone were numerous shoulder-launched SA-7 *Strela* missiles deployed with forward troops, over 100 of the tracked ZSU-23-4 quad 23-mm gun system, and more than 2,000 AAA sites with radar-directed cannons. Strela launchers were also mounted in a cluster of 12 on vehicles to allow salvo firing. The missile belt on the west bank of the canal commanded airspace up to 20 miles (32 km) deep over the Sinai. Although the air defense arrayed along the Golan front was smaller, it contained the same elements and was densely concentrated in a comparatively narrow zone.

Although the IAF faced formidable air defense systems, it had intelligence on all the elements and felt confident it could deal with them to perform effectively in any coming clash. The SA-7 had been encountered when one had struck an RF-4 in October 1971, but failed to explode.[98] However, the airmen failed to fully appreciate how, together, they increased the arrays' lethality. They possessed little intelligence about the new SA-6, but soon learned that it flew at very high speed and was exceptionally maneuverable. Its launch was difficult to detect visually and, more importantly, the system proved impervious to the ECM then in the IAF inventory.

The airmen had trained and studied hard and felt that they could defeat the SAMs. However, the Air Force reflected the same indolent attitude and under-estimation of enemy competence that pervaded the rest of Zahal. Since summer 1970, the investment in upgrading the defense suppression and EW systems had not kept pace with the expanding threat. The Air Force seldom trained with what suppression systems it did have in order to conceal the capabilities. The IAF seemed to feel that sound airmanship and bold action would compensate for any materiel deficiencies and permit effective missions.

As an element of *détente* with the West, the USSR greatly reduced its personnel footprint in Egypt beginning in summer 1972 while weapons deliveries continued. This purported "expulsion" gave Sadat a freer hand in preparing for the coming war while securing the military and monetary support of other Arab nations. The war was finally set to begin on October 6, 1973. The date was chosen

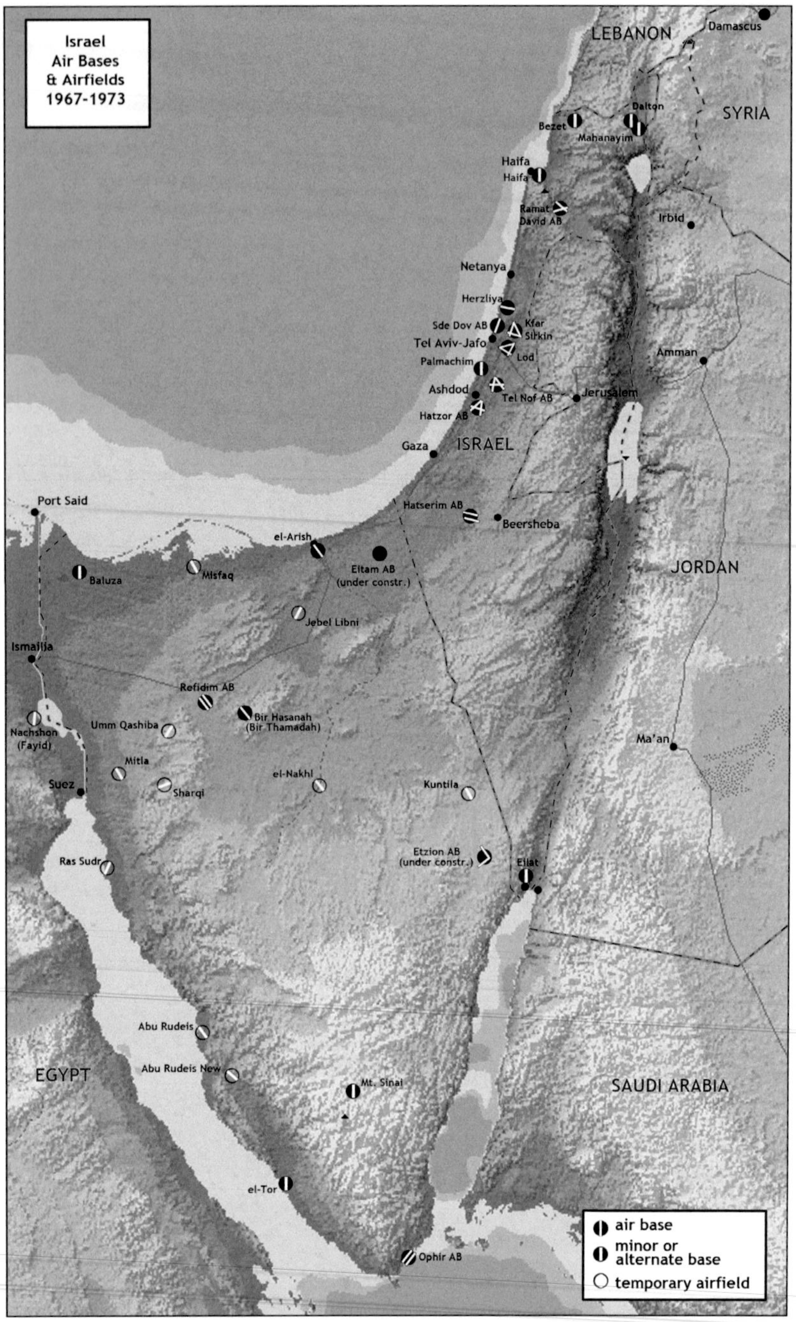

This map shows the locations of the Israeli air bases as they existed by October 1973, with Israeli names given. Egypt's Fayid (inactive) became Nachshon when occupied by the IAF during and immediately following the war. In this period, the IAF operated over the largest area of its existence. (Author)

because of the favorable meteorological and canal water conditions, but the Yom Kippur holiday also had Zahal at its lowest state of readiness. The entire nation was virtually shut down, including radio stations that were the principal means of summoning reservists to mobilize.

Explosion

The Egyptian and Syrian deception campaign was very successful, enabling one of the more effective surprise attacks in military history. Only hours before the attack did a Mirage reconnaissance mission bring back clear evidence to back-up other intelligence. The Israelis began mobilizing just five hours before fighting began.

When the Air Force was placed on alert, it made ready to launch a preemptive strike as the first step in securing air superiority. This was to have been the carefully crafted degradation of Egyptian and Syrian anti-aircraft defenses and interceptor bases. The IAF would then have made massive suppression strikes against the SAM and AAA belt the next morning. With heavy clouds over the north precluding pre-strike photo reconnaissance sorties and complicating the attack, the day-one missions were changed to just airfield strikes, presumably skirting the missile belt. As a consequence, aircraft weapons load reconfiguration had to be performed. However, the government decided against preemption because it might appear that Israel was the aggressor and cause the United States to limit its support.

On October 6, at 1200, the Egyptians and Syrians began a withering two-hour artillery barrage from about 4,000 guns. Their armies then began moving across the ceasefire lines at 1400. Tactical bridges were thrown across the canal at 11 points along its length under the cover of smoke screens. Simultaneously, 263 aircraft struck Israeli installations throughout the peninsula.[99] Air base facilities, runways, radar, Hawk missile sites, artillery batteries, EW posts, logistics sites, and command centers, all suffered serious damage. The air bases remained sufficiently operational to allow

In an effort to sustain a valuable asset in the evolving air war *milieu*, the Israelis re-engined the Super Mystère B2s with the American J52 engine from the A-4. The extended tail cone and external cable duct across the top of the jet (renamed Sa'ar) are witness to the major modification. The ability to fire AAM was also introduced. Only 18 jets were modified by the time of the 1973 war and they continued to equip 105 Squadron who lost three in combat and one to a mishap. (Yoav Efrati Collection)

Commander

8th Commander – Benjamin 'Beni' Peled was assigned as IAF commander just months prior to the great test of the Yom Kippur War. He served in the early Air Force as a mechanic before going through pilot training. He became a leading fighter pilot and was sent to the UK for several advanced courses while also serving as an instructor back home. Peled was a deputy commander within 117 Squadron when they began operating Meteors. He was sent to France to assess aircraft acquisition options and then led their introduction. During Peled's conversion training in France he became the first Israeli pilot to fly beyond the speed of sound. He led the formation of 113 Squadron with new Ouragans and then supervised delivery of Mystère IVAs before commanding the 101 as it took on the newest fighter. It was in this jet he was shot down during the Sinai Campaign, having the dubious distinction of becoming the first Israeli pilot to eject from an aircraft. He went on to lead the AHQ Training Department before taking command of the Hatzor wing which he led through the Six-Day War. An engineering degree and several technical projects made him suited for acquiring and integrating new technology to face the growing SAM threat. Peled subsequently headed the Air Department as the stepping stone to the top post to which he ascended in May 1973. The general commanded through the Yom Kippur War and the difficult period that followed, adjusting tactics and taking up new equipment. He also performed some restructuring to ensure commanders were given authority commensurate with their responsibilities. Peled set the template for the next three commanders with age in their mid-40s and serving for five-year terms.

Air Force CO Beni Peled (center) escorts Prime Minister Golda Meir and her entourage during a visit to an IAF installation. (Ofer Zidon Collection)

fighters to take-off and down several attackers. Egyptian Tu-16s fired about 23 Kelt missiles at various Israeli targets.[100] Egyptian FROG ballistic rockets were also launched against IDF command posts. Egyptian Mi-6 and Mi-8 troop transport helicopters carried hundreds of commandos deep behind IDF lines to wreak havoc.

The simultaneous Syrian assault on the Golan Heights met with similar early success. About 900 tanks and other armored vehicles, supported by 132 ground attack aircraft, penetrated up to 6 miles (10 km) into Israeli lines.[101] The small number of defenders fought heroically and managed to contain the attack until reinforcements began arriving the following morning. An assault by 500 commandos succeeded in capturing the critical Israeli observation and electronics listening post atop Mt. Hermon (Jebel Sheikh). The SyAAF also hit a few targets in northern Israel.

The IAF quickly reconfigured its strike jets again – downloading fuzed weapons – to repel the invaders and launch all its ready aircraft. Some were still loaded with bombs when enemy aircraft arrived and so dumped their stores into the sea following take-off so as to fight air-to-air. Most of the flights in Israel-proper did not launch as the enemy never appeared, and so the weapons were uploaded yet again for strike missions. Israeli AA assets downed two aircraft while aviation scored 31, including two Kelts and 14 troop helicopters. Pursuit of the remaining Egyptian commandos required the support of Hueys over the coming days. Given the scope of the enemy airstrikes opening the campaign, these IAF successes were meager attrition.

Before the end of the day the IAF attempted to hit Syrian armor and the Egyptian bridgehead but were greatly hampered by air

As soon as the IAF was approved to buy Phantoms they sought to acquire RF-4Es to greatly bolster their PR capabilities. They ultimately procured a dozen of the machines and lost only one in a long and hazardous career. One of the few examples finished in gray pigment, 497, bears 201 Squadron markings. This is probably a photo from the 1990s, though the refueling probe seen on the starboard side was initially introduced in 1970. (Ofer Zidon Collection)

Three days before the Yom Kippur War, 115 Squadron's CO, Colonel Ami 'Goldie' Gadish, had been killed in an accident. Giora Rom was named the new CO, immediately taking up the role at Tel Nof AB while his kit was collected from Hatzor AB. A Mirage pilot, Rom had no experience in the squadron's Skyhawks. His first flight was a combat mission on October 6 as he was talked through the details over the radio by the flight lead.

defenses and lack of FACs or reconnaissance imagery. In some cases the crews were simply told to go find targets, their search extending their exposure to the defenses and they risked hitting IDF elements. In some 200 sorties in the south they lost four aircraft and in the north two machines fell. Four crewmen were killed and two made prisoner.

The Egyptians achieved all of their first day objectives with minimal losses. Israeli fortifications on the waterway were either overrun or isolated as the enemy established beachheads along the Suez. Overnight, hundreds more tanks crossed into Sinai to protect against the certain counterattack from IDF mobilized reserves. They held against the initial Israeli response, their defenses including *Sagger* wire-guided anti-tank missiles and rocket-propelled grenades (RPG). The Egyptian forces were careful not to push beyond the cover of the air defense umbrella. The Syrians likewise pushed hard against the IDF armor and advanced towards the Golan escarpment.

The second day began with IAF attacks on the Egyptian anti-aircraft barrier and penetrations to hit seven air bases, these strikes comprising about 100 sorties.[102] Their inability to conduct comprehensive reconnaissance and the mobile SAM assets meant that the IAF was not even sure where all the batteries were located. Although firing Shrikes, other assets such as EW were unavailable or non-optimally deployed. The attacks proved costly and were broken off after the first of four waves before achieving decisive results.

The Israelis judged the northern front as critical and so frantically redirected resources to stabilize that situation. The Air Force attempted a hasty and moderate-sized initial raid against the Syrian AAA and SAM sites (113 sorties) to permit easier work supporting ground troops.[103] Here, again, many elements of a coordinated attack as had been planned in past years were unavailable and some crews were handed new mission packets as they strapped into their jets. The preparatory shelling did not occur because Zahal was in such dire straits. The Ivry missiles went unfired. The Chukar decoys were launched from Dalton airstrip based on the original timeline, uninformed that it had shifted, and so the effort was wasted. With dated intel, most of the batteries were found to have moved when the fighter-bombers popped up to make their attack. Seven of the Israeli attackers were lost while putting only one site out of operation. The shock of this outcome prompted termination of the operation after a single wave.

The grave situation on the southern end of the Golan, with the IDF armored forces so depleted that the path into Israel was open, meant airstrikes on enemy forces had to continue. Attacks in support of the increasingly desperate troops proceeded in the face of the intact air defenses, and they suffered as a consequence. However, the airmen helped buy the hours necessary for more reserves to enter the battle.

Attacks against the Egyptian bridges on the 6th and 7th also met with mixed success. These were difficult targets under the best of circumstances, but exceptionally so without the use of PGMs. The air defenses made photo reconnaissance very hazardous and turnaround of the imagery to the squadrons was lengthy. In the meantime, pilots were sent on missions against spans whose location and status were uncertain and the targets entirely unfamiliar. The pop-up and search method for attacking these and other targets was especially fraught given the air defense environment. Although the bridging equipment was hit several times, damaged segments were quickly replaced.

October 7, 1973, was the worst day in IAF history with 22 aircraft lost and 14 aircrew killed, 12 others captured. Yet, there was little materially to show for the sacrifices. They claimed 20

These 201 Squadron ground crew ready a Phantom in a hardened shelter for the October 7 attack on Syrian SAMs. The aircraft did not return from the mission and the crew was made POW. Aircraft 621 is armed with cluster bombs and carries an ECM pod. (Ra'anan Weiss Collection)

enemy aircraft downed, four by air defense assets, but this affected little the critical battlefield conditions.

Crisis

During the first two days of war 28 Israeli aircraft and 31 aircrew had fallen – more than a squadron of assets or nearly 10 percent of available attack aircraft. For every airplane shot down there were two others damaged and usually out of action for a day or more. With reservists still reporting for duty, the IAF could generate only half their peak sortie rates. During the same period, the enemy had lost twice that number of machines, but those air forces could more easily absorb such attrition. On the positive side, the IAF had kept the skies over Israel and the occupied territories sufficiently clear to permit unimpeded mobilization and deployment of ground forces, and air bases to operate with little fear of attack.

The Egyptian army held strong positions 5 miles (8 km) deep along almost the entire length of the canal and continued consolidating their beachheads. The Syrians continued their pressure on the sparse armored units facing them and who were slowly being worn-away to ineffectiveness. The IDF mobilization was only just taking hold. Hamstrung by the formidable enemy air defenses, the IAF could contribute little to assist the ground situation. Zahal found itself fighting without the air support it had come to expect and for which the nation had invested so heavily at the expense of artillery and armored personnel carriers (APC) whose lack were so desperately felt. In some cases, ground force commanders requested a cessation to airstrikes because watching Israeli aircraft being shot down was demoralizing their troops.

The weight of the surprise attack seriously unbalanced IDF responsiveness. Not being permitted to execute their preplanned attack strategy immediately placed the Air Force at a disadvantage. They simply had no other plans for situations where they did not initiate hostilities and, without 48 hours warning, had lacked all the expected resources.[104] The Army leadership failed to understand that they could not expect the usual support in the absence of air superiority that required two days of dedicated effort to establish. In the short-term, it was all the IAF could do to react without focus to the enemy initiative. They never had time to properly assess the situation and plan or execute accordingly. Weapon loads were changed as missions were altered, and pilots were given charts for revised sorties as they prepared to depart. Efforts were shifted from front-to-front and crisis-to-crisis, unable to mass its strength against a critical point for a decisive outcome. What reconnaissance could be performed did not keep up with the rapidly shifting battlefield or return BDA data in a timely manner. Without conducting a sustained counter-air campaign, defenses frequently undermined the IAF's effectiveness. It had still not created an efficient means of handling requests for air support, and a system had to be improvised to meet the urgent demands of combat. Forward command posts were established at regional headquarters to handle tactical coordination and offload the main control center.[105] Tactics and equipment were clearly deficient and unit leaders were being lost, but the pressure of combat meant lessons were not being assessed and acted upon. Direction from headquarters shifted frequently as personnel frantically reacted to changing commands from higher-up or to whomever shouted loudest. No one had the time or attention span for reports from the operational squadrons. Squadrons began to lose confidence in the AHQ planners such that some pilots executed missions in the manner they felt best rather than strictly adhering to orders.

The IDF has always been known for commanders "leading from the front" and sharing the risks of their personnel. This has been true for Air Force squadron commanders and their deputies as well. In the Yom Kippur War, they were counted among the casualties, but there was always a leader to step forward. A 110 Squadron deputy, Levi Bar-Ziv, was killed on the 7th when his A-4 was hit by a SAM. His commander was injured during a mission and another officer assigned to replace him. October 7 saw 101's deputy CO, Israel Bahara, suffer a ground mishap in a Shahak that left him injured and likely out of action for the duration. On October 9, 116's CO Lieutenant Colonel Ehud Shelach was killed when his A-4E was destroyed by an Egyptian SAM. One of 119's deputies, Shmulik Ben-Rom, took over. The 115 Squadron had gotten a new commander days before the war after their CO was killed in an accident, but then lost a deputy, Mickey Schneider, on the 11th when he came POW. Lieutenant Colonel Avi Lanir, 101's commander, was shot down on the 13th when his Mirage was struck by a SAM. He was captured by the Syrians and subsequently died under interrogation. The 201's CO, Iftach Zemer, was injured on October 13 ejecting from his F-4E. He was replaced by Eitan Ben-Eliyahu who had been Zemer's deputy until just before the war when he had been transferred to a staff posting.

A 100 Squadron Do.27 crew and support personnel standby for a call or meeting, possibly to fly a casualty to an aid station. The ground is suitable for off-field operations in which the Dornier excelled. The type also flew SAM launch spotter duties and one was shot down as a consequence. The double-slotted flaps and drooped ailerons enabling STOL operation are evident. (Ra'anan Weiss Collection)

Given the new elements added since summer 1970, the air defenses were unlike anything previously experienced and they took a terrible toll. Major-General Beni Peled ordered aircrews not to approach closer than 15 miles (24 km) east of the canal unless they were executing a priority mission. However, defense suppression operations on both fronts tended to be hastily assembled affairs. They employed Shrikes, with some ECM and chaff support, before going in with general purpose bombs. The ECM was not state-of-the-art and was largely ineffective against the SA-6 and ZSU-23 systems. The A-4s still lacked any RWR and only the Es had flare/chaff dispensers. Electronic Support Measures systems (to collect radar frequency data) aboard aircraft such as the C-97s and C-47s were either ineffective or the dangerous environment near the front kept them too far in the rear to perform optimally.

The attack on EAF airfields during the morning of the 7th, and on several occasions in the coming days, achieved little of consequence. The larger number of bases diluted the counter-air effect. The IAF had altered its airfield strike tactics to three elements with the first suppressing air defenses, the second cratering runways and bombing facilities, and the third providing a CAP – all requiring more aircraft than in 1967. However, each field had more than one runway, as well as taxiways that could serve as runways, and teams were prepared to quickly repair damaged surfaces. The HAS proved largely impervious to IAF ordnance. Only direct hits from large bombs ensured penetration of the hangarettes, but the service lacked sufficient technical means to consistently achieve such accuracy. Barrage balloons limited attack paths to those covered by AAA and discouraging low-level passes. At least a dozen attackers may have been lost on these missions, with about five on the 7th alone. Few bases were shut down, and then only briefly.

On the morning of the 8th, the Israeli attention remained largely centered on the Golan. The tide turned there as sufficient reserves were brought on line in an organized manner. Heavy armored punches began to push the enemy back. The failure of the Syrians to move their SAM umbrella forward in concert with armor penetrations left their advancing forces more vulnerable to air attack, and the IAF scored some telling blows. The service flew two-thirds of its missions on that front during the day. The situation lost its criticality for Israel but was becoming desperate for Syria who had stretched its forces to breaking. The IDF maintained pressure to keep the enemy off-balance, the Air Force continuing to attack air bases and interdict the movement of supplies.

Syria launched FROG missiles that fell into civilian areas of northern Israel, several striking Ramat David AB and killing a pilot plus injuring others.[106] In response, the IAF flew raids against military headquarters buildings in Damascus, Russian shipping in Latakia harbor, and the Homs oil refinery. The attackers over-flew Lebanese and Jordanian territory to skirt the missile belt. The subsequent damage disrupted landline communications – an objective also achieved in Egypt. These strikes and others on Syria's national infrastructure produced collateral damage and civilian deaths, earning Israel sharp rebukes from the international community. The Syrians dispersed their counter-air systems to protect high value assets throughout the country, thinning frontline defenses. Similar strategic operations in Egyptian may have been restrained owing to the Scud threat.[107]

With sufficient reservists and equipment then in the combat zone, a hastily organized Israeli armored counterattack was launched in the south on October 8. The IAF again redirected its efforts, flying 48 preparatory sorties and then 58 in support while losing 10 aircraft. With insufficient infantry support to deal with the Egyptian anti-tank teams, the attack was beaten back. Encouraged by this, the Egyptians attempted an advance beyond the air defense umbrella the following day but was badly mauled by IDF armor and aircraft (125 sorties). In the next few days, they worked to move their air defense screen forward.

The coming days became a grinding contest of wills and equipment attrition as both sides sought to contain the other and seek an advantage. The Israelis prioritized operations in the north from October 9 to throw the Syrians onto the defense in the short-term while holding in the south. On the 13th, the IDF pressure there eased while focus shifted south again.

Attacks in the face of dense and integrated air defenses employed a number of techniques improvised or emphasized. Loft-bombing and bomb-tossing, or pop-up direct bombing, were used to reduce aircraft exposure, driving into the area at as low as 100 feet (31 m) and usually dropping tanks before the pull-up. The slower-speed A-4s suffered the most with these tactics, especially being engaged by SA-7s and AAA. This tended to force the aircraft to a moderately higher altitude, depending upon targets, where they could still dive down when SAMs were launched. Efforts to evade missiles included a sharp split-S roll across the path of the rockets, but pilots were over-stressing their airframes. Changes were made to standard formation practices to ensure one or two pilots were looking for threats while other elements bombed, then the roles were switched.[108] The service also began employing standoff aircraft to provide verbal warning of missile launches, though this proved fatal for a few of the light-planes and helicopters. Some TA-4s performing this and artillery spotting missions were also shot down. Specific attack squadrons were assigned dedicated sectors in the hope aircrews would become familiar with the area and improve mission success.

Suppression of the air defense networks were more carefully planned and executed on a smaller scale as measures were improvised to increase effectiveness. Remaining Chukars were launched either in advance of a strike formation or one or two immediately leading a flight such that radar were activated and vulnerable to strike by ARM.[109] This contributed to attrition and the Chukar force was reduced to near irrelevance. Firebees were pressed into service as decoys after removing cameras, and so that reconnaissance asset was also rapidly depleting. Sometimes scores of missiles were fired against the drones and other formations, greatly reducing the store of ready missiles. Both the Syrians and the Egyptians had to cut back on the volume of SAM fire. Additional flare dispensers were affixed to bomb racks and lead aircraft in a formation would fire multiple expendables to decoy the SA-7s.[110] Chaff was also stuffed into the airbrake cavities of Skyhawks as an emergency expedient; a quick cycle of the airbrakes dispensing the countermeasure. These EW resources were not always used optimally owing to lack of training, or the expendables were not suitably matched to the threats. However,

This 116 Squadron TA-4H is actually in a post-war image but remains a good depiction of the model as it served during the war. The two-seat jets were mixed in with other aircraft on attack missions, but also served as spotters. In the latter role, looking for SAM fly-outs, it proved the end for a few aircraft. (Amos Dor Collection)

they generally allowed attackers to fly above the best effective range of AAA and SAM-7s, and return to more standard tactics with less chance of being struck by a SAM.

Attacks on the Suez front concentrated on the northern and southern ends of the defense line where mutually supporting fire from multiple batteries was much reduced and where the EAF could be drawn out into relatively clear skies. The very dense Syrian air defense system was somewhat limited by lack of full integration or long-range surveillance radar. This allowed attack jets to close within striking range of the batteries with little advance warning. These tactics began to erode the defenses and permitted greater freedom for interdiction and support of ground forces.

By the 10th, the Syrian invasion force had been pushed back beyond their starting point. Damascus came within artillery range of IDF lines before defenses firmed. The IAF hit additional strategic targets in Syria to increase the cost of the war and force the enemy to divert resources from the fronts. There were 20 such Phantom missions (130 sorties) from October 9 to the 23rd, the farthest nearly 200 miles (322 km) from Israel. Strikes denied electrical power to large portions of Syria for the better part of a week. Some targets, such as bridges and storage sites, sought to slow the movement of new Soviet equipment to the battle zone. After the 14th, these were meant to keep the enemy reeling and impede efforts to prepare for renewed large-scale operations.

Pressure on the Syrians was telling, especially in lost aircraft and thinned air defenses. Egyptian aircraft and crews were transferred there to bolster the force. Iraqi and Jordanian reinforcements could not reverse the situation but did contribute to the IDF halting its advance as focus again shifted south.

Using the new techniques, attacks on the canal bridges continued. According to some accounts, the IAF knocked out

The S-65/CH-53 fleet continued to be invaluable vertical replenishment and commando assault assets throughout the war. These roles were augmented with pilot rescue where night ingress into hostile territory was necessary to recover hiding aircrew. This emphasized the need for specialized medical equipment and defensive personnel aboard the chopper. Shown is a 118 Squadron machine with extended range tanks and an aerial refueling probe. (Ra'anan Weiss Collection)

This 101 Squadron Mirage, mounting Sidewinder missiles, carries kill markings from prior years and identification triangles added to the wings and tail during the Yom Kippur War. Libyan Mirage 5s operated from Egypt during the war and so recognition of friendly delta-wing types was facilitated by the hastily applied black-bordered yellow fields. (Ra'anan Weiss Collection)

each of the primary spans at least twice – with all claimed to have been put out of action by noon on the 8th – but they were usually operating again within a few hours. Sorties were also wasted on a number of dummy spans. The effort began to yield results as the number of replacement bridging segments ran low. Israelis stated that after the 8th only four of the remaining bridges were capable of handling heavy armor vehicles, and these were only used at night.

The IAF continued to launch air base attacks in a struggle to seize undisputed air superiority over the Suez. These typically consisted of 18 to 40 jets and directed against five primary fighter bases. Ultimately, they struck 10 air bases and 15 radar or communication facilities with 348 sorties. Although the IAF claimed to have destroyed 14 Egyptian aircraft in the open or in shelters during the war, these results were insignificant compared with the cost of the raids and their impact on the war.

Appreciating the inferiority in their equipment and proficiency, the Arab air forces flew only limited hit-and-run ground attack sorties after the 7th and generally avoided being drawn into IAF traps. They commonly restricted themselves to point-defense operations, leaving the IAF to smash itself against the deadly defense curtain. The IAF remained superior in air-to-air combat, but this contributed little immediately to the crucial struggle at the fronts.

Equipment losses and exceptionally high ordnance expenditure rates quickly approached critical levels for both sides. Soviet resupply efforts began almost immediately, reaching 100 cargo flights on the 9th alone, especially replenishing anti-aircraft missiles. Tanks and MiG-21 fighters were shipped by sea, some withdrawn from Warsaw Pact units.

Several days of heavy fighting and losses was stretching the IAF thin as well via attrition. Two-seat TA-4s were being sent on attack sorties as early as the 8th and Neshers, supposedly devoted to intercepts, began to be tasked for air-to-ground missions. Invaluable photo reconnaissance machines were sent on intercept sorties. Some units had to stand down or reduce operational tempo for a day when losses and damaged aircraft left them too depleted. In-country producers (principally IMI and Rafael) worked to replenish aircraft external tanks and Shafrir missiles.[111] The stock of tanks and bomb racks became so critical that pilots were ordered to retain them until combat was certain.

The Yom Kippur War consumed materiel at an unprecedented rate, demanding prodigious replenishment efforts. For the Air Force, aircraft drop tanks ran low very soon after initiation of hostilities and required an increase of domestic production as well as shipments from the USA. This 120 Squadron C-97 (4X-FPN 39), with a C-130 beyond, is taking on tanks at Ramat David AB for delivery to another base. (Ra'anan Weiss Collection)

On the 10th the IAF was down to 70 percent of its combat strength: 57 aircraft lost and as many rendered unflyable, 30 aircrew killed and 22 POW.[112] This approached the "Red Line" where it considered itself unable to ensure air superiority over Israel. These numbers and a report on October 12 that supplies remained for only four more days of fighting prompted a direct appeal to the USA by the Prime Minister. Given the mammoth Soviet resupply already underway and the Arab reticence regarding Israel's overtures for a ceasefire, the Americans agreed to assist. Mobilized El Al aircraft and leased Boeing 707s ferried 5,500 tons in 250 flights, but an emergency airlift by USAF transports was essential in augmenting sea replenishment with urgent deliveries.

American military transports began landing in Israel on the 14th. Among the priority cargo for the IAF were four different types of ECM and ECCM (Electronic Counter-Counter Measures) pods for the fighter-bombers, F-4 external tanks, TOW anti-tank missiles, AIM-9s, bombs and shells, and vital repair parts. The United States also supplied new flares for the fighter-bombers, large quantities of chaff with dispensers, plus a store devoted to dispensing bulk quantities of chaff.[113] Nineteen A-4 aft fuselage assemblies were shipped as the IR-guided Strela's 5.5-lb (2.5-kg) warhead was often insufficient to bring down an aircraft but did considerable damage to the engine exhaust and empennage.[114] Aircraft were laid-up for days undergoing extensive repair.

One particularly painful loss for the IAF during the Yom Kippur War was that of the Ramat David wing commander, Colonel Arlozor 'Zorik' Lev. He began flying as a Mosquito pilot but was so reckless that the CGS dismissed him from the service as a public example. After heartfelt appeals he was reinstated. In subsequent years, as a fighter pilot and commander, he enforced order and discipline among his personnel. Yet, he was always understanding and kind. Across his many assignments interacting with thousands of Air Force personnel, Zorik imprinted many of his fine personal qualities on younger service members. During the first days of the Yom Kippur War he was particularly worried about 110 Squadron after its leadership had suffered casualties, five aircraft were lost, and three pilots killed in just three days. On October 9 he joined a flight of their A-4Es to serve as an example in an attack on Port Said. He was last seen as his aircraft plunged into the sea during a diving attack. His outstanding example as a leader, aviator, warrior, instructor, friend, and father were impressed on the force that worked to be worthy of the lifeblood he had poured into it.

The large Skyhawk fleet was employed daily in relentless bombing of the enemy. This 102 Squadron A-4H shows a common loadout of bombs, by this period having begun adopting American ordnance. The aircraft was comparatively slow and its attack mission frequently brought it into range of enemy air defenses, costing the IAF 54 of the jets – more than any other type. (Ra'anan Weiss Collection)

Among the electronic warfare gear hastily supplied by the Americans was this QRC-490 mass quantity flare/chaff dispenser seen on an F-4. It was initially employed on October 19. (Asher Roth Collection via Ra'anan Weiss)

The pilot of 116 Squadron's Skyhawk 216 (see inset) was successful in bringing his jet back to base despite grave damage from a missile. Especially the SA-7 shoulder-fired SAM inflicted damage to the tail and aft fuselage that kept the aircraft on the ground for a day or two of repair. 216 is seen in depot undergoing rapid repair in the company of a unit mate plus a 109 Squadron machine. (Ra'anan Weiss Collection)

The need for precision strike and standoff capability was painfully evident from the first hours of the war. The Americans assisted with delivery of contrast-tracking Maverick missiles that the IAF quickly adopted and used to good effect. This Phantom, delivered during the war from a USAF operational unit, has the camera in the cylindrical housing projecting from the port wing leading edge, used to guide the multiple AGM-65s mounted on the aircraft. (Ofer Zidon Collection)

Israel's benefactor also replaced combat aircraft losses by flying machines directly from active units in Europe or off aircraft carriers. The first of 34 F-4Es began arriving on October 14, and six previously ordered Phantoms were also delivered during the war. Some of the USAF aircraft had the integral camera to cue Maverick missiles, also delivered. Of 28 A-4Es and 15 Fs, some were flown in on the 17th.[115] After a national markings change and Skyhawk repainting, plus radio and transponder swaps, these warplanes began to be pressed into combat as early as 17 October. A dozen USAF C-130Es were delivered from the 14th and these, along with 120's two Hs, equipped 131 Squadron created at Lod AB the same day.[116] New crewman then had to be trained during wartime missions. Also provided were 180 Chukar decoys and eight CH-53As, although none of these assets saw combat. Many more aircraft were delivered by sea, arriving only after the ceasefire.

Reversal

There was a lull in the war's intensity for several days during which the IAF regained its balance and considered how best to proceed. The brief respite ended on October 14 when, in an effort to relieve the pressure on their Syrian allies, the Egyptians committed their two reserve divisions from the west bank in an attempt to advance toward the Sinai mountain passes. Once they were beyond the protective aerial umbrella, however, the Egyptian formations were hit hard by tank fire and air attacks. They were forced to discontinue the offensive. The deepest penetration was about 5 miles (8 km).

Also on the 14th, the IAF made another concerted effort to break the back of the EAF fighter force, probably in preparation for the major counter-offensive that was to begin the following day. Large raids were flown against three air bases. Over 100 Phantoms and Skyhawks were committed to the three-wave attack. One base was shut down for a few hours and as many as 150 aircraft engaged in a battle that lasted 53 minutes with moderate losses on both sides. Up to this time the Egyptians had probably lost about 170 aircraft in air-to-air combat while the Israelis admit to only five lost in the same manner (referring only to air intercept sorties). The IAF also worked over the northern end of the air defense belt to open a corridor into the Egyptian interior, but the enemy restored the batteries as fast as they were knocked out. The Israel Navy also contributed with gunfire and missiles directed at the northern end of the SAM barrier. The large number of dummy SAM sites the Egyptians had erected complicated the work. It was October 16 before the efforts showed results.[117]

With the threat from Syria effectively neutralized, the IDF began a major offensive in the Sinai on October 15. They pushed through a gap between the Egyptian Second and Third Armies to reach the canal. The largest armor battle since the Second World War raged as the Egyptians counterattacked fiercely. However, Zahal was able to send a small element across the waterway that was rapidly increased over the coming days. This force spread out to attack and isolate the enemy from the rear. In so doing, they also eliminated SAM sites, radars, and other air defense elements.

The IAF exploited the gap to attack air bases and to progressively destroy air defense sites that no longer enjoyed mutually

Tel Nof AB was an important transport helicopter hub throughout the war. This photo shows a 124 Squadron Bell and three 114 Squadron Super Frelons ready to respond. All have flare dispenser tubes or mounts for these added by the Israelis. The background Frelon appears to have the Katef electronic warfare jammer suite mounted in the crew door entrance. The foreground Frelon has an unidentified object beneath the belly ahead of the loading ramp – possibly a radar altimeter. (Ra'anan Weiss Collection)

supportive zones of fire. The Israelis claim to have eliminated 56 missile "sites" out of the 62 adjacent to the canal, with perhaps 20 percent taken out by the ground forces. By another measure this was reportedly 32 batteries destroyed and 11 damaged, with 11 more destroyed by ground fire. The Egyptians credited ground fire for most of the damage to their air defense network.

With the air defense network badly fractured, the EAF now joined the battle in numbers not seen since October 6 to stabilize the situation. They flew up to 500 sorties during this period and 1,500 during the last week of the war. Everything was put into the air to destroy the Israeli bridgehead, including trainers and helicopters. The EAF ground attack sorties scored many good hits, but their fighter cover was badly mauled. Radar stations on the mountains in the Sinai easily tracked the movement of enemy aircraft and EW assets gave the Israelis a decided advantage in the air battles.

A number of large dogfights ensued, some involving upwards of 60 aircraft, and Egyptian losses rose. Along with the 84 aircraft lost during the first 10 days, this was creating a dire situation. Six foreign air arms had moved to reinforce the EAF and SyAAF with nearly 200 aircraft plus pilots and defense personnel.

American ECM pods and improvised tactics had helped to make Israeli aircraft less vulnerable to the air defenses and losses declined. The 19th was the first day of the war in which there were no IAF aircraft destroyed.

By October 20, the Israelis were firmly established on the west bank of the Suez Canal. They had captured the inoperative Fayid airfield and employed it as an emergency landing field to fly in supplies and extract casualties. This the IAF dubbed Wing 28 "Nachshon."[118]

Israel was determined to retake Mt. Hermon. Preparatory air attacks on the 19th and the 20th saw the first use of the Maverick and suitably equipped F-4Es in strikes on the outpost. Employing missiles and aircraft delivered just days before by the Americans, the first attack yielded 50 percent direct hit success despite no prior experience with the system.[119] The next afternoon, six Sea Stallions flew 27 flights from Mahanayim airfield in northern Israel, landing in trios on three sides of the summit fortress to offload 627 paratroopers.[120] Another force fought their way up the slope. It was a long and bloody battle throughout the night, with heavy causalities on both sides, but Hermon was again in Israeli hands.

Arab combatants had been seeking a ceasefire and, on the 22nd, the United Nations passed a resolution calling for a halt to the fighting that evening. Although both sides contributed to the ceasefire breaches, the IDF was clearly unwilling to stop until they had some firm gains to bargain with in postwar negotiations. Troops continued to advance along the canal destroying more enemy installations. The Egyptian Third Army was soon cut-off on the east bank as Zahal pushed south in an attempt to capture Suez City. Likewise, air activity carried on.

Two 103 Squadron Nords and a U206 were photographed at the captured Egyptian base of Fayid. It had not been an active airfield, but the IAF put it to use for logistics support of IDF forces operating on the west bank of the canal. Ingress and egress remained hazardous and aircraft flew at very low altitudes until well clear of the canal area. (Asher Roth Collection via Ra'anan Weiss)

The continued IDF advance and the risk of imminent collapse of the Arab forces brought a quick reaction from the Soviets. They threatened unilateral action to halt the Israelis. Red Army airmobile forces were placed on alert for deployment to the Middle East and there was suspicion that the USSR was moving FROG missile nuclear warheads into the region. The United States responded by moving its military forces to their highest state of peacetime alert since the Cuban missile crisis of 1962. The situation was tense and the Israelis were pressured to bring their offensive to a standstill. The war finally came to an end on October 24. Sporadic fighting continued for two more days.

Reflection

The October 1973 war ended better for Israel than the Arabs in terms of military advantage and condition. However, diplomatically it was a draw. The Arabs showed they could inflict great losses on their adversary, reduce the effectiveness of its much-vaunted air force, and compel world powers to intervene. Israel had fought with determination and daring, winning militarily significant gains. However, the ferocity and destructiveness of the war was enormously costly. The vast quantities of materiel consumed in the 18-day conflagration caused worldwide rethinking of combat requirements. The vulnerability of tanks and aircraft to precision-guided missiles would require many years and expanded budgets to answer adequately.

The superpowers had been brought to the brink of armed conflict in trying to support their allies. A dramatic escalation in the price of oil and cut in production, instigated by Arab producers, were followed by an embargo on oil to the USA after she announced the emergency shipment of arms to Israel. This threat to the economies of industrialized nations was particularly alarming. Stock markets fell and inflation rose around the globe. This compelled strenuous diplomatic efforts to separate the combatants, reopen the Suez Canal, resume the flow of oil, and move towards final resolution of the conflict.

The combat casualties were especially distressing to Israel. A total 2,838 personnel were killed with another 7,500 or so wounded and 500 captured. One third of the IDF's tanks were destroyed. Aircrew impact was 62 killed, 53 of these pilots, and 44 captured. Dozens of Air Force ground personnel and air defense force soldiers also died and still more wounded. The IAF lost 108 aircraft in combat or operational accidents and perhaps a few more destroyed on the ground. This was 28 percent of the fighter-bombers and 14 percent of the overall inventory.

The Arabs had shown much improved skills and a great willingness to fight. They were still not, in general, a match for Zahal once the IDF recovered from the surprise attack and adjusted for the new elements in the enemy arsenals. The IAF remained superior in all measures, although the Arab ground-based air defenses were a great impediment to operations throughout the war. Multiple measures had initially made IAF attacks on enemy air bases of little effective value given the cost. Later they served only to keep the Syrians reeling. The service showed considerable ability to compensate for its preparedness shortcomings and adapt to the new realities it faced in meeting combat obligations. New tactics and weapons were adopted in the heat of battle, and these adjusted based upon results. It persevered through heavy losses, which also depleted squadron leadership, and succeeded in winning sufficient air superiority in the final days to allow ground forces to succeed in offensives with reduced worry about enemy air attack. However, many capabilities and assets remained wanting.

Air-ground joint planning had been minimal before the war, and execution reflected this. The FACs, serving with ground forces down to the division level, were inadequately trained and poorly equipped. Ground commanders' requests for air

A 105 Squadron Sa'ar taxis at what is likely Hatzor AB in preparation for another strike during the war. Its weapons loadout includes two Shafrir 2 AAM and 100-kg bombs, plus 625-l drop tanks. The 105 maintained a detachment of four aircraft at Ophir AB in the Sinai. (Ra'anan Weiss Collection)

This A-4E carries two Walleye TV-guided bombs plus two Sidewinder AAM. The IAF had modest precision guided air-delivered munitions capacity going into the war, the AGM-62 Walleye being one. The aircraft carries the tail badge of 110 Squadron though operated by 116 because of the E's capability to deliver the Walleye. (Ra'anan Weiss Collection)

support required General Staff approval in a time-consuming process. The Air Force lacked a battle management center to quickly generate sorties in response to the requests, coordinate resources efficiently, and provide a rapid response to shifting priorities. Two officers improvised such a resource in the midst of battle. The early dysfunction in the AHQ in repeatedly generating conflicting strike plans and disputatious generals was disquieting and would need to be addressed postwar. Despite the central control, air battles developed at the instigation of individual pilots instead of resources being managed to the best advantage of the tactical situation as a whole. The lax adherence to specifics of orders and acceptance of personal courses of actions in meeting missions, all which had become a matter of some pride for the Air Force and reflecting Israeli society in general, did not meet the needs of the modern battlefield. The same was true for the general nature of the force with rugged individualism, lax adherence to standards, and "cowboy" aggressiveness, all that so many admired, no longer suiting modern aerial combat. Additionally, the IAF's assessment that it was days from running out of munitions and parts, prompting an urgent appeal to the Americans by national leadership, was flawed. The inventory control system was faulty and falsely indicated shortages.

The IAF was dependent on A'man to provide targeting information. This was not timely, sufficiently accurate, or meeting specific Air Force needs. Reconnaissance missions were tardy in generation and the results slow in being exploited. Imagery had to be processed through A'man before becoming available to IAF mission planners.[121] This was too lengthy in meeting the fast-changing tactical situation. Many vital opportunities were missed and aircrew placed at risk.

Compared with the more than 42,000 "dumb" bombs dropped, the contribution of PGMs was relatively minor owning to small stocks, operational inexperience, and possibly under-appreciation of their potential. Shrikes were well-employed from early on with 212 fired. However, the service was not well-prepared to use the TV-guided munitions. The Walleye was employed by only 116 Squadron with their A-4Es, beginning only on the 10th, though they ultimately released 118.[122] The first of just 30 HOBOS was not initially dropped until the 16th.[123] By this point the weapons were getting attention and the Mavericks delivered by the USA were put to quick use. In just four days the IAF fired 54.[124]

The IAF contributions to destroying tanks and affecting mechanized battles appears to have been minor. Such would generally require careful targeting and a direct hit by bomb or missile (possessing few), but the IAF had little ability to setup such attacks in the face of air defenses or to deliver such weapons with necessary precision. The armor-piercing unguided rockets of the past were less effective against the latest tanks and required dangerously close range. Many tank battles occurred at night and the IAF had minimal night combat capability (with very few missions flown in darkness), and certainly none on this tactical level. Accounts by armor battle participants make few reference to the influence of airpower. Instead, the aircraft interdicted concentrations of tanks, supply convoys, and disrupted replenishment by hitting infrastructure – with some of these significant blows.[125]

Aircraft such as Noratlases, equipped with Sarah, flew patrols concurrent with strikes to await survival radio signals.[126] The Bell 205s and S-65s performed numerous aircrew rescues on land and sea, with 53 saves. The Sikorskys normally recovered those behind

The delta-wing fleet continued to perform intercept duties and added to their large score of enemy aircraft destroyed. This 113 Squadron Nesher touches down at Hatzor AB after the war when a 5 prefix was added to the aircraft series. The aircraft was delivered following the war and so lacks kill markings, and the identification triangles are more regular given that they were applied at the factory. (Ed Okun Collection)

enemy lines, carrying armed personnel and medics. The IAF flew 890 wounded to rear aid stations on any available aircraft. The mobilized civilian transports performed yeoman service in this role.

The IAF effort was mammoth. It fought on two fronts with 200 miles (322 km) from central Israel to Suez and 120 miles (193 km) to the Golan – significant distances for some aircraft of the period and especially limiting interceptor time over their patrol areas given the essentially non-operational aerial refueling resources of the period. Of its total 11,223 fighter-bomber sorties, just 27 percent were in the north. The highlights were 46 percent devoted to ground attack, just 12 percent to SEAD, and 40 percent to patrols, escort, and intercepts.[127] The 119 Squadron flew 17 percent of its sorties as photo-recce.[128] Transport units contributed 1,218 sorties, rotorcraft approximately 2,818, and light-planes 2,000. Of the total for these three classes of aircraft, 42 percent were for patrol, 22 percent general personnel and materiel transport, 9 percent rescue and casualty evacuation, and a significant 25 percent for EW (excluding light-planes for which data is lacking). The 117 Squadron, flying Shahaks, averaged 37 sorties per pilot over the 18-day emergency, and this may be indicative of the average for most fighter-bomber pilots.[129] Those flying transports, light-planes, and helicopters likely averaged more.

The importance of the American airlift cannot be overstated. It continued through November 15, with 147 C-5A and 421 C-141A flights delivering 22,345 metric tons of freight, far outstripping the Soviet effort. Yet, only 40 percent of these supplies arrived before the final ceasefire. Although commencing after the fronts had been stabilized, the arrival of thousands of artillery and tank rounds allowed the IDF to undertake the Suez offensive with greater logistical confidence. It was less critical for the Air Force but was considered essential given that the end of the startlingly draining war was unknown. The Phantoms and Skyhawks delivered during the war contributed 480 sorties, just 85 of these from 30 of the A-4Es placed into service.[130] That is 7 percent of the total sortie types to which these aircraft would

The IAF escorted the American transports into Israeli airspace during the mammoth airlift that was so vital during the Yom Kippur War. One C-141A pilot (C-5A shown) remembered the fighter pilots finding the duty boring and so a pair amused themselves by performing opposing barrel rolls around the airlifters. A 119 Squadron F-4E is shown on October 23, 1973. (Author's Collection)

have been committed.[131] The dozen C-130Es flew 180 hours or 20 missions.[132]

The IAF leadership continued to be pleased by success in air-to-air combat that slowly wore away the Arab air defenses. Of 117 engagements with 175 Israeli formations (456 aircraft) and 780 enemy machines, the service claimed 287 aircraft destroyed for a loss of 15 of their own with six aircrew killed and five captured.[133] This number of 15 is hotly disputed by the opposition and refers perhaps only to aircraft on air-intercept missions and not those engaged by enemy aircraft while on other taskings. The F-4 claimed 29 percent of the kills; the delta wing jets the rest. The use of AAM increased again. The IR-guided missiles accounted for 150 or 59 percent of the air-to-air kills (of 416 fired or 36 percent success rate), radar-guided just three kills (49 launched or 14 percent success), and the rest to cannons. Israel claimed some 450 Arab aircraft destroyed from all causes including perhaps two dozen on the ground.[134] Israeli ground-based air defenses scored 55 kills or 16 percent of the total (twelve to Hawks for 40 to 50 fired).[135]

Despite energetic efforts, the IAF never achieved complete air superiority. There were many occasions when enemy interceptors significantly disrupted missions, forcing attack jets to dump their ordnance and defend themselves. Throughout the war, opposition aircraft executed repeated airstrikes on IDF elements, albeit quickly and not terribly effectively. Afterwards the exclamation "Where was the Air Force?" was heard.

Although Arab aircraft losses were much greater than those of the Israelis, the IAF was seriously impaired. The overall rate of attrition was actually less than in 1967, but with many more aircraft and aircrew sacrificed over a longer war. To the IAF losses of 110 machines should be added perhaps six or more Phantoms written off after returning. Readily accounted for are 52 A-4s, 33 F-4s (one shot down by a Nesher), eight Mirages (including four operational accidents and one fuel starvation after combat), five Neshers, six Sa'ars (one to an operational accident), one Do.27, one Do.28, two S-65s, two Bell 205s, plus 10 Firebees and 21 Chukars. The drones were reduced to just a few of each type.[136] Reports of aircraft destroyed on the ground by EAF airstrikes in the Sinai are not discussed by Israeli sources. A loss rate of one aircraft per 102 sorties has been offered, compared with an EAF rate of 1 in 24 and a SyAAF of 1 in 28.

> One of the IAF's precious RF-4Es, aircraft 194 with 119 Squadron, was downed over Egypt on November 9, 1973, by SA-2s. The crew ejected at Mach 1.7 and 48,000 feet (1,463 m) altitude. Although the navigator, Ofer Tsidon, was killed, the pilot, Gideon Sheffer, survived (though losing both hands) and held the dubious world record for the highest altitude ejection. Such missions were flown as high as 73,000 feet (22,250 m). Remarkably, this is the only loss from the small fleet of Israeli RF-4Es and F-4E(S) s in a long and hazardous career. The crew of aircraft 194 had survived near-death just a few months previously. On August 9, 1973, an AA-2 Atoll missile fired from an Egyptian MiG-21 struck it. Although one engine and to be shutdown, the men managed to recover to Ophir AB.

The light helicopter fleet was as busy as the light-planes throughout the war zone in ferrying personnel and small but vital items. This image captures the old and the new with a 125 Squadron French Alouette II and an American JetRanger, types the unit operated during the war. The Bell shows flare dispenser tubes the Israelis added to the fuselage. (Asher Roth Collection via Ra'anan Weiss)

More than 100 IAF aircraft fell during the war. The Skyhawk suffered especially given its relatively slower speed and meager EW defenses, plus its attack mission bringing it into range of more of the enemy air defenses. The tail section of this 110 Squadron machine is among the detritus of war photographed on the Golan Heights following the ceasefire. (Ed Okun Collection)

About 80 Israeli jets fell on both fronts to air defense systems. As many as 235 suffered combat damage and about 225 heavily damaged – with some aircraft meeting this fate more than once during the war. Some 81 machines were forced to execute emergency landings away from their home bases after being hit.[137] Most were repaired to fly again within a day or two, and all but 21 within a week. Even the 20 or so aircraft that had been severely damaged were flying again before the ceasefire.[138]

The Arab air defense forces may have fired as many as 2,100 to 2,600 missiles for perhaps 39 aircraft downed by these systems. The AAA and SA-7s became especially effective when the attackers were forced to low altitude in evading the SAMs. Despite the relatively low success rate for the number of missiles fired, there is no disputing that they severely disrupted IAF operations. Observing from the sidelines, Ezer Weizman commented metaphorically that, "The missiles left some dents in the wing of the airplane."[139] As a consequence, the Air Force's support to ground forces was much less successful than had been hoped. Although new tactics and weapons did greatly reduce the effectiveness of the enemy air defense network by the end, the time and cost was unacceptably high.

There was more hard work for the Israeli Air Force to address the deficiencies highlighted by the Yom Kippur War and prepare for any rematch with these adversaries. This spelled more costly investment by the small state and deeper beholding to the Unites States.

Bibliography

Aloni, Shlomo, "A Decade of Air Power: Israel 1950-1959," *Wings of Fame*, Vol.7 1997, pp.142-157.

Aloni, Shlomo, *Israeli A-4 Skyhawk Units in Combat*, Osprey Combat Aircraft 81 (Oxford, England: Osprey Publishing, 2005).

Aloni, Shlomo, *Israeli F-4 Phantom II Aces*, Osprey Aircraft of the Aces 60 (Oxford, England: Osprey Publishing, 2004).

Aloni, Shlomo, *Israeli Air Force Operations in the 1948 War, Israeli Winter Offensive Operation Horev 22 December 1948-7 January 1949*, Middle East @ War Volume 2 (West Midlands, England: Helion & Company, 2015).

Aloni, Shlomo, *Israeli Air Force Operations in the 1956 Suez War, 29 October 1956-8 November 1956*, Middle East @ War Volume 3 (West Midlands, England: Helion & Company, 2015).

Aloni, Shlomo, *The June 1967 Six-Day War, Volume A – Operation Focus: The Israeli Pre-emptive Strike of June 5, 1967*, Israeli Air Force Air Campaigns (Bat-Hefer, Israel: IsraDecal Publications, 2008).

Aloni, Shlomo, "La guerre du Six-Jours: les combats aériens, 1re partie: Les combats pour la supériorité aérienne," *Avions*, Hors-séries #30, May 2011, pp.1-96 (French).

Aloni, Shlomo, "Les "as" de l'aviation israélienne de 1948 à 1985," *Avions*, Hors-séries #44, February 2016, pp.1-96 (French).

Aloni, Shlomo, *Night Fighters in Israeli Service: Squadron 119, 1956-1963*, Israeli Airpower History Publications AISO0031 (E-publication: Shlomo Aloni, 13 June 2010).

Aloni, Shlomo, 'No. 105 Squadron, IDF/AF,' *Wings of Fame*, Vol.13 1998, pp.20-31.

Aloni, Shlomo, 'Ouragan, Mystère & Super Mystère en Israël 1955-1975,' *Avions*, Hors-séries #51 September 2019, pp.1-104.

Aloni, Shlomo, *Six-Day War 1967, Operation Focus and the 12 Hours That Changed the Middle East*, Osprey Air Campaign 10 (Oxford, England: Osprey Publishing, 2019).

Aloni, Shlomo, 'Trainers in Combat: Valour and Sacrifice in the Six Day War,' *Air Enthusiast*, No.94, July/August 2001, pp.42-55.

Aloni, Shlomo, *Vultures Over Israel, The Vautour in Israeli Service: Squadron 110 1957-1971* (Atglen, Pennsylvania: Schiffer Publishing, 2011).

Amir, Amos, *Fire in the Sky, Flying in Defence of Israel* (South Yorkshire, England: Pen & Sword Aviation, 2005).

Anon., 'Major-General Mordechai Hod,' Obituaries, *The Telegraph*, July 20, 2003 (online, https://www.telegraph.co.uk/news/obituaries/1434579/Major-General-Mordechai-Hod.html).

Asher, Dani (ed.), *Inside Israel's Northern Command, The Yom Kippur War on the Syrian Border* (Lexington, Kentucky: University Press of Kentucky, 2014).

Barkai, Aviram, *For Heaven's Sake, Squadron 201 and the Yom Kippur War* (Tel Aviv, Israel: ContentoNow, 2017).

Boyne, Walter J., *The Two O'Clock War, The 1973 Yom Kippur Conflict and the Airlift that Saved Israel* (New York, New York: St. Martin's Press, 2002).

Brugioni, Dino A., 'The Effects of Aerial and Satellite Imagery on the 1973 Yom Kippur War,' *Air Power History*, Fall 2004, pp.4-13.

Cohen, Eliezer, *Israel's Best Defense: The Full Story of the Israeli Air Force* (New York, New York: Crown Publishers, 1993).

Cooling, Benjamin F. (ed.), *Case Studies in the Development of Close Air Support (CAS)* (Washington, D.C.: Office of Air Force History, United States Air Force, 1990).

Cooper, Tom and Santana, Sergio, *Lebanese Civil War, Volume 1: Palestinian Diaspora, Syrian and Israeli Interventions, 1970-1978*, Middle East @ War Series No.21 (Warwick, England; Helion & Company, 2019).

Cull, Brian, Aloni, Shlomo and Nicolle, David, *Spitfires Over Israel* (London, England: Grub Street, 1994).

Cull, Brian, Nicolle, David and Aloni, Shlomo, *Wings Over Suez* (London, England: Grub Street, 1996).

Dor, Amos, *The F-4E Phantom II Kurnass*, The IAF Aircraft Series No.1 (Milano, Italy: AD Graphics, 1998).

Efrati, Yoav, *Colors & Markings of the Israeli Air Force* (Bat-Hefer, Israel: IsraDecal Publications, 2005).

Ginor, Isabella and Remez, Gideon, *The Soviet-Israeli War 1967-1973, The USSR's Military Intervention in the Egyptian-Israeli Conflict* (Oxford, England: Oxford University Press, 2017).

Habakuk, Motty, Leshem, Yossi and Weiss, Ra'anan, *The Israeli Air Force, Air Power as a Bridge to Regional Stability* (Israel: Israeli Air Force, Ministry of Defense, 2018).

Haloutz, Dani, *Eye to Eye* (Tel Aviv, Israel: ContentoNow, 2016).

Hartoch Noam and Warshai, Ilan, 'The Auster in Israel,' *Kne-Mida* No.65, July 2016, pp.4-15. (Hebrew).

Hartoch Noam and Warshai, Ilan, 'The Dakota in Israel,' *Kne-Mida – IPMS Israel Magazine* No.52, December 2009, pp.16-31. (Hebrew).

Hartoch Noam and Warshai, Ilan, 'From the Dart Herald to the DHC-7: Arkia's "British" Turboprop Airliners,' *Kne-Mida – IPMS Israel Magazine* No.49/50, December 2008, pp.4-19 (Hebrew).

Huertas, Salvador Mafé, *The Israeli Air Force 1947-1960: An Illustrated History* (Atglen, Pennsylvania: Schiffer Publishing, 1998).

IAF Magazine Staff, *Israeli Air Force – IAF Journal*, www.iaf.org.il/iaf.

Anon., *Israel Air Force Handbook, Volume 1 Strategic Information and Weapon Systems* (Washington, D.C.: International Business Publications, 2010).

Israeli Air Force official website (Israeli Air Force, http://iaf.org.il/2381-en/IAF.aspx).

Kaplansky, Eddy, *The First Fliers* (Israel: Israel Defence Forces, 1993).

Katz, Samuel M., *The Night Raiders, Israel's Naval Commandos at War* (New York, New York: Pocket Books, 1997).

Marszalkiewicz, Jakub, *Air Combat During the Arab-Israeli Wars*, Library of Armed Conflicts No.01 (Lublin, Poland: Kagero Publishing, 2017).

Newdick, Thomas and Zidon, Ofer, *Modern Israeli Air Power, Aircraft and Units of the Israeli Air Force* (Houston, Texas: Harpia Publishing, 2013).

Nordeen, Lon and Nicolle, David, *Phoenix Over the Nile, A History of Egyptian Air Power 1932-1994* (Washington, D.C.: Smithsonian Institution Press, 1996).

Powers, David G., 'Vultures & Young Lions,' *Dassault Mirage III/5*, Aviation Classics Issue 17, 2012, pp.70-83.

Pressfield, Steve, *The Lion's Gate, On the Front Lines of the Six Day War* (New York, New York: Sentinel, 2014).

Ronen, Ran, *Eagle in the Sky, One of the World's Greatest Fighter Pilots* (Tel Aviv, Israel: Contento De Semrik, 2013).

Rosen, Dan, "Air-to-Air Missiles Development in Israel" (Haifa, Israel: Rafael, 1998) technical paper presented at the 38th Israel Annual Conference on Aerospace Sciences, February 25-26, 1998.

Rosen, Yoav, 'The Order was: "Shoot Any Plane in Sight,"' *Israel Air Force Magazine* (English edition), January-February 2002, pp.94-98.

Spector, Iftach, *Loud and Clear, The Memoir of an Israeli Fighter Pilot* (Minneapolis, Minnesota: Zenith Press, 2009).

Warshai, Ilan, 'Fouga Magister and Tzukit in Israel,' *Kne-Mida IPMS Israel Magazine*, No.61, June 2014, pp.10-25. (Hebrew).

Warshai, Ilan, 'Sikorsky Helicopters in Israel,' *Kne-Mida – IPMS Israel Magazine*, No.54, December 2010, pp.9-17. (Hebrew).

Weiss, Ra'anan, *The Israeli AF in the Yom Kippur War, Facts and Figures* (Erlangen, Germany: IsraDecal Publications, 2014).

Weiss, Ra'anan, *Super Mystère and Sa'ar*, Israeli AF Mini Photo Album No.4 (Kefar-Tavor, Israel: IsraDecal Publications, December 2019).

Weiss, Ra'anan and Aloni, Shlomo, *McDonnell Douglas F-4E Phantom Kurnass in IAF Service, Part 1*, Aircraft in Detail 4 (Israel: IsraDecal Publications, 2008).

Weiss, Ra'anan, Ben-Yosef, Nir and Bar-Shalom, Ofer, *First in the Negev – Hatzerim Air Force Base Jubilee, 1966 –2016* (Israel: Ministry of Defense, 2016).

Weiss, Ra'anan and Efrati, Yoav, *McDonell Douglas A-4 Skyhawk*, Aircraft of the Israeli Air Force 3 (Bat-Hefer, Israel: IsraDecal Publications, 2001).

Weizman, Ezer, *On Eagles' Wings* (New York, New York: Macmillan Publishing Company, 1976).

Yonay, Ehud, *No Margin For Error: The Making of the Israeli Air Force* (New York, New York: Pantheon Books, 1993).

Zidon, Ofer, *The Israeli Air Force, An Inside Look at IAF Structure and Operations* (Jerusalem, Israel: IsraelDefense and Fisher Institute, 2014).

Zidon, Ofer, *Israeli Air Force Yearbook 2015-2016*, Modern I.A.F. Series 6 (Israel: Wizard Publications, 2015).

Zidon, Ofer and Aloni, Shlomo, *Israeli Air Force Cutting Edge*, Modern I.A.F. Series 4 (Israel: Wizard Publications, 2009).

Zidon, Ofer and Aloni, Shlomo, *Israeli Air Force Yearbook, IAF at War*, Modern I.A.F. Series 2 (Israel: Wizard Publications, 2007).

Endnotes

1 Salvador Mafé Huertas, *The Israeli Air Force 1947-1960: An Illustrated History* (Atglen, Pennsylvania: Schiffer Publishing, 1998), p.10, and Brian Cull, Shlomo Aloni, and David Nicolle, *Spitfires Over Israel* (London, England: Grub Street, 1994), p.53.

2 Noam Hartoch and Ilan Warshai, 'The Auster in Israel,' *Kne-Mida* No.65, July 2016, p.15, show how each aircraft was placed into service. Previously it was believed that some of these Austers were cannibalized or otherwise too damaged to be restored to airworthiness.

3 IAF Magazine Staff, *Israeli Air Force – IAF Journal*, www.iaf.org.il/iaf, March 9, 1948 entry 'Sherut Ha'avir submits a 'plan for increasing the power of the Sherut' to General Yigael Yadin.'

4 The 900 figure, with breakdown, is from Huertas, The Israeli Air Force 1947-1960, p.43. It conflicts with Eliezer Cohen, *Israel's Best Defense: The Full Story of the Israeli Air Force* (New York, New York: Crown Publishers, 1993), p.26, offering 675 in administration. The aircrew breakdown are from a variety of sources but most especially Brian Cull, Shlomo Aloni, and David Nicolle, *Spitfires Over Israel* (London, England: Grub Street, 1994), and Eddy Kaplansky, *The First Fliers* (Israel: Israel Defence Forces, 1993), with this author's own weighing of veracity.

5 Huertas, *The Israeli Air Force 1947-1960*, p.43.

6 Huertas, *The Israeli Air Force 1947-1960*, p.65.

7 Huertas, *The Israeli Air Force 1947-1960*, p.43.

8 Huertas, *The Israeli Air Force 1947-1960*, p.43, and Cull, *et al*, *Spitfires Over Israel*, p.201.

9 Cohen, *Israel's Best Defense*, p.39. What became of this post is unclear.

10 Huertas, *The Israeli Air Force 1947-1960*, pp.39 and 44, counting tons as multiples of 2,000 lb.

11 Huertas, *The Israeli Air Force 1947-1960*, p.58.

12 Huertas, *The Israeli Air Force 1947-1960*, p.59, and Cull, *et al*, *Spitfires Over Israel*, p.237.

13 Huertas, *The Israeli Air Force 1947-1960*, p.71.

14 Huertas, *The Israeli Air Force 1947-1960*, and Cull, *et al*, *Spitfires Over Israel*, p.247.

15 Huertas, *The Israeli Air Force 1947*-1960, pp.67-68, and Cull, *et al*, *Spitfires Over Israel*, p.273.

16 Shlomo Aloni, *Israeli Air Force Operations in the 1948 War, Israeli Winter Offensive Operation Horev 22 December 1948-7 January 1949*, Middle East @ War Volume 2 (West Midlands, England: Helion & Company, 2015), p.71. This gives the 226-ton figure and the Spitfires sorties by counting of the sorties summary throughout the reference. This very detailed account post-dates Cull, *et al*, *Spitfires Over Israel*, p.330, that gives the tonnage as 267.

17 Huertas, *The Israeli Air Force 1947-1960*, p.79.

18 IAF Magazine Staff, *Israeli Air Force – IAF Journal*, www.iaf.org.il/iaf, October 9-21, 1950 entry.

19 Huertas, *The Israeli Air Force 1947-1960*, p.82.

20 Huertas, *The Israeli Air Force 1947-1960*, p.82.

21 Shlomo Aloni, 'A Decade of Air Power: Israel 1950-1959,' *Wings of Fame*, Vol.7, 1997, p.143.

22 The Israel MoD has never publicly released a comprehensive organizational chart for the Air Force. The diagrams depicted within this volume were compiled from a number of incomplete references, but most especially Huertas, *The Israeli Air Force 1947-1960*, pp.153-155, Shlomo Aloni, *Night Fighters in Israeli Service: Squadron 119, 1956-1963*, Israeli Airpower History Publications AISO0031 (E-publication: Shlomo Aloni, June 13, 2010), p.20, several annually released summaries such as *Jane's World Air Forces*, and the official IASF website. When it comes to the headquarters, nothing below the higher staff offices are shown and references to branches below too scattered and incomplete, apart from occasional changes and translation inconsistencies, to draw a complete organizational chart.

23 Huertas, *The Israeli Air Force 1947-1960*, pp.147 and 156.

24 Shlomo Aloni, *The June 1967 Six-Day War, Volume A – Operation Focus: The Israeli Pre-emptive Strike of June 5, 1967*, Israeli Air Force Air Campaigns (Bat-Hefer, Israel: IsraDecal Publications, 2008), p.50, and Ofer Zidon and Shlomo Aloni, *Israeli Air Force Cutting Edge*, Modern I.A.F. Series 4 (Israel: Wizard Publications, 2009), p.70.

25 Huertas, *The Israeli Air Force 1947-1960*, p.149, and Aloni, *Wings of Fame*, p.142.

26 Cohen, Israel's Best Defense, p.164.

27 *Israel Air Force Handbook, Volume 1 Strategic Information and Weapon Systems* (Washington, D.C.: International Business Publications, 2010), p.95.

28 Aloni, *Night Fighters in Israeli Service*, p.6.

29 Huertas, *The Israeli Air Force 1947-1960*, p.83.

30 It has been occasionally stated that the IAF never contained "reserve" units. These examples were rare in the history. There were other examples of units, with second-tier aircraft, that had but a skeleton of regular personnel and were ineffective without reservists.

31 Such figures are difficult to pin down. Some references upon which the numbers provided were drawn include Salvador Mafé Huertas, *The Israeli Air Force 1947-1960: An Illustrated History* (Atglen, Pennsylvania: Schiffer Publishing, 1998), p.148, and Eliezer Cohen, *Israel's Best Defense: The Full Story of the Israeli Air Force* (New York, New York: Crown Publishers, 1993), p.105.

32 Shlomo Aloni, *Israeli Air Force Operations in the 1956 Suez War, 29 October 1956-8 November 1956*, Middle East @ War Volume 3 (West Midlands, England: Helion & Company, 2015), p.3., gives the total strength of 100 Squadron Cubs as 30. The distribution into four flights is shown on p.9 though with only serviceable aircraft enumerated except for Flight C (the largest detachment) that did not report. Likewise, Brian Cull, David Nicolle, and Shlomo Aloni, *Wings Over Suez* (London, England: Grub Street, 1996), pp.108-109, gives a list of serviceable aircraft that disagrees and omits some of the detachments. The author has attempted to piece together the distribution at the start of hostilities from these primary references with the sum of 30 machines.

33 Aloni, *Night Fighters in Israeli Service*, p.24.

34 Ehud Yonay, *No Margin For Error: The Making of the Israeli Air Force* (New York, New York: Pantheon Books, 1993), p.167.

35 Cull, Nicolle, and Aloni, *Wings Over Suez*, p.154, and Ofer Zidon, *Israeli Air Force Yearbook 2015-2016*, Modern I.A.F. Series 6 (Israel: Wizard Publications, 2015), p.83.

36 Aloni, *The June 1967 Six-Day War, Volume A*, p.176.

37 Ofer Zidon, *The Israeli Air Force, An Inside Look at IAF Structure and Operations* (Jerusalem, Israel: IsraelDefense and Fisher Institute, 2014), p.122, and Motty Habakuk, Yossi Leshem, Ra'anan Weiss, R., *The Israeli Air Force, Air Power as a Bridge to Regional Stability* (Israel: Israeli Air Force, Ministry of Defense, 2018), p.241.

38 Aloni, *The June 1967 Six-Day War, Volume A – Operation Focus*, p.27.

39 Benjamin F. Cooling (ed.), *Case Studies in the Development of Close Air Support (CAS)* (Washington, D.C.: Office of Air Force History, United States Air Force, 1990), e-book p.10275.

40 Cooling, *Case Studies in the Development of Close Air Support*, p.10442.

41 Aloni, 'A Decade of Air Power: Israel 1950-1959,' *Wings of Fame*, p.154, and Shlomo Aloni, *Vultures Over Israel, The Vautour in Israeli Service: Squadron 110 1957-1971* (Atglen, Pennsylvania: Schiffer Publishing, 2011), p.24.

42 Aloni, *The June 1967 Six-Day War, Volume A – Operation Focus*, p.49.

43 Amos Amir, *Fire in the Sky, Flying in Defence of Israel* (South Yorkshire, England: Pen & Sword Aviation, 2005), p.78.

44 Aloni, *The June 1967 Six-Day War, Volume A – Operation Focus*, p.17.

45 The Western code designations for such systems as the SA-2 will be employed throughout this book, as it was at that time by the Israelis.

46 Dan Rosen, 'Air-to-Air Missiles Development in Israel' (Haifa, Israel: Rafael, 1998) technical paper presented at the 38th Israel Annual Conference on Aerospace Sciences, 25-26 February 1998, proceedings, pp.S9-S24.

47 Aloni, *The June 1967 Six-Day War, Volume A – Operation Focus*, p. 57, and Yoav Efrati, *Colors & Markings of the Israeli Air Force*, (Bat-Hefer, Israel: IsraDecal Publications, 2005), p.30.

48 Efrati, *Colors & Markings of the Israeli Air Force*, p.77.

49 Thomas Newdick, and Ofer Zidon, *Modern Israeli Air Power, Aircraft and Units of the Israeli Air Force* (Houston, Texas: Harpia Publishing, 2013), p.122.

50 Aloni, *Night Fighters in Israeli Service*, pp.36 and 73, and Aloni, *Vultures Over Israel*, pp.93-94.

51 Aloni, *The June 1967 Six-Day War, Volume A*, p.48.

52 Aloni, *The June 1967 Six-Day War, Volume A – Operation Focus*, p.43.

53 Ilan Warshai, 'Sikorsky Helicopters in Israel,' *Kne-Mida – IPMS Israel Magazine*, No.54 December 2010, p.unknown.

54 Aloni, *The June 1967 Six-Day War, Volume A – Operation Focus*, calculated from the squadron personnel summary presented at the end of that book.

55 Ra'anan Weiss, *Super Mystère and Sa'ar*, Israeli AF Mini Photo Album No.4 (Kefar-Tavor, Israel: IsraDecal Publications, December 2019) p.3. Until this publication, only seven seized SMB2s were discussed in the English-language literature. However, Weiss summarizes the eight by tail number on p.86.

56 This number of armed and unarmed Fouga Magisters is the subject of some dispute. Cohen in *Israel's Best Defense*, p.238, reports that "The training squadron had 45 Fouga Magister, and the lack of equipment brought about, after deliberations, the altering of 20 of them to combat missions." The IAF was then a small force and Cohen, a pilot and squadron commander, would have been familiar with such subjects even apart from research for his book. In Steve Pressfield, *The Lion's Gate, On the Front Lines of the Six Day War* (New York, New York: Sentinel, 2014), p.312, Zvi Kanor, then a young pilot assigned to 147 Squadron, wrote "The air force had about 50 Fouga Magisters, the planes we trained on at the flight school. It will make 24 into warplanes." This is a firsthand account that is difficult to dismiss, even 50 years on. However, Kanor also states in his account that the number of fellow pilots in the squadron was 24 which is inaccurate. It had 21 regular (possibly what the author was referring to) and 29 reserve officers as detailed in Aloni, *The June 1967 Six-Day War, Volume A – Operation Focus*, pp.200-202. On p.54, Aloni lists the number of fighter aircraft available on June 5 as including 44 Magisters. Yet, Aloni lists 60 Magisters as assigned to 147 Squadron in 'La guerre du Six-Jours: les combats aériens, 1re partie: Les combats pour la supériorité aérienne,' *Avions*, Hors-séries #30, May 2011, p.6. Additionally, in Shlomo Aloni, *Six-Day War 1967, Operation Focus and the 12 Hours That Changed the Middle East*, Osprey Air Campaign 10 (Oxford, England: Osprey Publishing, 2019), p.19, he lists 44, as he does in 'Trainers in Combat: Valour and Sacrifice in the Six Day War,' *Air Enthusiast*, No.94, July/August 2001, p.44, and 'Ouragan, Mystère & Super Mystère en Israël 1955-1975,' *Avions*, Hors-séries #51, September 2019, p.78. Most official Israeli accounts appear to mix the armed and unarmed numbers or fail to count trainers altogether. For example, a detailed summary produced by the Air Force (Hebrew translation of the tables from the unspecified reference provided to the author) records 44 Magisters (at 100 percent serviceability) with 147 Squadron but does not list any trainers or light aircraft. Ilan Warshai, 'Fouga Magister and Tzukit in Israel,' *Kne-Mida IPMS Israel Magazine*, No.61, June 2014, p.15, states that the Air Force operated 45 armed Fougas out of a force of 60 airplanes. This appears to be the most thoroughly researched account of Israeli Magisters, yet still conflicts with the official number of 147 Squadron aircraft. Additionally, the 147 Squadron had a high sortie rate, with as many as five per day per pilot and a high of 170 sorties on June 5 (Aloni, *The June 1967 Six-Day War, Volume A – Operation Focus*, pp.200-202). Several accounts attribute a like number of flights per aircraft per day. With 45 machines and 170 sorties, this would round to an average of four flights per aircraft on that day, but seven for 25 aircraft. Seven is not inconceivable given the simplicity of the machine, even with arming, and with the short duration of the missions. The first Israeli Magister was an introductory airplane from France. The next four were assembled from French-manufactured assemblies. Israel Aircraft Industries was contracted to build just 34 Magisters, presumably all armed. They ran behind (just 20 delivered between 1960 and 1963) and so additional French and German aircraft were bought, more still later. Assemblies from France and Germany production were also acquired to help meet the IAI production schedule. It is reasonable to believe that only the Israeli-production had weapons. However, statements in literature suggest that all French-manufactured Magisters had accommodations for weapons, with gun mounts and hardpoints (and so not an IAI innovation), but it is unclear whether the German machines were so-equipped. Work would still have been required to actually complete the weapons installations.

57 Noam Hartoch, 'From the Dart Herald to the DHC-7: Arkia's "British" Turboprop Airliners,' *Kne-Mida - IPMS Israel Magazine* No.49/50, December 2008, p.8. However, in Aloni, *Six-Day War 1967, Operation Focus and the 12 Hours That Changed the Middle East*, p.19, and 'Ouragan, Mystère & Super Mystère en Israël 1955-1975,' *Avions*, Hors-séries #51, p.78, places 145 Squadron at Sde Dov.

58 Jakub Marszalkiewicz, *Air Combat During the Arab-Israeli Wars*, Library of Armed Conflicts No.01 (Lublin, Poland: Kagero Publishing, 2017), p.63.

59 Aloni, *The June 1967 Six-Day War, Volume A*, p.74. Shlomo Aloni, 'Trainers in Combat: Valour and Sacrifice in the Six Day War,' *Air Enthusiast*, No.94, pp.49, mentions the plans to move 147 Squadron forward. The IDF was so rapid that even El Arish would have been too far to the rear given the Magister's short range. However, a huge stock of 80-mm aerial rockets found at the base was airlifted back to Israel aboard Nortalases and put to immediate use.

60 Shlomo Aloni, 'No. 105 Squadron, IDF/AF,' *Wings of Fame*, Vol.13 1998, pp.27, records the Super Mystére loss to the SAM.

61 Here and throughout this book the references to SAM "sites" and "batteries" reflect the imprecise sources from which the accounts are drawn. A battery may consist of several radar and launch facilities, each with several launchers. Therefore, a "site" may be one launcher or the radar and control facility, or the entire complex. Consequently, the significance of such imprecise measures are difficult to gage – which may have been precisely the intent of such report verbiage.

62 Dino A. Brugioni, 'The Effects of Aerial and Satellite Imagery on the 1973 Yom Kippur War,' *Air Power History*, Fall 2004, p.6.

63 Shlomo Aloni, 'Les "as" de l'aviation israélienne de 1948 à 1985,' *Avions*, Hors-séries #44, February 2016, p.94.

64 Cooling, *Studies in the Development of Close Air Support*, p.10460.

65 Cooling, *Studies in the Development of Close Air Support*, p.10460.

66 Dani Haloutz, *Eye to Eye*, (Tel Aviv, Israel: ContentoNow, 2016), p.48.

67 Weiss, *Super Mystère and Sa'ar*, pp.3 and 88.

68 Weiss, *Super Mystère and Sa'ar*, p.3. A number of 25 was previously referenced.

69 David G. Powers, 'Vultures & Young Lions,' *Dassault Mirage III/5*, Aviation Classics Issue 17, 2012, pp.77-78. There is likely still more to this story to tell or refute.

70 Iftach Spector, *Loud and Clear, The Memoir of an Israeli Fighter Pilot* (Minneapolis, Minnesota: Zenith Press, 2009), p.208.

71 Rosen, 'Air-to-Air Missiles Development in Israel', pp.S9-24.

72 Ra'anan Weiss, and Yoav Efrati, *McDonell Douglas A-4 Skyhawk*, Aircraft of the Israeli Air Force 3, (Bat-Hefer, Israel: IsraDecal Publications, 2001), p.10.

73 Shlomo Aloni, *Israeli A-4 Skyhawk Units in Combat*, Osprey Combat Aircraft 81 (Oxford, England: Osprey Publishing, 2009), p.34.

74 Haloutz, *Eye to Eye*, p.78.

75 Ra'anan Weiss, *The Israeli AF in the Yom Kippur War, Facts and Figures* (Erlangen, Germany: IsraDecal Publications, 2014), p.161, has a photograph of a Noratlas performing this operation (reproduced herein).

76 Anon., 'Major-General Mordechai Hod,' Obituaries, *The Telegraph*, 20 July 2003 (online, https://www.telegraph.co.uk/news/obituaries/1434579/Major-General-Mordechai-Hod.html). There is no mention of such action in the account of the confrontation found in Cooper, Tom and Santana, Sergio, *Lebanese Civil War, Volume 1: Palestinian Diaspora, Syrian and Israeli Interventions, 1970-1978*, Middle East @ War Series No.21 (Warwick, England; Helion & Company, 2019), p.29.

77 Samuel M. Katz, *The Night Raiders, Israel's Naval Commandos at War* (New York, New York: Pocket Books, 1997), p.225.

78 Shlomo Aloni, *Israeli F-4 Phantom II Aces*, Osprey Aircraft of the Aces 60 (Oxford, England: Osprey Publishing, 2004), p.12.

79 Lon Nordeen and David Nicolle, *Phoenix Over the Nile, A History of Egyptian Air Power 1932-1994* (Washington, D.C.: Smithsonian Institution Press, 1996), p.249.

80 Nordeen and Nicolle, *Phoenix Over the Nile*, p.250.

81 Isabella Ginor and Gideon Remez, *The Soviet-Israeli War 1967-1973, The USSR's Military Intervention in the Egyptian-Israeli Conflict* (Oxford, England: Oxford University Press, 2017), p.401, note 34, cites well-researched sources. However, the 120 figure conflicts with the commonly quoted 118 from such authoritative sources as the Israeli Air Force official website (Israeli Air Force, http://iaf.org.il/2381-en/IAF.aspx) War of Attrition page.

82 Ginor and Remez, *The Soviet-Israeli War 1967-1973*, p.175.

83 Spector, *Loud and Clear*, p.247, and Aviram Barkai, *For Heaven's Sake, Squadron 201 and the Yom Kippur War* (Tel Aviv, Israel: ContentoNow, 2017), e-book p.479.

84 Ra'anan Weiss, and Shlomo Aloni, *McDonnell Douglas F-4E Phantom Kurnass in IAF Service, Part 1*, Aircraft in Detail 4 (Israel: IsraDecal Publications, 2008), pp.7 and 36.

85 Ginor and Remez, *The Soviet-Israeli War 1967-1973*, p.244.

86 Ginor and Remez, *The Soviet-Israeli War 1967-1973*, p.401 note 34.

87 Cohen, *Israel's Best Defense*, pp.312 and 396.

88 Nordeen and Nicolle, *Phoenix Over the Nile*, p.255, shows some figures from both the Egyptian and American perspective. All such numbers remain suspect.

89 Aloni, *Israeli A-4 Skyhawk Units in Combat*, p.29.

90 Barkai, *For Heaven's Sake*, e-book p.3204.

91 Ginor and Remez, *The Soviet-Israeli War 1967-1973*, p.245.

92 Weiss, *The Israeli AF in the Yom Kippur War*, p.25, and Aloni, *The June 1967 Six-Day War, Volume A*, p.173.

93 Barkai, *For Heaven's Sake,* p.3213 describes 26 decoys fired on the morning of October 7 and indicates on p.3523 that six remained. On p.4082 Barkai indicates 12 Chukars fired with four remaining. The author has added the four to the 26 for an assumed original number of Chukars and which appears an operationally reasonable number.

94 Ra'anan Weiss, Nir Ben-Yosef, and Ofer Bar-Shalom, *First in the Negev – Hatzerim Air Force Base Jubilee, 1966 –2016* (Israel: Ministry of Defense, 2016), p.34.

95 Weiss, *The Israeli AF in the Yom Kippur War*, pp.16 and 88.

96 Weiss, *The Israeli AF in the Yom Kippur War*, pp.99, 145, and 161. The addition of the three Netevei Nepht Dakotas is revealed by Noam Hartoch and Ilan Warshai in 'The Dakota in Israel,' *Kne-Mida – IPMS Israel Magazine* No.52, December 2009, p.unknown.

97 Ofer Zidon and Shlomo Aloni, *Israeli Air Force Yearbook, IAF at War*, Modern I.A.F. Series 2 (Israel: Wizard Publications, 2007), p.14.

98 Amos Dor, *The F-4E Phantom II Kurnass*, The IAF Aircraft Series No.1, (Milano, Italy: AD Graphics, 1998), p.25.

99 Barkai, *For Heaven's Sake*, e-book p.2426.

100 The number of AS-5 Kelt missiles fired at Israel and its assets in the Sinai, and the number shot down by ground and airborne defenses, remains unclear. Several were destroyed, some malfunctioned or exhausted their fuel short of the target, and some struck their aim points. Ginor and Remez, *The Soviet-Israeli War 1967-1973*, p.290, says that 23 missiles were launched throughout the war. The authors go on to detail on p.448 the shoot down of a missile just off the coast of Tel Aviv by a Mirage and the successful hit on a radar station in the Sinai. Nordeen and Nicolle, *Phoenix Over the Nile*, p.279, says that more than a dozen AS-5 missiles were launched on October 6 with at least five striking their targets, giving an American journal article as the source. This report of five successful hits is repeated in other sources but its origin is unclear. Weiss, *The Israeli AF in the Yom Kippur War*, p.174, lists three Kelts downed by anti-aircraft systems on the 11th but none on the 6th. On p.29, he details the downing of two of the missiles by fighters on the 6th. Appendix II of Volume 3 of this series reflects these kills but no others have come to light, suggesting five AS-5s downed by Israeli air defenses out of the 23 launched.

101 Barkai, *For Heaven's Sake*, e-book p.2426.

102 Weiss, *The Israeli AF in the Yom Kippur War*, p.34, says 87 sorties while Aloni, *Israeli A-4 Skyhawk Units in Combat*, p.41, says more than 100 sorties and eight air bases.
103 Barkai, *For Heaven's Sake*, e-book pp.3713, 4013, and 4079.
104 Ran Ronen, *Eagle in the Sky, One of the World's Greatest Fighter Pilots* (Tel Aviv, Israel: Contento De Semrik, 2013), p.371. Barkai, *For Heaven's Sake*, p.3373, and Dani Asher (ed.), *Inside Israel's Northern Command, The Yom Kippur War on the Syrian Border* (Lexington, Kentucky: University Press of Kentucky, 2014), pp.64, 72, and 578, all describe the Scratch order that was a response to urgent ground support requests, presumably stationary targets for which suitable intelligence could be conveyed. This, however, was not a plan, as such, meeting the demands of a major campaign responding to the joint Arab offensive of unprecedented scale.
105 Cohen, *Israel's Best Defense*, p.349.
106 Weiss, *The Israeli AF in the Yom Kippur War*, p.54.
107 Ginor and Remez, *The Soviet-Israeli War 1967-1973*, p.322.
108 Aloni, *Israeli A-4 Skyhawk Units in Combat*, pp.46, 48, and 61.
109 Weiss, *The Israeli AF in the Yom Kippur War*, pp.137 and 144, and as related by witnesses.
110 Weiss, and Efrati, *McDonell Douglas A-4 Skyhawk*, p.15.
111 Weiss, *The Israeli AF in the Yom Kippur War*, p.86.
112 Barkai, *For Heaven's Sake*, e-book pp.4888 and 5132.
113 Weiss, *The Israeli AF in the Yom Kippur War*, p.138.
114 Walter j. Boyne, *The Two O'Clock War, The 1973 Yom Kippur Conflict and the Airlift that Saved Israel* (New York, New York: St. Martin's Press, 2002), p.279.
115 Weiss, *The Israeli AF in the Yom Kippur War*, p.135.
116 Weiss, *The Israeli AF in the Yom Kippur War*, pp.107 and 116-117.
117 Weiss, *The Israeli AF in the Yom Kippur War*, p.116.
118 Weiss, *The Israeli AF in the Yom Kippur War*, pp.123 and 144.
119 Weiss, *The Israeli AF in the Yom Kippur War*, p.139.
120 Weiss, *The Israeli AF in the Yom Kippur War*, pp.144 and 168. Cohen, *Israel's Best Defense*, p.398. Asher, *Inside Israel's Northern Command*, pp.433, 437-438, and 596, gives this as five helicopters, 10-minute relays of pairs of helicopters, four LZs, and 626 paratroopers.
121 Cohen, *Israel's Best Defense*, p.401.
122 Weiss, *The Israeli AF in the Yom Kippur War*, pp.71 and 166, and Aloni, *Israeli A-4 Skyhawk Units in Combat*, p.49.
123 Weiss, *The Israeli AF in the Yom Kippur War*, pp.117 and 166.
124 Weiss, *The Israeli AF in the Yom Kippur War*, p.166.
125 Spector, in *Loud and Clear*, p.322, describes at attack on October 9 by his brace of Phantoms in which senior North Command personnel credited their action with breaking a Syrian advance into the Jordan Valley. Asher, *Inside Israel's Northern Command*, a book prepared and approved by the MoD, describes this event on pp.314 and 599 as an interdiction of Syrian reinforcements reacting to an Israeli armored advance, the strikes causing these elements to withdraw. By this point, the threat of the Syrians crushing Israeli defenses and overrunning home territory was considered past.
126 Newdick and Zidon, *Modern Israeli Air Power*, p.117.
127 Weiss, *The Israeli AF in the Yom Kippur War*, p.160, via calculation.
128 Zidon and Aloni, *Israeli Air Force Yearbook, IAF at War*, p.40.
129 Weiss, *The Israeli AF in the Yom Kippur War*, p.183.
130 Weiss, *The Israeli AF in the Yom Kippur War*, pp.108 and 157.
131 Weiss, *The Israeli AF in the Yom Kippur War*, p.164, via calculation summing 6,667 relevant sorties.
132 Zidon, *Israeli Air Force Yearbook 2015-2016*, p.24.
133 Aloni, *Israeli F-4 Phantom II Aces*, p.77, and Cohen, *Israel's Best Defense*, p.390, are sources for these figures. However, there were many such summaries that conflict. Those presented are the seemingly more complete and authoritative given assumed access to official documents.
134 Newdick and Zidon, *Modern Israeli Air Power*, p.15, gives what is perhaps the most recent summary by the IAF but still appears inflated, especially the number of aircraft destroyed on the ground. The figures on radar-guide missiles derive from Weiss, *The Israeli AF in the Yom Kippur War*, p.167 and counting from the tables on pp.175-185.
135 Weiss, *The Israeli AF in the Yom Kippur War*, p.174, provides the 12 Hawk kill figure with tabulated enumeration. Earlier sources differ greatly, such as Yoav Rosen, 'The Order was: "Shoot Any Plane in Sight,"' *Israel Air Force Magazine* (English edition), January-February 2002, p.95, with a 24 kill figure.
136 Weiss, *The Israeli AF in the Yom Kippur War*, pp.156 and 160.
137 Cohen, *Israel's Best Defense*, p.426.
138 Cohen, *Israel's Best Defense*, p.426.
139 Ezer Weizman, *On Eagles' Wings* (New York, New York: Macmillan Publishing Company, 1976), p.280.

ABOUT THE AUTHOR
BILL NORTON

William J. Norton is retired from a flight test engineering career that spanned 40 years, including 20 years as a US Air Force officer. This included serving as aircrew aboard test aircraft. He has held numerous positions in many organizations on dozens of aerospace programs spanning all aircraft types. He has penned scores of technical papers, seventeen books, and a multitude of magazine articles. Bill holds a Masters in Aeronautical Engineering and has taught technical courses at the college-level. In addition, he is a civil pilot with numerous ratings, restored and operates a DHC-1 Chipmunk, and built a Rutan Long-EZ.